LIVING
WITH
MIRACLES

Oct. Mt. Madena

3

Nov Seliman

5 End of Nov.

LIVING

WITH

MIRACLES

A Common-Sense Guide to

A Course in Miracles

D. PATRICK MILLER

JEREMY P. TARCHER/PENGUIN
a member of Penguin Group (USA) Inc.
New York

JEREMY P. TARCHER/PENGUIN
Published by the Penguin Group
Penguin Group (USA) Inc., 375 Hudson Street, New York, New York 10014, USA •
Penguin Group (Canada), 90 Eglinton Avenue East, Suite 700, Toronto, Ontario M4P 2Y3,
Canada (a division of Pearson Penguin Canada Inc.) • Penguin Books Ltd, 80 Strand,
London WC2R 0RL, England • Penguin Ireland, 25 St Stephen's Green, Dublin 2, Ireland
(a division of Penguin Books Ltd) • Penguin Group (Australia), 250 Camberwell Road,
Camberwell, Victoria 3124, Australia (a division of Pearson Australia Group Pty Ltd) •
Penguin Books India Pvt Ltd, 11 Community Centre, Panchsheel Park, New Delhi–110 017,
India • Penguin Group (NZ), 67 Apollo Drive, Rosedale, North Shore 0632,
New Zealand (a division of Pearson New Zealand Ltd) • Penguin Books
(South Africa) (Pty) Ltd, 24 Sturdee Avenue,
Rosebank, Johannesburg 2196, South Africa

Penguin Books Ltd, Registered Offices: 80 Strand, London WC2R 0RL, England

Most Tarcher/Penguin books are available at special quantity discounts for bulk purchase
for sales promotions, premiums, fund-raising, and educational needs. Special books or book
excerpts also can be created to fit specific needs. For details, write Penguin Group (USA) Inc.
Special Markets, 375 Hudson Street, New York, NY 10014.

Library of Congress Cataloging-in-Publication Data

Miller, D. Patrick, date.
Living with miracles: a common-sense guide to A Course in Miracles / D. Patrick Miller.
p.   cm.
ISBN 978-1-58542-879-3
1. Course in Miracles.   I. Title.
BP605.C68M57   2011   2011003813
299'.93—dc22

Printed in the United States of America
1   3   5   7   9   10   8   6   4   2

Book design by Meighan Cavanaugh

Neither the publisher nor the author is engaged in rendering professional advice or services
to the individual reader. The ideas, procedures, and suggestions contained in this book are
not intended as a substitute for consulting with a physician. All matters regarding your health
require medical supervision. Neither the author nor the publisher shall be liable or responsible
for any loss or damage allegedly arising from any information or suggestion in this book.

While the author has made every effort to provide accurate telephone numbers and Internet
addresses at the time of publication, neither the publisher nor the author assumes any responsibility for errors, or for changes that occur after publication. Further, the publisher does not
have any control over and does not assume any responsibility for author or third-party websites
or their content.

CONTENTS

INTRODUCTION

A NEW KIND OF COMMON SENSE

A Course in Miracles (ACIM) is a modern spiritual teaching, self-described as a "mind training," which leads its students toward a radical view of reality based on an intense discipline of forgiveness. It was first published as a three-volume set of books in the United States in the mid-1970s and has since sold more than two million copies in twenty languages around the world. Now published as a three-in-one compendium by the Foundation for Inner Peace in California, the standard edition of ACIM comprises about twelve hundred densely packed pages, divided between a lengthy Text, which lays out the basic philosophy; a shorter Workbook of 365 daily meditation lessons; and a brief Manual for Teachers that includes a "Clarification of Terms" and other explanatory material.

The Course was originally written down in shorthand by a Columbia University psychology professor named Helen Schucman by a process she identified as "inner dictation," and she consistently refused to take credit for its message or ideas. The prose itself is expressed in a first-person voice clearly identified with Jesus Christ, offering a major revision of some fundamental principles of modern Christianity. Not surprisingly, the mysterious nature of this authoritative voice has sparked much discussion and controversy over the real authorship of ACIM. Schucman worked for seven years in secret with her supervisor at Columbia, William Thetford, to complete the recording and transcription of the Course, but only spoke about it once in public before her death in 1981. Thetford also declined to become a spokesman for ACIM before he passed away in 1988.

While not the basis of a "religion" in the usual sense, ACIM has at least several million students and countless study groups devoted to it, and hundreds if not thousands of self-appointed teachers. It has strongly influenced a wide array of thinkers, writers, activists, and business leaders, including Marianne Williamson, Oprah Winfrey, Wayne Dyer, and John Mackey, the cofounder of the Whole Foods supermarket chain. Its influence was central to the founding of such research and service organizations as the Institute of Noetic Sciences and the Attitudinal Healing Centers (also known as CorStone).

Although often identified as a centerpiece of the so-called New Age, ACIM actually contradicts key elements of New Age thinking and has deeper philosophical similarities to eastern Vedantism, western Gnosticism, the eighteenth-century "immaterialism" of philosopher George Berkeley, and modern transpersonal psychology. While it frequently uses Christian terms such as *God*, *the Father*, *the Son*, and *the Holy Spirit*, the message of ACIM often contradicts conventional Christianity, which has led to vehement criticism of the teaching in conservative Protestant and Catholic circles.

In practical terms, the Course is designed to serve as a self-study handbook of personal transformation. It provides both a comprehensive theory and a demanding daily practice of surrendering ordinary perceptions, conventional thinking, and comforting beliefs in favor of living by the moment-by-moment wisdom of an instinctive goodness. The Course calls that active wisdom the Holy Spirit, and suggests that anyone can learn to be constantly guided by the Holy Spirit through the means of forgiveness. What the Course means by "forgiveness" goes well beyond popular usage of the term—but more about that later.

A Different Take on Love

In the broadest sense, *A Course in Miracles* is a teaching of love, but its aim is not to persuade more people to "believe" in love. Plenty of people believe in love already while continuing to suffer loneliness, bewilderment, or desperation as they seek for the great healing force that always seems to disappoint or elude them. By contrast, ACIM calls love our "natural inheritance," and aims to displace everything within the student's mind that gets in the way of recognizing that inheritance. As a recurring motif of the Course Workbook asserts, *"God is but love and therefore so am I."*

What's in our minds that's getting in the way of the love that is really our nature? It's not primarily hate or selfishness, as one might expect. According to ACIM, those negative energies are only the symptoms of what's actually in the way: *our fundamental beliefs that the everyday world around us is real, that we all live and die in separate bodies with individual minds, and that time and space limit our existence.* Those beliefs seem like common sense to almost everyone.

The Course asserts that such beliefs are not only mistaken, but in fact constitute madness.

To know what love is—and to live by its truth rather than merely believe in it—we must gradually surrender the root beliefs that feed our collective insanity. In other words, we must learn to see ourselves and relate to each other as spiritual rather than physical beings. The Course asserts that we live in our minds, not our bodies, and even the conviction that you have a mind separate from everyone else's is an illusion. Where other spiritual paths may urge the "surrender" of our individual egos, the Course suggests that you need not surrender or fight against something that doesn't exist to begin with. You need only recognize that your ego, like the body it calls its home, is a profound delusion.

As the Introduction to the ACIM Text summarizes, *"Nothing real can be threatened. Nothing unreal exists. Herein lies the peace of God."* Translation: What is real about us cannot be endangered. Since everything that is physical is threatened by decay or death, that means the entire material world is *unreal* and therefore does not exist. Understanding this is the key to recognizing our spiritual reality—that is, *we are love itself, and nothing else.* This realization eventually brings us real and permanent peace in the midst of the shifting, chaotic illusions of the everyday material world.

As radical as this diagnosis and prescription may sound, they're not new ideas. Both Hinduism and Buddhism have long suggested that our most profound goal as human beings is to "wake up" to a higher order of reality than the web of illusion in which we are habitually snared. But *A Course in Miracles* has an uncanny way of bringing this kind of teaching home for the modern seeker. It's much more than an intellectual philosophy to be pondered and discussed, then set aside while we deal with the everyday challenges and opportunities of the so-called real world. ACIM is intended to serve as an uncompromising guide to *a new way of life* based on a profoundly different grasp of reality. Over time, the Course delivers startling experiences of psychological challenge, spiritual insight, and healing in relationships. And it does so without requiring students to join a religion or move to a monastery, ashram, or lonely cave.

This doesn't mean that ACIM exactly meshes with a modern lifestyle. It's not easy to accept that you're crazy, or to submit to a demanding "mind training" that aims to overturn all your ordinary perceptions. As I'll be commenting later in this book, even the most devoted Course students find themselves needing to take a break from the discipline from time to time (even for months or years). There is also a tendency to space out on the teaching, which has contributed to popular misperceptions of ACIM students as brainwashed cultists. As most veteran students will attest, the Course can be exceptionally difficult to comprehend, even after years of study and practice. That's because it's focused less on intellectual education than on a genuine transformation of the human mind and heart. And transformation is often a sloppy, unpredictable, and emotionally riotous process.

The Purpose of This Book

The aim of this book is to help Course students at any level of experience, including beginners, negotiate some of the teaching's mysteries, hairpin turns, and ego-dropping challenges with a bit more ease than they might otherwise. With a quarter-century of ACIM study behind me, I don't claim to have a perfect or even advanced understanding. But I have worked through some of the early misconceptions and thorny developmental stages that often confuse newer students. I have written and spoken for many years about the Course with the combined perspective of a journalist and a student, and I've coached students privately. I've also interviewed leading teachers and hundreds of other students, as well as scholarly observers and critics of ACIM.

Much of that work is summarized in my previous book, *Understanding A Course in Miracles: The History, Message, and Legacy of a Spiritual Path for Today* (Celestial Arts/Random House). Readers can refer to that book for a more detailed history and critical commentary on ACIM than I will present in this volume. This book is a "how-to" guide with just enough history and background to introduce the Course to newcomers, while providing some novel perspectives and insights to veteran students.

To tell the truth, I often have the feeling that no one currently alive understands the Course entirely. That's why I cut a lot of slack for myself, and for other students who may not seem to be "getting it" in the same way I am. The Course is clearly not for everyone, and even those who gravitate to it as a lifelong path are pointed toward an understanding of life, self-awareness, and the cosmos that may well take several more generations of students to reach maturity. ACIM has only been with us for thirty-odd years now, which means it's in its infancy as a spiritual path. Given that novelty, it's remarkable that the Course already has millions of students worldwide and exerts as much cultural influence as it does.

The apparent purpose of a "course in miracles" surfacing in our times is to familiarize a growing number of people with a deeply healing perspective on their lives. Just as a foreign language curriculum gradually makes us familiar with a vocabulary and a culture that may at first seem exotic and impenetrable, this spiritual curriculum intends to make us conversant in a new, surpassing language and culture of love. When we can naturally speak that language and act reflexively on the basis of love, then we will be living in an entirely different world, even if it is unimaginable from our current point of view. If this book helps even a few students grasp the Course as a new kind of common sense, then all my years of study, periodic bewilderment, and occasional breakthroughs will have been doubly worthwhile.

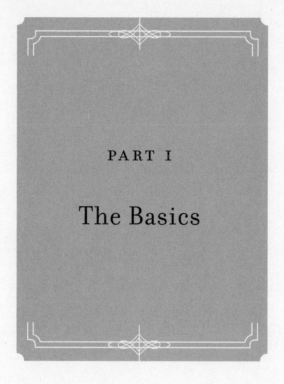

PART I

The Basics

1.

What Is *A Course in Miracles*?

Think not that happiness is ever found by following a road away from it. This makes no sense, and cannot be the way. . . . If this be difficult to understand, then is this course impossible to learn. But only then. For otherwise, it is a simple teaching in the obvious.

—*Chapter 31, IV: 7*

In the winter of 1985, I was very ill and dispirited. In early August I'd fallen prey to something that felt like the flu, but had only gotten worse as the weeks stretched into months. Exhausted, constantly sick to my stomach, and sleeping for up to sixteen hours a day without feeling rested, I had been diagnosed with a brand-new malady called "chronic fatigue syndrome," for which there was no specific treatment. Some doctors believed it wasn't even a genuine disease. But I was certainly sick, and this vague diagnosis was all I had to go on.

Desperate for a cure and not finding one in conventional medicine, I had turned to psychology and spirituality, topics I hadn't paid much attention to since my days in college over ten years earlier. As part of this exploration of the inner life, I began studying a strange book called *A Course in Miracles* (ACIM), which I'd found in a bookshop across the street from my doctor's office. Initially put off by its religious language and metaphysical propositions, I was unexpectedly drawn into daily study of its dense Text and peculiar Workbook of 365 meditation lessons. Fearing for my sanity as well as my health, I hadn't told anyone that I was studying the Course. I was trusting myself to catch on if the book proved to be dangerous, and in fact I was beginning to worry about its effect on my subconscious. In the six or seven weeks since I had begun my study, my dreams had grown increasingly powerful and sometimes disturbing.

One night I dreamed that I was driving an old white van owned by my father, the same one in which I had awkwardly learned to drive a stick shift as a teenager. In the dream, the beat-up truck was lurching and steering poorly; on top of that, I was driving into a dense fog that obscured everything in front of me. As I struggled to find my way forward, I realized that I had a passenger in the other seat, none other than former president Jimmy Carter. Now, on top of my frustration with driving, I had to deal with the embarrassment of having an important guest whom I respected highly, and whose safety was in my hapless hands.

Finally, too anxious to keep driving, I braked harshly to a stop and apologized to my passenger for the rough ride. "On top of that, Mr. President," I added sheepishly, "I have no idea where I'm going."

President Carter smiled graciously and said, "Don't worry," as he opened the glove compartment and reached inside. "I have a map right here." He handed me my blue softcover edition of *A Course in Miracles*, and at that point I awoke.

After this dream I felt better about the safety of ACIM as my guide through a perilous stage of life; it seemed that my unconscious had given me an "okay" signal. A couple weeks later, I was discussing with my therapist possible new avenues for our sessions. I'd felt for a while that I had been doing a lot of talking without gaining any sense of direction from the "talking cure" of psychotherapy. He asked what I might want to do differently, and I confessed my involvement with the Course. I was half-expecting a warning about getting involved in cultish belief systems. Instead he smiled and said, "If you can handle the Course, you probably don't need me."

In fact, I soon quit therapy and thereafter relied on the Course as my central guidance in negotiating the daunting journey of my illness, which would last about seven years. Having talked to many other people with chronic fatigue syndrome, I am convinced that my struggle would have lasted much longer by any other route.

For me, then, *A Course in Miracles* was at first an unexpected form of *intervention* at a time when my deeply ingrained habits of anger and pessimism had contributed to an overall collapse of my immune system. The Course first helped me to realize how and why I had become ill, which in my case had to do with a profound and unrecognized resentment that had been sapping my energy. Thereafter, ACIM gave me explicit and unrelenting instruction in an advanced form of forgiveness that would prove key to my healing. While the effects could be called miraculous over the long term, there were many times when I continued to suspect the value of the teaching. And I often resisted the discipline that the Course conveyed—all while I continued to study voluntarily, egged on by a powerful instinct that felt both new and strangely ancient.

As I would learn from researching the history of the Course, I was not the first person to relate to ACIM in such a conflicted way. That distinction belonged to the brilliant and troubled woman who spent seven years writing it down, only to proclaim, near the end of her days, "I know the Course is true, but I don't believe it."[1]

---

1. From Robert Skutch, *Journey Without Distance* (Berkeley: Celestial Arts, 1984).

Where the Course Came From

The year 1965 was a time of intense ferment in the cultural consciousness of the Western world. Martin Luther King, Jr., began leading protest marches in Selma, Alabama, as the Voting Rights Act became law. In the United Kingdom, a British band known as the Beatles was overtaking the pop music charts, and the miniskirt was launched in Chelsea by Mary Quant. U.S. forces began carpet-bombing North Vietnam in the operation known as Rolling Thunder, while the first American combat troops landed in Da Nang. In San Francisco, the *Chronicle* reported the rise of the hippie movement in the Haight-Ashbury section of the city. A rogue Harvard professor named Timothy Leary coined the subversive suggestion "Tune in, turn on, and drop out" and poet Allen Ginsberg floated "flower power" as a slogan for America's growing counterculture.

Meanwhile, a private exchange between two academics at Columbia University in New York City would seed a mystical process, the significance of which would unfold over the next several decades. In the fall of the year, the head of the psychology department of the Columbia–Presbyterian Medical Center, a laconic forty-two-year-old professor named Bill Thetford, invited his acerbic assistant Helen Schucman, then fifty-six, into his office. He wanted to discuss the deteriorating relations between themselves and with the rest of the department, all awash in petty bickering and competition. Later admitting that his words felt mawkish at the time, Thetford told Schucman that he felt "there must be another way" to manage the academic workload they faced. Usually inclined to disagree with her boss, Schucman instead felt moved to cooperate.

Their agreement did result in some improvement in departmental operations, although Schucman and Thetford would never really learn to get along. They would cooperate without fail, however, on a mystical undertaking that was about to get under way. On the evening of October 21, not long after their discussion about departmental politics, Schucman heard a voice in her head say, *"This is a course in miracles. Please take notes."* Prone to mystical experiences since she was a child, Schucman had heard this voice before and even accepted guidance from it, but she had never received a specific instruction like this. Afraid that she might be losing her mind, she anxiously called Thetford and asked him what she should do. He calmly suggested that she take notes as directed, and they would look over the notes the next morning to see if they made any sense.

Schucman did take down some initial notes, which proved to be the start of a seven-year "inner dictation" that would ultimately result in the published twelve-hundred-page teaching known as *A Course in Miracles*. It comprises a massive Text that lays out the fundamental philosophy, a Workbook of 365 daily lessons, and a relatively short Manual for Teachers. Schucman and Thetford kept the recording and editing of their massive manuscript mostly secret until it was complete, believing along the way that the Course was only an elaborate answer to their private, mutual quest for "another way." But as they gingerly shared the completed project with friends and confidants, the pressure for publication began growing.

Released in a three-volume hardcover edition in 1975, ACIM is currently available as a single volume in both hardcover and paperback, and has two million copies in print in twenty languages around the world. No longer under copyright, the Course is available in several editions from various publishers. The Standard Edition, the only one approved for publication by Schucman and Thetford, is still distributed by the original publisher, the Foundation for Inner Peace. (See Appendix: Recommended Resources for Further Course Study.)

A New Vision of Christianity?

Perhaps the most controversial element of the Course is its authorship. Although Helen Schucman wrote it down with the support and editorial assistance of Bill Thetford, neither of them ever claimed to be the source of its ideas. In the text of the Course, there are unmistakable first-person references to the author as Jesus Christ. "If the Apostles had not felt guilty," says the Text in Chapter 6, "they never could have quoted me as saying 'I come not to bring peace but a sword.' This is clearly the opposite of everything I taught." There are many other passages where Jesus claims to be speaking, often flatly contradicting the Bible and offering substantially new definitions of such standard Christian terminology as the Father, the Son, and the Holy Spirit.

There have been widely varying interpretations of these claims of authorship. Many students believe that the historical Jesus Christ somehow "channeled" a new vision of Christianity through Helen Schucman's mind. Others are more comfortable with Bill Thetford's opinion that Schucman accessed a high-level "Christ consciousness"—potentially available to everyone—that she felt compelled to articulate. I have even met avid ACIM students who believe that Schucman was a brilliant schizophrenic who originated the Course herself, but unconsciously disguised its authorship because she was afraid of her own message.

Regardless of how one views the source of the Course, its import remains clear: *A Course in Miracles* is a radical and sophisticated revision of Christian theology, joined to an experiential discipline of constant forgiveness designed to produce deep personal change. As this book will explain in coming chapters, the Course's concept of forgiveness goes far beyond the conventional understanding, ultimately challenging the student's fundamental grasp of reality. When we forgive someone, we are not dismissing his or her failures, flaws, or insults; instead we are letting go of our own beliefs about that person and ourselves. The ultimate aim of forgiveness as taught by ACIM is to let go of what we believe about the world in general—or as Workbook Lesson 132 suggests, to "loose the world from all I thought it was." By progressively letting go of the world as we're used to seeing it, we become "teachers of God"—the kind of people who perform miracles on a regular basis.

What Is a Miracle?

However, it's important to understand that the Course definition of a "miracle" is also different from the conventional understanding. This can be a stumbling block for new students, who may expect ACIM to be a guidebook to performing physical healing, experiencing visions, or solving the big problems of their lives instantaneously. As northern California student Scott Schnurman told me, "Originally I had thought that the word *miracles* related to psychic experiences and a path to financial abundance." Over time and with concentrated study, which involved going through the Workbook of daily lessons twice, Scott came to understand that ACIM is instead "a path to retraining one's mind to know God and to experience God's peace . . . a program that is teaching me peace, joy, simplicity, and compassion."

In that regard, the Course is both less and more than what it might seem to be at first. It is not, in a New Age sense, a guide to remaking the world into a brighter, happier place where all human beings live in peace and everyone's desires are fulfilled. In countless passages in both the Text and Workbook, the Course adamantly declares that the everyday material world is not real and that trying to change it to bring about physical healing, personal happiness, or global justice is only attempting to make adjustments to an illusion. "Seek not to change the world," ACIM advises in Chapter 21 of the Text, "but choose to change your mind about the world." And Workbook Lesson 128 directs the student to meditate upon the thought, "The world I see holds nothing that I want."

If a miracle is not a physical transformation of our everyday circumstances, then what is it? Although the Course offers many definitions of the miracle, one of its key qualities is a "shift in perception" that transforms one's way of *looking* at the world. If you are reflecting on the past with bitterness, the Course urges you to accept that "the past can touch me not" and that only the present moment matters. If you look on someone else as an opponent or victimizer, you are encouraged to see him or her instead as the key to your peace and happiness. If you feel lonely and abandoned, you are reminded that you are the source of love yourself, always united to everyone at the level of mind.

Finally, if you fear death, the Course suggests not that this life will be followed by an eternal life in heaven, but instead that you have *always* had eternal life—yet you have mistaken the time-bound, worldly trap of physical incarnation and decline for your real existence. Your real existence is in a totally abstract, infinite, and timeless realm of spirit, and you are there now, in fact. But you are tragically distracted from knowing your true self, and experiencing total happiness, by your false and temporary ego-identification as an individual human being.

If taken seriously, all these shifts of perception are quite profound and utterly contradictory to our everyday experience in the world. They confront our common sense, to say the least. So the "miracles" that the Course teaches about are not primarily intended to heal the sick or alter other worldly circumstances, although such changes are entirely possible. Instead, miracles are the means by which we begin waking from the dream that ACIM says we are caught in: "All your time is spent in dreaming. Your sleeping and your waking dreams have different forms, and that is all. Their content is the same" (Chapter 18, II: 5).

From Religion to "Mind Training"

Because *A Course in Miracles* uses many religious terms and ideas, it is natural to assume that it's meant to serve as the basis of a new religion. In fact, there are a handful of small churches using the Course as their gospel and training and certifying "ministers" in its name. Yet two of the largest and most influential teaching centers, the Foundation for A Course in Miracles in southern California and the Circle of Atonement in Arizona, treat the Course instead as an esoteric curriculum. Even in well-established

Course churches like the Community Miracles Center in San Francisco, California, the figures of Jesus Christ and God are not "worshipped" in the traditional way. Instead they are studied and celebrated as models for enlightenment that anyone can emulate.

In Course groups of every kind, both God and Christ are seen as powerful *ideas* that students are aspiring to make paramount in their consciousness and the everyday conduct of their lives. Since the Course redefines all forms of sin as "errors" that can be corrected through a new way of thinking, the ideas of sinfulness, guilt, and redemption associated with so many religious traditions are retranslated in Course study.

For instance, ACIM speaks often of "Atonement," by which it does not mean the expiation of sin. Instead, the Atonement is a realization that the student is "at one" with all other human beings, and with God, at the level of mind. Rather than convincing anyone else of the correctness of any religious ideals, the goal of Course study is always to "accept the Atonement" for oneself. Thus, atonement is not an act of contrition, but acceptance of the idea that "I am one Self, united with my Creator" (Lesson 95).

All these radical ideas add up to what the Course describes as a "mind training." The aim is not to indoctrinate students with a new or different set of religious beliefs, but to change the way their minds habitually work. That would mean responding to everyday challenges with a consistently forgiving demeanor, instead of the more common responses of fear, anger, or vengeance. Lesson 34 exemplifies the ACIM style of mind training when it suggests that the student can learn to regard any difficulty with the attitude "I could see peace instead of this."

Thus the Course can be seen as a provocative handbook for personal transformation based on a fundamental process of forgiveness, but not a catechism for religious behavior or moral correctness. The Course doesn't provide commandments, prescribe rituals, or forbid any behaviors, and it has nothing to say about such hot-button issues as abortion, homosexuality, extramarital sex, or any left- or right-wing politics. Although some prominent Course popularizers like Marianne Williamson make no secret of their personal politics, the Course itself cannot really be politicized, as it is difficult to make a solid case for improving a world that doesn't really exist. On the other hand, one shouldn't mistake the Course as strictly a form of "personal spirituality" that has no effect beyond oneself. For as one of the fifty "miracle principles" that open the Text suggests, a miracle "may touch many people you have not even met, and produce undreamed-of changes in situations of which you are not even aware."

A Guide to Transforming Relationships

Although *A Course in Miracles* is generally referred to as a "self-study" discipline because it is entirely contained within a three-part book that anyone can study without supervision, it's important to understand that you are unlikely to learn from the Course entirely on your own. First of all, virtually every student sooner or later looks for a study group or teacher for help in understanding ACIM, as well as consulting guides written by a host of authors in the field. Many people have made the Course the focus of their lives, becoming dedicated teachers and students and spending a lot of their time with like-minded people. The worldwide Course "community" is diverse and difficult to characterize, but there is nonetheless a sense of recognition and belonging that arises among people who have taken on this challenging discipline over the long term.

More to the point, this discipline that begins with privately reading a book ends up being about relating to other people. Forgiveness is always relational; even though the process may begin with a silent meditation or prayer, the effects of forgiving are eventually experienced in relationships. One studies the Course by reading the Text and following the Workbook lessons as directed and that work can be done alone or in a group. ACIM itself does not prescribe how one should undertake or continue study, except to say that each student will increasingly receive guidance from the "internal teacher" known as the Holy Spirit. But the *effects* of study will eventually arise within the student's relationships, and often in unexpected ways.

When I began studying ACIM, I rapidly became aware of how angry I was at my parents, who lived three thousand miles away. We had limited contact and thus I did not tell them about my involvement with the Course for many months. But I was applying many of the Course lessons with them in mind, particularly Lesson 21, "I am determined to see things differently."

The next time I saw my parents, when they came to California out of concern for my health, I found them unexpectedly different: more open and responsive, more honest about their difficulties and limitations. I was stunned at the degree of their seemingly sudden changes, and at first I did not connect this transformation to my "solo" forgiveness work. When I did begin to sense the connection and how it worked, I became aware that a substantial part of the change that had occurred had to do with how I was looking at my parents. In fact, I couldn't be sure who had actually changed more, myself or them. Regardless, this change proved to be one of the first important turning points in the cure of my illness.

This was also one of my first lessons in the working of a Course-style miracle. The point was not that all my problems were suddenly solved or things were going exactly the way I wanted, but that a key relationship had taken a significant step toward healing. And that healing was proceeding in a different way, and to a more significant degree, than I would have ever managed to plan or execute on my own. As ACIM suggests, "Miracles are habits, and should be involuntary. They should not be under conscious control. Consciously selected miracles can be misguided" (Chapter 1, I: 5).

The miracle with my parents seemed to have come about simply because I took on the intention and discipline of perceiving an important aspect of my life differently. I was responsible for initiating the process of change, but I was not in charge of exactly where it went or what happened as a result; in a very real sense, that result was "involuntary." Who was in charge of the change? An intelligence that seemed to be both within me and far beyond my personal resources was in charge of the change. For lack of a better identification, I had to assume that intelligence was what the Course identifies as the Holy Spirit.

Meeting Your Internal Teacher

One of the most startling theological departures of the Course is the idea that God did not create the world we see, and in fact has no concern for it because it's a perceptual illusion we made up ourselves. While there are frequent references to a loving, all-creative God who does love us and wishes us only perfect happiness, he is in fact unaware that we have fallen asleep and drifted into a dream ruled by time, matter, and death. God cannot act in a world that doesn't exist, so he does not directly intervene in human affairs or earthly events. (For anyone who has ever wondered how there could be any love or logic behind such massively fatal "acts of God" as earthquakes, tsunamis, and hurricanes, this radical cosmology may evoke a shock of recognition.)

Within our troubled dream, we are at least dimly aware that something has gone terribly wrong. We seem to be trapped in a realm where beauty is always countered by horror and happiness is known only in contrast to grief and suffering. No matter what we believe or how we conduct our lives, we are all condemned to die. On top of that, we secretly blame ourselves for our predicament. In fact, we feel guilty for abandoning the limitless reality of God and fear his punishment. This is the Course's explanation for the conventionally religious ideas of a strict, judgmental, and even vengeful God:

> For this world is the symbol of punishment, and all the laws that seem to govern it are the laws of death. Children are born into it through pain and in pain. Their growth is attended by suffering, and they learn of sorrow and separation and death. Their minds seem to be trapped in their brain, and its powers to decline if their bodies are hurt. They seem to love, yet they desert and are deserted. They appear to lose what they love, perhaps the most insane belief of all. And their bodies wither and gasp and are laid in the ground, and are no more. Not one of them but has thought that God is cruel.

If this were the real world, God *would* be cruel. (Chapter 13, Introduction: 2–3)

All of which is utter nonsense, says ACIM, for in fact we have never separated from God—nor from our ultimate reality in spirit—and could not possibly do so. Thus there is no reason for us to suffer death or any other kind of punishment. But we continue to believe in our dream of being separated from our Creator, and this belief literally makes the material and often painful world we see. We would truly be lost, without any hope of recognizing truth or finding happiness, were it not for a part of our minds that reminds us of our home.

That home is not "heaven" in the Christian sense, nor any place within the physical universe, but rather an awareness of belonging to an infinite and eternal consciousness. The "reminding" part of our mind is what the Course calls the Holy Spirit: a kind of ambassador from God who translates God's infinite and essentially *impersonal* love into personal terms of care and specific guidance that we can comprehend. One might also say that the Holy Spirit is our own loving memory of our divine reality beyond time and space. By constantly forgiving the illusory world we see all around us, we remember more and more of what's true and real. In one of the more lyrical passages of the Text, occurring in Chapter 21, the Course describes this memory in metaphorical terms as an "ancient song":

Listen,—perhaps you catch a hint of an ancient state not quite forgotten; dim, perhaps, and yet not altogether unfamiliar, like a song whose name is long forgotten, and the circumstances in which you heard completely unremembered. Not the whole song has stayed with you, but just a little wisp of melody, attached not to a person or a place or anything particular. But you remember, from just this little part, how lovely was the song, how wonderful the setting where you heard it, and how you loved those who were there and listened with you.

The notes are nothing. Yet you have kept them with you, not for themselves, but as a soft reminder of what would make you weep if you remembered how dear it was to you. You could remember, yet you are afraid, believing you would lose the world you learned since then. And yet you know that nothing in the world you learned is half so dear as this. Listen, and see if you remember an ancient song you knew so long ago and held more dear than any melody you taught yourself to cherish since. (Chapter 21, I: 6–7)

The Preface to the Course refers to the Holy Spirit as an "Internal Teacher," which may clarify its role. While the Holy Spirit of ACIM bears some resemblance to the same figure in the Holy Trinity of Christianity, it does not perform the theological duties ascribed to it in Catholic or Protestant traditions, and it does not enable "speaking in tongues" or other unusual abilities ascribed to it by Pentecostals. In the simplest terms, the Holy Spirit of the Course might best be understood as an "awakened conscience"— not just an internal sense of right and wrong, but an instinctive guide to thinking, acting, and relating based on love instead of fear.

According to ACIM, the choice to hear and follow the Holy Spirit is always available to us, and so is the choice to live in fear. Fear is literally the default mode of humanity; automatically and consistently choosing fear is what keeps our self-awareness trapped in the body with a nearly constant foreboding of death.

But the more we can learn to listen to the guidance of the Holy Spirit and choose love, the less we will feel trapped by our apparent incarnation and the more we will sense ourselves as timeless, limitless, and sinless. That doesn't necessarily mean we will appear to others as "enlightened" or otherwise special; in fact, the difference in our presence may be quite subtle:

> There is a way of living in the world that is not here, although it seems to be. You do not change appearance, though you smile more frequently. Your forehead is serene; your eyes are quiet. And the ones who walk the world as you do recognize their own. Yet those who have not yet perceived the way will recognize you also, and believe that you are like them, as you were before. (From Lesson 155)

Undoing the Ego

Besides offering a contrarian theology and a challenging guide to personal transformation, *A Course in Miracles* provides a radical analysis of the human ego that is perhaps unsurpassed in modern literature. Both Helen Schucman and Bill Thetford were clinical psychologists of considerable training and accomplishment, and their background is everywhere present in the psychological passages of the Course. Schucman herself often said that the form of ACIM was very much her own, while she almost completely dissociated herself from its message. One has to wonder how different the Course might have sounded were it not scribed by a psychologist. The fact that it was resulted in a profound and startling study of the human psyche, well-suited to a post-Freudian era in which a spiritualized or "transpersonal" psychology would arise.

For all its loving encouragement about our potential to realize our universal consciousness, the Course is unrelentingly harsh about our normally egocentric condition, in which we experience ourselves as separate from that consciousness:

> The ingeniousness of the ego to preserve itself is enormous, but it stems from the very power of the mind the ego denies. . . . The ego draws upon the one source that is totally inimical to its existence *for* its existence. Fearful of perceiving the power of this source, it is forced to depreciate it. This threatens its own existence, a state which it finds intolerable. Remaining logical but still insane, the ego resolves this completely insane dilemma in a completely insane way. It does not perceive *its* existence as threatened by projecting the threat onto *you*, and perceiving your being as nonexistent. This ensures its continuance if you side with it, by guaranteeing that you will not know your own safety. (Chapter 7, VI: 3)

In passages such as this, the Course makes it clear that its view of the human psyche departs significantly from the Freudian structure of id, ego, and superego, in which the ego represents a battleground of relentless struggle between the uncivilized urges of the id and the moral oversight of the superego. (In fact the terms *id* and *superego* never appear in ACIM.) Rather, the Course consistently speaks to "you" (the student) as an intelligent being who always has a choice between fear (the consistent if chaotic counsel of the ego) and love (the unwavering message of the Holy Spirit). The point of daily mind training as outlined by the Course

Workbook is not to overpower the ego, but gradually displace it through new habits of mind and heart. As Chapter 30 explains in a section entitled "Rules for Decision":

> Decisions are continuous. You do not always know when you are making them. But with a little practice with the ones you recognize, a set begins to form which sees you through the rest. It is not wise to let yourself become preoccupied with every step you take. The proper set, adopted consciously each time you wake, will put you well ahead. And if you find resistance strong and dedication weak, you are not ready. *Do not fight yourself.* But think about the kind of day you want, and tell yourself there is a way in which this very day can happen just like that. Then try again to have the day you want. (Chapter 30, I: 1)

Summary

There is no simple answer to the question, "What is *A Course in Miracles?*" ACIM offers a thoroughgoing revision of Christian theology, but is not a religion in itself; it provides a map for personal transformation, but does not offer a program for changing or saving the world. It issues a complete denial of the everyday reality we all experience, but also urges that we forgive that reality instead of hating it or sinking into nihilistic despair. The Course comprises one of the most exacting and critical analyses of ego psychology ever recorded, but proposes a spiritual rather than psychoanalytic or therapeutic solution for all the problems of egocentricity. Finally, the Course is a healing prescription for the human condition in the form of a "mind training" that aims to replace our fear-driven habits of thinking, feeling, and behaving with instinctive responses of love in action.

And for many who encounter it and become dedicated students, *A Course in Miracles* is what it was for this writer: an unexpected intervention in the course of a life that isn't working too well. Like addicts who can't break free of drinking, smoking, or abusive relationships, many people find themselves in the grip of an unproductive mindset that seems impossible to release even though its negative effects are perfectly clear. As the next chapter will illustrate, the Course tends to show up in people's lives when they are ready, at some level, to confront their unproductive mindset—even if it's the last thing they expect to do.

2.

How (and Why)
to Start the Course

This is a course in miracles. It is a required course. Only the time you take it is voluntary. Free will does not mean that you can establish the curriculum. It means only that you can elect what you want to take at a given time . . .

—*From the Introduction to ACIM*

In twenty-plus years of interviewing ACIM students, I've heard two people report that they discovered the Course when it fell off a towering stack of books in a used-book store and hit them on the head. With two million copies circulating worldwide since the original publication date of 1975, perhaps the odds of this kind of initiation occurring twice are not so improbable. The chances improve when you consider that there has probably been a substantial number of Course books abandoned by frustrated readers who either gave up on understanding the teaching or became too angry with it to continue.

Ironically, many of those same readers likely took up the Course again; the stories of how people began their study are often linked to stories about how they started over, months or even years later. A student once complained to me that he was "probably making the Foundation for Inner Peace rich" by buying seven copies over his years of on-and-off studying. He certainly wasn't the first person to attempt to escape from the teaching. Helen Schucman, the Course scribe, can be heard on a rare audiotaped interview admitting that "no matter what I did, I couldn't get rid of this course. And believe me, I tried."[1] In fact, Schucman once tossed the working manuscript into the trash at Columbia University, leading to a frenzied rummaging through the nearest dumpsters by her and Bill Thetford the next morning. They found the work, and Schucman apparently did not try to dispose of it again.

Such tales of attempted rejection may seem paradoxical for a teaching that is beloved by most of its followers, occasionally to the point of fanatical attachment. I know a student who devised a "total immersion" method of study, wearing headphones all day and night to listen to the audio version of the Course while keeping his printed copy, bulging with scores of paper clips attached to the pages, always by his side. While there are no doubt countless people who have briefly encountered and quickly discounted the Course without having an emotional reaction, it does inspire powerful feelings for those who engage with it over the long term. Perhaps that's because getting seriously started with *A Course in Miracles* is not unlike getting hit on the head.

Discovering a "Universal Experience"

"Nothing I see in this room (on this street, from this window, in this place) means anything." So says Lesson 1 of the Course

---

1. From "Rare Interview with Helen Schucman," a DVD available from the Foundation for Inner Peace, www.acim.org.

Workbook of 365 daily lessons, inaugurating at least one year of confrontational, revelatory, and potentially life-altering meditations. The early lessons all have to do with alerting novice students to their psychological projections ("I have given everything I see . . . all the meaning it has for me"; "I see only the past") and shortly move on to raising the possibility that there is an entirely different way of seeing ("Above all else I want to see differently"; "God is in everything I see"). Thus the Course wastes no time in providing a shock to the psychic system of most students, as it attempts to dislodge their established habits of perception and prepare their minds for a different way of seeing.

For me, however, one of the most significant instructions comes just before the lessons begin, in the introduction to the Workbook:

> Some of the ideas the workbook presents you will find hard to believe, and others may seem to be quite startling. This does not matter. You are merely asked to apply the ideas as you are directed to do. You are not asked to judge them at all. You are asked only to use them. It is their use that will give them meaning to you, and will show you that they are true.
>
> Remember only this; you need not believe the ideas, you need not accept them, and you need not even welcome them. Some of them you may actively resist. None of this will matter, or decrease their efficacy. But do not allow yourself to make exceptions in applying the ideas the workbook contains, and whatever your reactions to the ideas may be, use them. Nothing more than that is required. (Workbook, Introduction: 8–9)

By suggesting that the student "need not believe the ideas" put forth in the Workbook because using them "will show you that they are true," the Course distinguishes itself from conventional religious systems that threaten damnation or disfavor if certain key ideas are not accepted as beliefs. Instead, ACIM relies on the student's own direct experience to verify the ideas it puts forth, acknowledging that some of those ideas may initially incur the student's disagreement or resistance.

Although the Course speaks only of spiritual matters, this approach is essentially an application of the scientific method to the exploration of one's own consciousness. Each Workbook lesson can be seen as a hypothesis which the student is instructed to test in his or her own experience, regardless of any prior belief, prejudices, or the seeming unlikelihood that the hypothesis is true. The confirmation or failure of these hypotheses will be assessed by each student through such direct testing, for as long as each one decides to continue study.

Since there is no single, authoritative institution enforcing this spiritual discipline, no requirements for undertaking it, and no punishment for not finishing it, ACIM appears to be an entirely voluntary experiment in transforming one's own consciousness. Elsewhere the Course refers to itself as only one form of a universal curriculum, suggesting that there are many other legitimate forms, each of them designed to "save time" for the particular students attracted to them. As the Clarification of Terms in the Teacher's Manual of ACIM explains, "A universal theology is impossible, but a universal experience is not only possible but necessary. It is this experience toward which the course is directed."

For beginners, then, the most important thing to understand about *A Course in Miracles* is that its aim is not to change one's religion or indoctrinate anyone with a particular or exclusive set of beliefs. (In fact, I know of Course students who continue to practice an established religion while also studying ACIM; I have also met agnostic and atheist students.) Instead, the dense Text and didactic Workbook are both directed toward inducing a particular kind of experience—or, more precisely, a series of evolving experiences—that change one's consciousness at a deeper level than that of "believing."

This experience may not always seem profound at first. For me, the typical "Course experience" often starts with a subtle shift in my habitual point of view that gradually unfolds and deepens in the following days, months, and years. Not long after starting the Course, I was driving through the streets of my hometown of Berkeley, California, thinking about nothing in particular, when it suddenly occurred to me that the road I was driving on was only a few inches thick. That may sound like a common-sense perception. But to me it was revelatory, because I next realized that my "mental map" of the urban surroundings was imbued with a false permanence. Until that moment, I had unconsciously assumed that the road was an eternal and unchanging feature of the landscape, as if it extended to the core of the earth and couldn't possibly be altered. The same went for the buildings, the sidewalks, even the trees lining the streets.

Intellectually, I knew that roads get repaved, buildings are eventually demolished or rebuilt, and trees grow larger, die off, or get cut down. But that moment of recognizing how thin the roadway was immediately led to the realization that I had an emotional *attachment* to seeing the immediate physical world as solid and unchangeable. In Course terms, I had given a meaning of permanence to things that actually didn't have that quality. Since I had assigned that meaning to everything I saw around me, the realization of impermanence rapidly began repeating and reverberating.

Before long, this realization was taking on a new and even more challenging resonance. I soon became aware that I had many prejudices, resentments, and suspicions that had long seemed just as inevitable and immutable as the "eternal asphalt" in my mental map of the town. If the physical environment was temporary and subject to change, then so were many more of my fixed convictions about myself, other people, and the world in general.

As disconcerting as this internal shift was at times, there was also an encouraging sensation of release and relief involved with it. Lesson 6 of the Workbook directs the student to consider that "I am upset because I see something that is not there." If the world you see every day seems harsh or cruel, and also seems fixed with no hope of change, then it can be an enormous relief to entertain a lighter point of view. Of course, anyone's view of the world can lighten or darken in accordance with passing moods. But ACIM points its students toward an entirely new perception of reality on a permanent basis, by training them to question their habitual way of seeing. This is the inception of the "universal experience" that the Course says we are all destined to have, regardless of the particular curriculum that brings us to it. For anyone who encounters *A Course in Miracles*, the salient question is whether it's the right curriculum for them.

The Last Alternative

Although it's impossible to describe a "typical" student of the Course, a common theme among many students is their discovery of ACIM as the culmination of a long search for personal salvation. "Even as a child I seemed to feel things more acutely than many," says writer Susan Dugan of Colorado, "and I'd tried everything—including traditional therapy, psychic healing, yoga, various forms of meditation, and Zen Buddhism—in my quest for peace and happiness. All offered temporary relief. But the gnawing sense of loneliness, the despair and self-loathing that had me constantly second-guessing every choice I made, magnifying every perceived failure, and blaming others for my problems would not subside. I needed help but didn't know where to turn. So I started to pray to some vague, benevolent force I sensed on good days and hoped to hell I had not invented. I offered the only prayer I really believed in: *help me, help me, help me.* In a synchronistic series of events, *A Course in Miracles* appeared as my answer."

Three elements of Susan's story echo the reports of many people who have come to the Course:

- a heightened sensitivity that contributes to an acute psychological crisis of will and self-worth;
- a dissatisfaction with previous religious paths or healing methods; and
- a prayerful surrender that leads to an unexpected encounter with the teaching.

This surrender can be especially dramatic because the dissatisfaction with previous religions or therapeutic techniques has often led people to a kind of world-weariness, or a suspicion of any perspective that promises salvation or healing. As a rule, potential Course students are neither naïve nor inexperienced by the time they encounter the teaching—and it's safe to say that many of them are a bit jaded.

My surrender came after I had been ill with chronic fatigue

syndrome for several months and had exhausted every medical approach I could afford, to no effect. Increasingly unable to work, I had spent some of my dwindling money on a weekend at a therapeutic hot springs, hoping for a salutary detoxification from a mud bath. Instead, the treatment made me feel deathly ill, and I spent a long afternoon and evening in bed with the room completely darkened, trying to get through a terrifying migraine headache without calling for emergency medical help. No one knew where I was, and my sensation of isolation and defeat was complete. At age thirty-two, I felt that my life had come to a dead stop and that my prospects for the future were bleak, to say the least.

Ambivalent about the idea of God and totally skeptical of prayer, I found myself waking from a fitful nap in that dark room and saying out loud, "I give up. I will make no further decisions by myself. I give my life to you." I had no idea of who the "you" I was speaking to might be. Like Susan Dugan, I was hoping there was some kind of "vague, benevolent force" to which I was surrendering, something more substantial and effective than my own wishful thinking. Although I would feel a little silly about the surrender by the next morning when I awoke and felt functional again, the moment itself was utterly sincere and a deeper acknowledgment of my own sense of inadequacy than I had ever admitted before.

Within a week, I would read a description of *A Course in Miracles* that piqued my interest. At the time, however, ACIM was available only in a hardcover edition for forty dollars, which aroused my suspicion. Not long after, I dropped into a small metaphysical bookshop across the street from my physician's office, where the owner was stocking two shelves of the first paperback edition of ACIM. This edition had just been released, and was half the price of the hardcover. I was struck by how quickly and conveniently my initial reservation about ACIM was dissolved, and I bought my first copy.

This was the first of many synchronistic "pushes" I would receive as a Course student; thankfully it was a softer introduction than getting hit on the head by a falling book. But the Course's strange language and outrageous propositions were difficult to take at first, and I don't know that I would have stuck with it had it not been for the powerful sensation that it was my last alternative for a cure to my illness. My life situation was precarious, and thus I was open to an exceptional approach for putting it right.

"Tolerance for pain may be high, but it is not without limit," the Course suggests. "Eventually everyone begins to recognize, however dimly, that there *must* be a better way. As this recognition becomes more firmly established, it becomes a turning point. This ultimately reawakens spiritual vision, simultaneously weakening the investment in physical sight. The alternating investment in the two levels of perception is usually experienced as conflict, which can become very acute. But the outcome is as certain as God" (Chapter 2, III: 3).

How the Course Finds Its Students

Although the Course has been widely available in the United States for more than thirty years and nineteen translations have carried its presence worldwide, it has never shown up on national best-seller lists or become a household term. Sales peaked at about 75,000 copies annually during the mid-1990s when Course popularizer Marianne Williamson, author of *A Return to Love* and a number of subsequent books on spirituality and progressive politics, was frequently in the news. ACIM has experienced other increases in public notice after books by such writers as Jerry Jampolsky, Wayne Dyer, and Gary Renard made mention of it. But the original publisher, the nonprofit Foundation for Inner Peace, has never pursued direct advertising or conventional public relations for the book, preferring to let it spread by the same word-of-mouth popularity that initially sparked the formal publication of the original manuscript.

From 1996 to 2001 the Course was licensed to a major publishing house with extensive national distribution and did briefly receive more conventional exposure in the bookstore market. I remember visiting a chain bookstore where a number of copies of the new edition of ACIM were featured in a large display near the front of the store and watching people encounter it for the first time. Without exception, the five or six customers who picked up the dark blue, unassuming volume during the twenty minutes I was watching all opened it with a curious squint, read a page or so at random with either a frown or a look of increasing puzzlement on their faces, then replaced the book on its stand and moved on. I knew then that the Course was never going to fly off bookstore shelves as a result of direct marketing.

In fact, when you have heard many stories of how people began their Course study, a very different picture of how ACIM gets around begins to emerge: it seems to find its most likely readers, rather than the other way around. Unlike self-help books that promise step-by-step assistance with such common issues as finding love, losing weight, or building self-esteem, the Course does not immediately offer solutions for the most popular problems of human beings. If you flip the book open to the Text Introduction to get a clue to the book's offerings, you learn only that the Course can be summed up "very simply" by these statements: *"Nothing real can be threatened. Nothing unreal exists. Herein lies the peace of God."*

Since this assertion immediately makes sense to almost no one, it's a wonder that the book finds any readers who will stick with it over the next few pages, much less all twelve hundred of them. After many years of my own study and countless discussions with other students and teachers, it's my conclusion that the initial appeal of ACIM is largely unconscious. The abstruse and often challenging language of the teaching connects not with the everyday, egocentric self looking for quick solutions to everyday problems, but to a deeper part of the psyche that might properly be called the soul. This aspect of our self-awareness instinctively seeks wholeness and communion, long-term objectives that don't necessarily jibe with the more ordinary goals of the ego.

The deep-seated and challenging appeal of ACIM may explain one of the most curious phenomena associated with its study, the fact that some students don't become seriously engaged soon after they've acquired the book. "I bought it and it sat on my bookshelf for at least a year," admits student Toni Neal, "until one day I made a decision just to read it through from cover to cover to get the gist of it. It was love at first read! Not that I got that much out of it at the time, but there were a number of 'ahas!' and an inner knowing that this was true."

I have also heard countless stories of students who began reading the Text or following the Workbook Lessons as soon as they acquired the book, only to become so bewildered or disturbed that they put the Course away for a very long time—sometimes ten years or more. Often for no particular reason that they are aware of, these students eventually take their dusty ACIM off the shelf, read a few passages, and suddenly recognize a theme or lesson that appeals to them. Others are brought back to study by other books that simplify or summarize ACIM's main themes. In every case, there seems to be a sensation of "readiness" that readers must feel before they can become seriously and continuously engaged with the discipline.

For some, readiness may be immediate. Perhaps because I had reached a precarious state of ego-surrender just before I encountered the Course, my engagement with it was intense from the start. Even though I paused a few times in my study, sometimes uncertain of whether I would finish, I did get through the Text, Workbook, and Manual for Teachers in about eighteen months. In retrospect, that seems like an almost dizzying pace; I have rarely heard of students completing ACIM for the first time in a year. Almost without exception, those who do complete it return for more Text reading and Workbook practice, generally for many years. I have been a student for twenty-five years, and though I never went through the entire book from beginning to end again, I have probably reread different portions of it enough times to constitute three or four completions. I also use Workbook lessons on a random basis, usually starting the day with one that comes to my mind unbidden. After many years of intensive involvement, the Course has become a touchstone of my self-awareness.

Despite the fact that I write about *A Course in Miracles* and coach students on understanding it, I seldom explicitly recommend it to anyone who is not already familiar with it. My writing has been focused on making sure that accurate information about ACIM is available to the public, rather than overtly promoting it. In fact, very few ACIM teachers or organizations have been evangelical, and those that have been are generally regarded as aberrations from the mainstream of Course studies.

Most veteran students and teachers came to the teaching gradually, often overcoming significant personal skepticism in the process of accepting a teaching that is far outside the cultural mainstream. The Course is just too difficult and demanding to fit into a simplistic sales pitch, although there is no doubt that some aspects of it have been distorted or oversimplified in order to sell workshops with some kind of New Age or self-help focus.

Books that achieve a popular following without extensive advertising are generally believed to spread by "word of mouth," a description that fits the Course, albeit in a peculiar way. I have seldom heard people saying they undertook the teaching because one friend directly recommended it; more often students recall hearing something about the Course from a number of people before they became curious enough to look into it themselves.

In a very real sense, it seems that *A Course in Miracles* simply shows up in people's lives when they are ready for it. And it's impossible to say how many people have been influenced by a brief or partial encounter, reading some of the Text or trying a few of the Workbook lessons before moving on. Despite its orderly presentation as a complete curriculum ending with a concise "Manual for Teachers," the Course offers no hard-and-fast rules about how—or even where—a new student should begin his or her study.

Text, Workbook, or Manual?

In fact, it is only near the end of the Course's three volumes, in the concluding section of the Manual for Teachers entitled "As for the Rest," that ACIM suggests "in some cases, it may be helpful for the pupil to read the manual first. Others might do better to begin with the workbook. Still others may need to start at the more abstract level of the text. . . . The curriculum is highly individualized, and all aspects are under the Holy Spirit's particular care and guidance. Ask and He will answer."

One might wonder why this kind of advice, however unspecific, is not offered near the beginning rather than the end of this long and complex teaching. I think the answer to that lies in the assertion that all aspects of the curriculum are "under the Holy Spirit's particular care and guidance." From the Course point of view, we are always privy to the guidance of the Holy Spirit whether we know it or not, and we have encountered ACIM only because we have already heard its direction at some level of our self-awareness. From this perspective, coming upon the Course is no accident; it is the version of the "universal curriculum" that we have been directed to find.

There can also be no mistake in how we begin or continue our study, even if we lapse or permanently discontinue it. The point of studying the Course is not to become a lifelong devotee of the book itself, but to gain a more ready and reflexive access to the Holy Spirit, which might also be called our better nature. As we become more attuned to that higher voice of instinctive wisdom, our study will become easier and our lives less troubled. Thus, starting or following the Course "correctly" is simply a matter of remembering to ask for guidance at every opportunity and trusting that guidance is active in our study and our lives overall even if we are not always aware of it.

When I look back on my own history with ACIM, I believe that I opened myself to spiritual guidance in the "surrender" experience described earlier and that guidance led me to discover and begin the Course even though I did not immediately make the connection. For whatever reason, it seemed obvious to me to begin following the Workbook and reading the Text simultaneously, which I did in a very intense fashion for at least the first six months of my study. Some of this concentration owed to my circumstances at the time; I was quite ill and usually at home, capable of doing little more than reading and studying during my sporadic waking hours. Prone to extended stretches of "nonrefreshing" sleep (a primary symptom of chronic fatigue syndrome), I often awoke to an extended borderline state of awareness, in which the difference between the conscious and unconscious was not so clearly drawn as it would have been otherwise. This provided me with an unprecedented opportunity to integrate the Course at a level deeper than mere intellect.

However, part of the brilliance of *A Course in Miracles* is the way in which it affects different levels of any student's consciousness, sometimes confusing the purely conscious, intellectual aspect in order to penetrate to greater depths. How it achieves this has a lot to do with the remarkable prose style of the work, which is at turns analytical, lyrical, stern, and profoundly loving. The next chapter will contemplate the mysterious interplay between the language used by the scribe, Helen Schucman, and the underlying message that she steadfastly insisted was not her own.

Summary

Although *A Course in Miracles* comprises an explicit and challenging discipline for the transformation of consciousness, there are no specific guidelines for how it is to be undertaken, and no institution that administers or enforces its self-contained curriculum.

Many readers begin reading the Course only to put it aside for a while, sometimes for years. Although the sequential structure of the philosophical Text, experiential Workbook of daily meditations, and brief Manual for Teachers implicitly suggests an order of study, the Manual allows that students may choose different starting points according to their own intuition. The Course does not offer immediate rewards for study and may in fact appear impenetrable to those who chance upon it. The reasons that people take it up seem to have to do with an unconscious calling toward deeper and longer-term goals than the typical egocentric rewards of most "self-help" techniques.

And unlike conventional religious teachings, *A Course in Miracles* is not focused on inculcating a certain set of beliefs within its followers. Rather, it aims to generate a "universal experience" that it claims is both necessary and inevitable for the progress of human consciousness toward wholeness, communion, and peace. When a potential student is ready for ACIM's particular approach to that experience, then the teaching will appear. Whether the student completes the Course in an efficient manner—or repeatedly stops and restarts for years to come—is up to the guidance of the Holy Spirit, or "internal teacher" that is always within human consciousness. To begin the Course is to start learning how to hear that voice of wisdom more clearly and consistently.

3.

Getting Through the Language

God does not understand words, for they were made by separated minds to keep them in the illusion of separation. Words can be helpful, particularly for the beginner, in helping concentration and facilitating the exclusion, or at least the control, of extraneous thoughts. Let us not forget, however, that words are but symbols of symbols. They are thus twice removed from reality.

These words from Section 21 of ACIM's Manual for Teachers indicate the fundamental challenge of understanding the dense and sometimes disorienting language of the Course. They also explain the impossibility of "literally" interpreting this teaching—or the Bible or any written document for that matter. For words can only *symbolize*, that is, provide a verbal sign or emblem that makes us think of a particular thing, person, concept, or situation. Exactly what we think of next—and especially what we think *about* it—will be an individualized reaction, based on our unique upbringing, social and cultural influences, and personal prejudices.

Another way to put it is that words are the labels we place on our ideas, so that ideas can be shared with some confidence that we are talking about the same things. But when the Course uses the phrase "symbols of symbols," it is suggesting that whatever a word points our attention toward is an idea as well—and that includes human beings:

> You do not find it difficult to believe that when another calls on God for love, your call remains as strong. Nor do you think that when God answers him, your hope of answer is diminished. On the contrary, you are more inclined to regard his success as witness to the possibility of yours. That is because you recognize, however dimly, that God is an idea, and so your faith in Him is strengthened by sharing. What you find difficult to accept is the fact that, like your Father, *you* are an idea. And like Him, you can give yourself completely, wholly without loss and only with gain. Herein lies peace, for here there *is* no conflict. (Chapter 15, VI: 4)

In this brief passage, *A Course in Miracles* asserts a startling proposition as "fact": that not only is God just an idea within our minds, but *we* are only ideas as well. Each of us believes that he or she is a separate, physical being with an individual consciousness. But from ACIM's point of view, our individuality is only a *symbol* of the separation that we fervently believe in, a separation that has actually never occurred. As the text following Workbook Lesson 161 teaches:

> One brother is all brothers. Every mind contains all minds, for every mind is one. Such is the truth. Yet do these thoughts make clear the meaning of creation? Do these words bring perfect clarity with them to you? What can they seem to be but empty sounds; pretty, perhaps, correct in sentiment, yet fundamentally not understood nor understandable. The mind that taught itself to think specifically can no longer grasp abstraction in the sense that it is all-encompassing. We need to see a little, that we learn a lot.

In such passages, one begins to sense the transcendent authority of *A Course in Miracles*. It seems to be speaking to the reader from a vantage point high above the human perspective—not just proposing a radically different view of reality, but also providing a disciplined approach to changing how our minds work. To achieve all this, the Course uses a complex literary form that can be both bewildering and entrancing, sometimes simultaneously. That form is the product of the teaching's very human scribe, even though she never claimed credit for the message. Understanding the difference between the form and the message of ACIM is key to making use of it in a practical manner.

Where Did the Words Come From?

When new readers of the Course learn that its self-identified author is Jesus Christ, they react with varying degrees of scorn, ambivalence, or acceptance. Those who do accept the idea of this extraordinary authorship sometimes conclude that the teaching's transmission via Helen Schucman must have been perfect—e.g., that she heard and wrote it down word for word from Jesus, just as it appears in the standard published version. But that is not how the Course came to be. The real story is a fascinating study in the interplay of mystical inspiration and human creativity.

Although it's generally reported that Helen Schucman heard a "voice" that dictated the Course, she struggled to clarify exactly what that meant in a 1976 audiotaped interview: "I call it a voice, but a 'voice' has sounds . . . And I didn't hear anything. I think it's the sort of hearing that you can't really describe. . . . I think 'knew' may be a better word than 'heard.'" Schucman was sure about one thing, however: "It wasn't my voice. It couldn't have been because it talked about a whole area with which I am entirely unfamiliar."[1]

"Jesus does not speak words," explains Kenneth Wapnick, Ph.D., in a lengthy article about the editing of *A Course in Miracles* that appears in the online Archives of the Foundation for Inner Peace, the Course publisher.[2] Wapnick worked directly with Helen Schucman on the last round of editing that was done to the original Course manuscript; previous rounds had been done by Schucman herself under the guidance of the dictating Voice, with assistance from Bill Thetford. It should also be remembered that Schucman wrote down the original "dictation" that she heard in her mind in a personalized form of shorthand, which she then read aloud to Thetford, who typed it up as she translated her own notes aloud.

Thus, there was never an occurrence of automatic writing or any form of direct word-to-word transmission of the Course. In fact, the first five chapters of the Text underwent significant changes before being published in FIP's standard edition of ACIM. (Those chapters revealed an ongoing dialogue that Schucman had with her inner voice, frequently involving personal issues of herself and her helper Bill Thetford, before the Text settled into the consistent monologue that characterizes the rest of ACIM.)[3]

In the essay referenced above, Wapnick delineates some of the major characteristics that mark the form and structure of the Course as products of Helen Schucman's mind, including the fact that its original language is English with an American idiom. For instance, in the text following Lesson 76 ("I am under no laws

---

1. From "Rare Interview with Helen Schucman," a DVD available from the Foundation for Inner Peace, www.acim.org.
2. See http://acim-archives.org/Publishing/editing_history.html.
3. *Ibid.*

but God's"), the Course says "You really think that you would starve unless you have stacks of green paper strips and piles of metal discs"—an obvious reference to the American greenback form of currency. Wapnick also points out that the curricular form of ACIM—an explanatory Text, lesson-driven Workbook, and Manual for Teachers—fits the logical format that a professional educator like Helen Schucman would likely prefer.

Additionally, Schucman was a lover of Shakespeare, and substantial portions of the Course adhere to the Shakespearean rhythm of iambic pentameter (that is, five "iambic feet" in a single line; an iambic foot is a pair of syllables, the second of which is stressed or emphasized when spoken aloud). Consider, for instance, this paragraph of text following Lesson 107, which can be broken into perfectly metered lines of verse:

When truth has come it does not stay a while, to disappear or change to something else. It does not shift and alter in its form, nor come and go and go and come again. It stays exactly as it always was, to be depended on in every need, and trusted with a perfect trust in all the seeming difficulties and the doubts that the appearances the world presents engender. They will merely blow away, when truth corrects the errors in your mind.

When truth has come it does not stay a while,
to disappear or change to something else.
It does not shift and alter in its form,
nor come and go and go and come again.
It stays exactly as it always was,
to be depended on in every need,
and trusted with a perfect trust in all

the seeming difficulties and the doubts
that the appearances the world presents
engender. They will merely blow away,
when truth corrects the errors in your mind."

The fact that roughly one-fourth of the Text (Chapters 24–31) and two-thirds of the Workbook (Lessons 98–365) adhere to this rhythm make the Course a remarkable literary accomplishment in itself, especially considering that the prose began taking shape this way before Schucman and Thetford were aware of it. Thus, this rhythm must have been unconsciously rooted, for as Wapnick notes, Schucman normally "wrote in an almost Spartan style, appropriate for scientific writing, in contrast to the more poetic and grammatically loose sentence structure one finds in the *Course*, which incidentally used to drive Helen up a wall."

Thus, *A Course in Miracles* comprises over twelve hundred pages of intense and often poetic instruction in a psychospiritual philosophy that its human recorder largely disavowed, even as the structure of the document drew on major aspects of her training and literary predilections. Yet its style was perhaps not under her control any more than its content, which she clearly found vexatious: "I think the thing that I found upsetting about it was that it went against everything I believe."[4]

Although the "channeling" of divine inspiration is an unusual and questionable phenomenon, what Helen Schucman described as an "inner dictation" is not essentially different from the creative inspiration experienced by writers and artists of all kinds. Many writers can attest to the inspired feeling of being "in the flow"

---

4. From "Rare Interview" DVD.

and having words form effortlessly in their mind. If such fortunate periods of creative flow last long enough, they can result in lengthy works that the human author may be amazed by upon their completion, wondering if he or she was really the source of the material. The eighteenth-century visionary poet William Blake, for instance, reported that he wrote his longest epic poem, "Jerusalem," from an inner dictation, rapidly setting down twenty or thirty lines at a time without planning or premeditation.

What's unusual about *A Course in Miracles* is that not only did its recorder deny being the source of its message, she felt mostly at odds with it during and after its transmission. In her unpublished autobiography, Schucman wrote that she found herself in the position of "not believing in my own life's work, a situation that was clearly ridiculous as well as painful."[5] The Urtext, or unedited transcript of Schucman's original notes for ACIM, includes actual arguments that she had with the author, all of which were edited out for the standard published version.[6] But here and there one can still hear echoes of Schucman's dogged resistance to the message that she faithfully recorded even as her ego—"the teacher who could not possibly give you what you want"—fought against it:

> You may insist that the Holy Spirit does not answer you, but it might be wiser to consider the kind of questioner you are. You do not ask only for what you want. This is because you are afraid you might receive it, and you would. That is why you persist in asking

---

5. From an eighty-page version of Helen Schucman's unpublished autobiography in my possession.

6. For commentary on the Urtext and other early versions of ACIM, see Richard Smoley's report "A Comparison of Miracles" appearing in *Understanding A Course in Miracles* by D. Patrick Miller (Berkeley: Celestial Arts/Random House, 2008).

the teacher who could not possibly give you what you want. Of him you can never learn what it is, and this gives you the illusion of safety. Yet you cannot be safe *from* truth, but only *in* truth. Reality is the only safety. Your will is your salvation because it is the same as God's. The separation is nothing more than the belief that it is different. (Chapter 9, I: 7)

In sum, it's important to understand that the language of *A Course in Miracles* is not a holy writ that students should regard as perfect or infallible because its source is presumably divine. Rather, the Course represents the translation of a profound and timeless message into the language of a twentieth-century academic whose resistance to the teaching she transcribed resulted in a paradoxical purity. The more one studies ACIM and its history, the more it becomes clear that its message was flavored by Schucman and her editorial helpers, but its source was beyond their ken. If that source was indeed Jesus Christ, one can safely say that he's not exactly the same savior one may have learned about in Sunday school.

Meeting a New Father, Son, and Holy Spirit

For most new students, the chief barrier presented by the language of the Course is its religious terminology, especially *God* (or *the Father*), *the Son*, and *the Holy Spirit*. Traditional Christians come to the Course with prior assumptions about what all these terms mean, generally that they refer to the three divine "persons" who variously judge, forgive, and offer guidance to a fallen and sinful humanity. People from agnostic, Jewish, or other religious perspectives are often put off by these names, assuming that the Course is just a thinly disguised rewrite of the Bible. But the more one reads of ACIM, the more it becomes clear that it makes dramatic departures from biblical philosophy, beginning with substantially new identities for the principals of the Holy Trinity.

As suggested earlier, the Course view of God as an "idea" instead of a divine person is radically different from what most people are accustomed to. Rather than an all-powerful being who rules the universe from a faraway perch in heaven, dispensing love, justice, or punishment as he sees fit, the God of the Course is an omnipresent, creative consciousness that is immanent in all things, yet is obscured by our choice to see those "things" rather than the energetic reality behind them. Lesson 29 suggests that "God is in everything I see" and then directs the student to apply this idea to everything in one's immediate environment, such as:

God is in this coat hanger.
God is in this magazine.
God is in this finger.
God is in this lamp.
God is in that body.
God is in that door.
God is in that waste basket.

"You will probably find this idea very difficult to grasp at this point," comments the text accompanying Lesson 29. "You may find it silly, irreverent, senseless, funny and even objectionable. Certainly God is not in a table, for example, as you see it. Yet we emphasized yesterday that a table shares the purpose of the universe. And what shares the purpose of the universe shares the purpose of its Creator."

That is not to say that God actually created tables, wastebaskets, doors, and bodies. To the contrary, the Course asserts that the entire physical world is of our making—or more correctly, the world *seems to exist* only as a vast and insane error of our perception. For "God made it not," declares the text following Lesson 152. "Of this you can be sure. What can He know of the ephemeral, the sinful and the guilty, the afraid, the suffering and lonely, and the mind that lives within a body that must die? You but accuse Him of insanity, to think He made a world where such things seem to have reality. He is not mad. Yet only madness makes a world like this."

To know the God of the Course, then, it is not necessary to follow the Ten Commandments, pray five times a day, perform rites of atonement, or otherwise curry favor with a Creator who is always watching us and, like Santa Claus, keeping a list of who's been naughty or nice. Rather, we have to pierce the veil of illusion that we have draped over God's real creation:

> Sit quietly and look upon the world you see, and tell yourself: "The real world is not like this. It has no buildings and there are no streets where people walk alone and separate. There are no stores where people buy an endless list of things they do not need. It is not lit with artificial light, and night comes not upon it. There is no day that brightens and grows dim. There is no loss. Nothing is there but shines, and shines forever." (Chapter 13, VII: 1)

What "shines forever" is what the Course identifies as our true reality; it is essentially the same as God, and it is where we are right now, even though everything in our experience tells us something quite different. At this point, one can easily see why words can only fail to encompass what the Course means by "God"; words describe specifics, and the God of the Course is an absolute and infinite abstraction.

"Ego illusions are quite specific," explains ACIM, "although the mind is naturally abstract. Part of the mind becomes concrete, however, when it splits. The concrete part believes in the ego, because the ego depends on the concrete. The ego is the part of the mind that believes your existence is defined by separation" (Chapter 4, VII: 2).

Does that mean, then, that we are hopelessly exiled from God by our own delusions of separateness? In a section of the Manual for Teachers entitled "Can God Be Reached Directly?" the answer is given in no uncertain terms: "God indeed can be reached directly, for there is no distance between Him and His Son. His awareness is in everyone's memory, and His Word is written on everyone's heart. Yet this awareness and this memory can arise across the threshold of recognition only where all barriers to truth have been removed" (Manual, 26).

In the Course, the key to removing the barriers to truth is forgiveness of the world we see around us. As we learn to forgive, we become more and more attuned to the moment-by-moment guidance of the Holy Spirit, which can be seen as a kind of liaison or personalized connection between the fractured consciousness of our distracted, ego-driven selves and the limitless abstraction of God. In the Clarification of Terms, a glossary in essay form that ends the Manual for Teachers, the Holy Spirit is defined this way:

The Holy Spirit is described as the remaining Communication Link between God and His separated Sons. In order to fulfill this special function the Holy Spirit has assumed a dual function. He knows because He is part of God; He perceives because He was sent to save humanity. He is the great correction principle; the bringer of true perception, the inherent power of the vision of Christ. He is the light in which the forgiven world is perceived; in which the face of Christ alone is seen. He never forgets the Creator or His creation. He never forgets the Son of God. He never forgets you. And He brings the Love of your Father to you in an eternal shining that will never be obliterated because God has put it there.

The Holy Spirit abides in the part of your mind that is part of the Christ Mind. He represents your Self and your Creator, Who are One. He speaks for God and also for you, being joined with Both. And therefore it is He Who proves Them One. He seems to be a Voice, for in that form He speaks God's Word to you. He seems to be a Guide through a far country, for you need that form of help. He seems to be whatever meets the needs you think you have. But He is not deceived when you perceive your self entrapped in needs you do not have. It is from these He would deliver you. It is from these that He would make you safe. (Clarification, 6-C, 6: 4)

The latter part of this passage provides an important clue to the nature of the Holy Spirit, which may seem to be "whatever meets the needs you think you have" while actually steering us away from our false needs. This is not a distinction easily grasped by novice Course students, and one could make the argument that learning to hear the Holy Spirit's advice is truly a lifelong discipline. It is a very common temptation, for instance, to think that the Holy Spirit will guide us toward material prosperity, romance, or better health because we so often think that we desperately need these things.

Instead, the Holy Spirit exists within our minds as a reminder of the transcendent reality of God, which is far beyond all the material and temporal conditions of life on earth as we currently perceive it. Our one real need is to wake up and recognize that reality, not necessarily to become more comfortable with our daily illusion in the meantime. On the other hand, we are not called upon to suffer in the name of waking up. The Course makes it clear that any struggle we endure is of our own making, and is neither ordained by God nor required for salvation.

With experience, one learns that becoming more attuned to the Holy Spirit's guidance *does* make one's life go more smoothly, but not because we are magically guided to get the material things or conditions of life that we want. Instead, by constantly forgiving the conditions of our illusory existence as individual, embodied persons, we become more loving and powerful regardless of our circumstances, gradually slipping our material bonds to claim more and more of our authenticity in spirit. What we think we need on a daily basis then becomes less important as our minds gradually recognize who we really are: *"God is but love, and therefore so am I."*

Relating to Our Elder Brother

While Helen Schucman was never comfortable with a public acknowledgment of the invisible source of the Course, referring to it in her unpublished autobiography only as the "Voice," there are a number of unmistakable self-identifications in the ACIM Text itself, including these three remarkable passages:

> If the Apostles had not felt guilty, they never could have quoted me as saying, "I come not to bring peace but a sword." This is clearly the opposite of everything I taught. Nor could they have described my reactions to Judas as they did, if they had really understood me. I could not have said, "Betrayest thou the Son of man with a kiss?" unless I believed in betrayal. . . .
>
> As you read the teachings of the Apostles, remember that I told them myself that there was much they would understand later, because they were not wholly ready to follow me at the time. (Chapter 6, I: 15, 16)

> Your resurrection is your reawakening. I am the model for rebirth, but rebirth itself is merely the dawning on your mind of what is already in it. God placed it there Himself, and so it is true forever. I believed in it, and therefore accepted it as true for me. Help me to teach it to our brothers in the name of the Kingdom of God, but first believe that it is true for you, or you will teach amiss. My brothers slept during the so-called agony in the garden, but I could not be angry with them because I knew I could not *be* abandoned. . . .
>
> I elected, for your sake and mine, to demonstrate that the most outrageous assault, as judged by the ego, does not matter. As the world judges these things, but not as God knows them, I was betrayed, abandoned, beaten, torn, and finally killed. It was clear that this was only because of the projection of others onto me, since I had not harmed anyone and had healed many. (Chapter 6, I: 7, 9)

. . .

"No man cometh unto the Father but by me" does not mean that I am in any way separate or different from you except in time, and time does not really exist. The statement is more meaningful in terms of a vertical rather than a horizontal axis. You stand below me and I stand below God. In the process of "rising up," I am higher because without me the distance between God and man would be too great for you to encompass. I bridge the distance as an elder brother to you on the one hand, and as a Son of God on the other. (Chapter 1, II: 4)

The last passage refers to one of the most significant differences that the Course has with traditional Christianity: the idea that Jesus Christ is not "in any way separate or different from you except in time." In the Clarification of Terms, this innate equality of Jesus with all humanity (which ACIM often refers to as the "Sonship") is further explained:

The name of *Jesus* is the name of one who was a man but saw the face of Christ in all his brothers and remembered God. So he became identified with *Christ*, a man no longer, but at one with God. The man was an illusion, for he seemed to be a separate being, walking by himself, within a body that appeared to hold his self from Self, as all illusions do. . . .

Is he the Christ? O yes, along with you. His little life on earth was not enough to teach the mighty lesson that he learned for all of you. He will remain with you to lead you from the hell you made to God. (Clarification, 5: 2, 5)

In sum, *A Course in Miracles* refers to "God" as the creative force or intelligence behind all creation; to "Jesus Christ" as a being who was once human like us, but became an eternal part of our collective mind when he saw through the illusion of the material universe; and to the "Holy Spirit" as an intuitive communication link between our seemingly limited minds and the unlimited consciousness of God. As the Voice behind the Course, Christ gives us a written curriculum designed to help us learn how to live by the instinctive guidance of the Holy Spirit, guidance that will be necessary until we have recognized our identity with God.

While the Course does make frequent references to these entities as if they were separate beings, it's important to remember that all three of them are actually *ideas* within our minds. Which of these ideas we refer to or rely upon most in our spiritual growth is a matter of personal (and temporary) preference, for ultimately all these ideas are one. Likewise, our own sense of self is just an idea—an idea that happens to separate us from the awareness that "I am one Self, united with my Creator" (Lesson 95).

ACIM is essentially a guidebook for learning which ideas we want to live by and then training our minds to choose those ideas consistently. We are used to thinking in symbols and specifics, so the Course gives us names and words that we can use as long as we need them. But its explanations are not always crystal clear, and there may be a cunning psychological strategy behind its more challenging uses of language.

A Deliberate Mystification?

New students of the Course can find plenty not to like in its characteristic means of expression, from the radical redefinitions of

Christian terminology to the consistently masculine references. I've met at least a few female students who reported that they would make gender substitutions like "Mother" for "Father" as they read early in their study, until that particular aspect of the language didn't bother them anymore. "I quickly got over my initial resistance to ACIM's gender terms," recalls Australian student Rowan Hagen. "I had already been irritated by the growing use of 'Father-Mother God,' 'Divine Parent,' the clumsy and unpronounceable He-She-ing and S/He-ing of modern Christian liturgies. If we are all Sons, part of the Sonship, what could be more inclusive?"

But a bigger hurdle for most students is that the language of the Course, especially in the thirty-one chapters of the Text, sometimes grows so dense that it can seem incomprehensible. The passage below is typical of the Course's occasional convoluted syntax that challenges understanding:

> Since you believe that you are separate, Heaven presents itself to you as separate, too. Not that it is in truth, but that the link that has been given you to join the truth may reach to you through what you understand. Father and Son and Holy Spirit are as One, as all your brothers join as one in truth. Christ and His Father never have been separate, and Christ abides within your understanding, in the part of you that shares His Father's Will. The Holy Spirit links the other part—the tiny, mad desire to be separate, different and special—to the Christ, to make the oneness clear to what is really one. In this world this is not understood, but can be taught. (Chapter 25, I: 5)

Such prominent Course philosophers as Ken Wapnick have suggested that ACIM may sometimes be confounding on purpose, in

order to defeat our ego-driven minds' attempts to fit the logic of the
Course into our own. Since the Course often states that it is proposing a system of thought that is totally and profoundly opposed to
the ego's, its aim is not really to convince or persuade us of its right-
ness on an intellectual basis. Instead, it is trying to uproot or totally
disorient the ego, which it calls "perfectly logical but clearly insane."
While the Workbook pursues this disorientation by explicit mental
exercises that are generally expressed in a straightforward way, the
Text uses an often challenging prose style that is at turns reassuring,
perplexing, adamant, and maddeningly mysterious.

One of the axioms of so-called brainwashing is the disruption
of a subject's belief system, coupled with a gradual wearing down
of normal ego defenses, in order to bend someone to the agenda of
a different religious or political system, or to the will of a cult leader
or group. *A Course in Miracles* has occasionally been criticized as
a form of brainwashing. Yet as a stand-alone teaching contained
in a book, it lacks a crucial element: the presence of a powerful
personality, coercive group, or restricted environment to force the
teaching on an unwilling or unsuspecting participant. While there
have been a few cults and controversial teachers associated with
ACIM, the overwhelming majority of students encounter it on
their own, and decide to pursue or reject it independently.

One "miracle" of Course study is that so many people of high
intelligence and considerable life experience—often disillusioned
with previous religious affiliations—elect to take on a daunting
spiritual discipline that is not only difficult to decipher on the
page, but also demands years of study to yield its most significant
benefits. For many students, their allegiance is strengthened by
accepting the authority of the self-identified source, Jesus Christ,
as unimpeachable.

Yet the Course itself teaches that each student's ultimate authority must be the Holy Spirit, the "internal teacher" whom we can learn to hear through the consistent practice of forgiveness. The veracity of inner guidance is not always clear-cut, and in fact people can hear voices whose counsel is dangerous or delusory. The next chapter will explore what it means to hear an inner voice of genuine wisdom.

Summary

A key to understanding *A Course in Miracles* is distinguishing between the *form* and *content* of its message. The curricular form, comprising a complicated and often lyrical language, is largely a product of scribe Helen Schucman's professional background and literary leanings, including her love of Shakespeare. While the inner "Voice" of the Course clearly identifies itself as Jesus Christ, that does not mean that the content is to be taken as an infallible scripture or holy writ. The Course itself comments on the symbolic nature of language, noting that words are "twice removed" from reality and thus cannot be taken as literal truth in themselves.

Additionally, the Course uses words to direct its students toward a transcendental experience rather than the acceptance of fixed religious beliefs. Along the way, it radically redefines the traditional holy trinity of Father, Son, and Holy Spirit as profound *ideas* within our consciousness, rather than distinct and divine "persons" as they are seen in traditional Christianity. Jesus Christ is further identified as an "elder brother" to the rest of humanity, which comprises the Son of God (or Sonship), along with him. The Holy Spirit functions as a kind of liaison, or "Communication

Link," between the infinite and abstract intelligence of God and the seemingly separated mind of each human being.

While the traditionally Christian and patriarchal language of the Course presents initial barriers to understanding for many students, those who stick with it over the long term learn to interpret its unusual style and vocabulary for themselves. In fact, getting through the language of the Course may be seen as a first step in getting past the resistance of the ego to tap the wellspring of instinctive spiritual guidance.

4.

Hearing an Inner Voice

If you cannot hear the Voice for God,
it is because you do not choose to listen.

—*Chapter 4, IV: 1*

I had just arrived at a San Francisco ACIM conference in the
year 2000 when I was approached by a couple who recognized
me and asked, "So you're the reporter, right?"

"Yes, I guess I am," I replied tentatively, always a little wary
about what's coming next after someone identifies me as "the
reporter."

"Great!" said the female half of the pair. "We wanted to talk
to you because we think that you, of all people, might understand
what we're thinking."

"All right," I said, intrigued. "I'll try."

"It's this thing about Jesus," she continued, almost breathless.
"We've been Course students for a long time and we think it's
wonderful. It's completely changed our lives. But we just can't buy
this stuff about Jesus being the author. I mean, what seems more
likely to you: that the historical Jesus Christ somehow dictated

this giant book inside Helen Schucman's head, or that Helen herself was this crazy, brilliant woman who made it all up, but just couldn't admit it to herself?"

"Well . . ." I said hesitantly, not sure myself which was the more likely of the two choices as stated.

"Come on," challenged the woman's partner, "the man's been dead for two thousand years!"

Now I couldn't help laughing. "Shh," I responded, "you better watch out with that kind of talk around here. You might get us kicked out."

"Tell me about it," the woman sighed. "We've been asked to leave our study group just for bringing it up."

This exchange illustrated two important points for me. First, it is not necessary to believe in the paranormal authorship of ACIM to benefit from its teaching, and agnostics or even atheists can find their way through its thicket of religious language to a practical understanding. On the other hand, Course students who do believe in the authorship of Jesus Christ can become just as righteous and discriminatory as the followers of any conventional religion. On the whole I've found Course students to be a tolerant bunch over the years, but that's not to say they've all escaped the surlier bonds of human nature.

Ultimately, the aim of the Course teaching is not to bring more followers to the fold of a new and improved Jesus Christ, but rather to awaken an "internal teacher" in each student that always gives reliable spiritual guidance on the spot, in any circumstance, without having to rely on religious rules or commandments. ACIM calls that internal teacher the Holy Spirit; it could just as well be called one's "higher self" or an enlightened conscience. Regardless of what you call it, distinguishing between a genuinely transcendent inner voice of wisdom and the more mundane impulses of the self-serving ego is not a simple matter. Faithfully reading the Course and following its lesson plan is no guarantee of getting God on the line—nor is it a foolproof means of avoiding delusion. To understand what it means to be truly and beneficially guided from within, it's helpful to look first at the reasons so many people seek an authority higher than their own common sense.

Religion as Transcendental Parent?

My lifelong friend Jack Wathey, a career scientist, is writing a book about his hypothesis that some aspects of religion can be understood as a search for a wiser and more reliable parent than the ones who conceived us. He believes that as our childish, unquestioning faith in our progenitors inevitably disintegrates during adolescence (if not before), some people begin an innately rooted search for a belief system, symbol, or embodied religious figure to take their place.

Jack asserts that this search for a new and better parent is biologically driven. He surmises that we have an innate propensity to experience the presence of an unconditionally loving "other being," an expectation arising from a part of the brain concerned with mother-infant bonding immediately after birth. Not everyone will seek out this loving presence, but under certain circumstances, this "search for God" can be triggered in anyone. Nonetheless, from Jack's scientific point of view, it is an essential function of human maturity to recognize that there is no divine or infallible successor to our earthly parents. Thus we must each learn to take full responsibility for our own existence, preferably with a rational, empirical perspective informing our behavior and decisions.

But Jack allows that a belief in God can be largely salutary, even if it is fundamentally mistaken:

> For some people, the loss of loved ones, debilitating disease or the cruelty of others leaves them desperate for a source of comfort, strength and unconditional love. If their God is *only* that—if it does not shackle them to archaic and intolerant dogma, if it does not compel proselytizing and restrict the freedom of others, if it does not denigrate this life in deference to some imagined afterlife—then I see little harm and potentially great benefit in it. Even if their God is only an illusion, as I am convinced it is, it can nonetheless be a highly therapeutic illusion. For some people, it may be the only way they can cope with life.[1]

I think Jack's argument about the origin of the religious search has a lot going for it, particularly when you consider the deeply irrational and often childish behavior of religious devotees of all stripes. Vicious wars have begun with religious strife rooted in little more than a "my God is better than your God" attitude, and it is easy to see this perspective operating in the fundamentalist wings of virtually every major religion.

On the other hand, the highly ethical and selfless motivations that are suggested by the better side of most religions often surpass the practical life lessons taught to children by their parents. If one is looking for an inner comforter and role model, Jesus Christ is arguably a wise and honorable successor to most

---

1. Reprinted by permission of the author from the working manuscript for *Why Does God Seem So Real? A Biological Explanation for the Sense of God's Presence* by John C. Wathey.

parents—depending, of course, on which sources you choose to believe about the real life and significance of that great teacher.

In addition, a purely rational or scientific view of life provides little in the way of moral guidance. The reigning scientific theory of human evolution is Darwinism, whose "survival of the fittest" ethos leaves little room for the higher human values of compassion, community, and cultural progress. Granted, there are many studies suggesting that altruism and cooperation are just as important to human survival as competition, but it is not the role of science to provide moral direction. Instead, that role is to develop and test hypotheses about reality.

With some minor permutations (and against loud protests from the "Intelligent Design" wing of Christian-oriented research), classic Darwinism remains the primary scientific theory of humanity's development. But to believe that the purpose of an individual human life is to serve as a tiny, temporary, and probably insignificant cog in the great machine of natural selection doesn't really tell one much about how to live an ethical or satisfying life.

And while the scientific method is an excellent method for investigating the immediate physical world, producing awesome technological progress as a byproduct, it has also generated more puzzling questions than convincing answers about the universe and the ultimate nature of reality. Witness this basic overview of what comprises the universe from the website of NASA's Goddard Space Flight Center:

Remarkably, it turns out there is five times more material in clusters of galaxies than we would expect from the galaxies and hot gas we can see. Most of the stuff in clusters of galaxies is invisible and, since these are the largest structures in the Universe held together by gravity, scientists then conclude that most of the matter in the entire Universe is invisible. This invisible stuff is called "dark matter." There is currently much ongoing research by scientists attempting to discover exactly what this dark matter is, how much there is, and what effect it may have on the future of the Universe as a whole.[2]

Another way to put it is that a couple hundred years after setting aside the mythos of religion for explanations of the cosmos, science has so far concluded that most of what's out there is invisible, and frankly, we don't know what it is! As quantum physics has made more or less clear over the last century, even what we *can* see is not as cut-and-dried as it appears. There may well be more spatial dimensions than the three we take for granted, although that hypothesis is so counterintuitive as to be virtually incomprehensible to anyone but advanced mathematicians. Even the apparent fundamentals of space and time aren't exactly what they seem—an earthshaking line of thought that has been developing since Einstein advanced his theories of relativity. The leading-edge work in physics increasingly suggests that space and time do not even *exist* as verifiable phenomena independent of our own flawed perceptions—a conclusion echoed by *A Course in Miracles*. (For more on this perspective, see Chapter 7, "Recognizing What's Real—and What Isn't.")

Thus, if conventional religion is not a reliable parental surrogate for those who seek knowledge and guidance through all the mysteries of daily life, science offers even fewer answers. One can be meaningfully engaged in the scientific exploration of life

---

2. See http://imagine.gsfc.nasa.gov/docs/science/know_11/dark_matter.html.

and the universe, but it would be folly to rely upon the scientific method to divulge how we should make critical moral decisions, choose friends and mates, find meaningful work, and so on. Most people either choose a religious or humanistic system of beliefs they can live with, or they just muddle through somehow. But when they least expect it, some people get advice and information from an unexpected source.

Inner Voices Through History

The role of mystical inner voices in religion, philosophy, the arts, science, and even politics has been greater than many people may suspect. Roger Walsh, a veteran Course student and professor of psychiatry and philosophy at the University of California at Irvine, says that "it seems pretty clear that some of the Bible was produced through channeling, as well as part of the Koran. In Judaism there have been scores of mystics who produced works by the process of inner dictation, and in Buddhism, many Indian and Tibetan texts were produced this way. The Greek oracle of Delphi—actually a series of priestesses who supposedly spoke on behalf of the god Apollo—stayed in business for 900 years."

In his book *With the Tongues of Men and Angels*, channeling researcher Arthur Hastings cites such examples as Srinivasa Ramanujan (1887–1920), a major contributor to modern number theory who claimed that he received many of his mathematical concepts from the Indian goddess Namagiri, and Edgar Cayce (1877–1943), the noted modern psychic who became famous for giving over sixteen thousand readings, mostly on health matters, while speaking in a trance state. Hastings also notes that the

modern spiritual community of Findhorn in northern Scotland
was originally inspired by the messages that its founders claimed
to hear from "devas," or angels of the forces of nature.

According to psychiatrist Mitch Liester, who has studied the
psychology of those who hear inner voices, other beneficiaries
of the phenomenon included the mystic Hildegard of Bingen,
the French patriot Joan of Arc, and the early twentieth-century
poet Amy Lowell. Even Sigmund Freud, the scientifically minded
founder of modern psychology, related experiences of an inner
voice: "During the days when I was living alone in a foreign city—
I was a young man at the time—I quite often heard my name suddenly called by an unmistakable and beloved voice." Civil rights
leader Martin Luther King, Jr., reported that an inner voice helped
him stay the course through protests, arrests, and death threats: "In
the midst of lonely days and dreary nights I have heard an inner
voice saying, 'Lo, I will be with you.'"

Inner voices have apparently changed the course of history as
well. During World War II the British prime minister Winston
Churchill was about to get into a car in London during a German
air raid. As he approached the side of the car where he usually sat,
he heard a disembodied voice clearly say "Stop!" As Churchill would
later recount, "It then appeared to me that I was told I was meant to
open the door on the other side and get in and sit there—and that's
what I did." Moments later a bomb exploded near the car, nearly
causing it to turn over. Had Churchill been sitting in his accustomed
place, it certainly would have caused him serious or mortal injury.

But it cannot be concluded from such stories that inner voices
always have humanity's best interests at stake. During World War
I a young soldier was eating dinner with his comrades in a trench
when a disembodied voice commanded him to "get up and go

over there." Without thinking the soldier picked up his tin-can dinner and moved twenty yards away.

"Hardly had I done so," the soldier later wrote, "when a flash and deafening report came from the part of the trench I had just left. A stray shell had burst over the group in which I had been sitting, and every member of it was killed." The soldier—who would rely heavily on the inner voice he called "Providence" throughout his military career—survived to become a major force in twentieth-century history, and the archnemesis of Winston Churchill. His name was Adolf Hitler.[3]

Distinguishing the Value of an Inner Voice

Inner or disembodied voices can be as dangerous as they are convincing. The notorious "Son of Sam" serial killer David Berkowitz heard a demonic voice that told him to murder, and cult leaders from Jim Jones to David Koresh have led their followers into group suicides while claiming to be directed by God. Further, many diagnosed schizophrenics hear seemingly disembodied voices that offer them anything but higher wisdom.

"There's quite a difference between the contents of pathological hallucinations and transcendent voices," explains Mitch Liester. "Delusory voices tend to be very demanding, critical, or judgmental whereas transcendent voices are uplifting, supportive, and encouraging." Liester adds that the states of mind in which the two kinds of voices are heard are also quite different. The sustained reception

---

3. Adapted from M. B. Liester, "Inner Voices: Distinguishing Transcendent and Pathological Characteristics," *Journal of Transpersonal Psychology* 28, 1.

of a transcendent voice tends to occur in "an altered state of consciousness that is profoundly transpersonal. The channeler's sense of identity changes from that of an individual to someone connected with something beyond themselves. There's an altered perception of space and time that differs from hallucinations, in which people lose track of time or are disoriented within time. Hearing transpersonal voices, people transcend time; that is, they still know it's there but they aren't trapped within it."

Finally, delusory voices will tend to have a divisive or negative message, issuing warnings or portents of doom instead of instruction or insight. "Transcendent voices have a unitive nature," comments Liester. "They come from a perspective that sees both sides of paradoxes and integrates them into a larger whole. From the perspective of the divine there is no doom and gloom; a divine voice will guide us past the dualities of life and lift us into a transcendent outlook."

A Course in Miracles doesn't give explicit guidelines about exactly how the beneficial inner voice of the Holy Spirit may manifest, besides suggesting that a state of inner calm and equanimity can be a helpful prerequisite: "Let me be still and listen to the truth" (Lesson 106); "In quiet I receive God's word today" (Lesson 125); "Let every voice but God's be still in me" (Lesson 254). But the actual experiences that Course students have with the reception of an inner voice vary widely and may even change over time, as the following report from student April Walton attests. She had been an on-and-off student of ACIM for a number of years when an unexpected personal crisis abruptly intensified her study:

My husband of eleven years told me he had been seeing other women for several years and was in love with someone else. I had no clue. It was enough to send me into a deep crisis. I decided to go to a canyon near our home and burn the Course because I felt it was all lies. I was distraught, crying, screaming to myself in the canyon and cursing Jesus Christ and the Course. I had my matches lit and was getting ready to torch it when suddenly I heard the Voice that was talked about in the Course. It was more of an impression of a voice than a literal voice, but it was clear, it was gentle, it was real! I could distinguish it from my own self-talk in my head or a voice I might have imagined by its quality of energy. It was not from me.

I spent four hours in that canyon arguing with the Voice. The Voice never argued with me, however; there was just silence. By the end of that time I was exhausted, but the Course had come alive. God was not a belief any longer but real to me. I knew from that day forward I could die anytime and I would die happy because God was real. The state wherein I could hear the Voice lasted for nearly eight months. During that eight months I never mentioned I heard the Voice to anyone except my husband. I wanted to appear normal, but I wasn't. There was little need to sleep (I averaged three hours a night); little need to eat (I lost thirty pounds in thirty days and never felt better); and little need to plan (every morning I asked about my day and was given instructions). In a word, I was sustained by the Love of God. . . .

Every unhealed relationship I had came to me to be healed. I told my husband if he had to leave then so be it, but I could not live a lie. I didn't beg him to stay as I might have earlier, but told him he had to make a decision as to what he wanted to do. He ended up staying for another two years. I knew what I had to do and that was simply to get out of the way, keep my ego at bay and I'd know what to do or say. It was a miracle on a daily basis. The fact that I remained in that state while being a mom and wife for over eight months is extraordinary.

Eventually the Voice became harder to hear and I started to panic. In one of my morning meditations I asked why everything was fading, what had I done wrong? The Voice explained that I'd been given a gift to show me that God was real, and Jesus was real, but now it was my responsibility to get to that state of guidance by my own volition. Shortly thereafter I stopped hearing the Voice clearly. I did feel a bit abandoned at first, but the Course remains my guiding light to this day. I cry and laugh and I'm normal, except that I'm constantly on the lookout for forgiveness, knowing that is the key to my guidance. It's not an easy path, and I still get a good belly laugh when I hear about someone new to the Course wallowing in bliss. . . .

While April's story of hearing or sensing a "Voice" is not uncommon among Course followers, there are also many students like myself who never hear a voice but do begin to experience powerful intuitions, mystical dreams, and peculiar synchronicities soon after beginning their study. Early in my work with ACIM, when I was ill and often experiencing altered mental states of a dreamlike nature, I would experience odd intuitive "pushes" that led me toward healing resources of which I had no conscious knowledge.

For instance, one day when I was barely functioning, I forced myself to go to a grocery store for necessary supplies and upon exiting felt seized by the impulse to walk two extra blocks to a nearby bookstore. This was a significant physical challenge at the time. I had no idea what I was looking for and certainly didn't have the energy to be browsing, but upon entering the store, I walked straight to the psychology bookshelf and picked up a new book by an author unknown to me, Arnold Mindell's *Working with the Dreaming Body*. The book had no direct bearing on my Course study or my health problems, and I could not immediately grasp what it was about from reading the cover. Nonetheless, the impulse to buy it was irresistible. That book would shortly provide a significant turning point in both my psychological and physical healing from chronic fatigue syndrome. In retrospect, it seemed that I had been silently told to go and find it precisely when I needed it the most. But I had no prior conscious knowledge of its existence, and I was not accustomed to such powerful intuitive hunches before undertaking the Course.

Without overmystifying the circumstances, it seems reasonable to assume that my study of ACIM was producing exactly the results it promises: the awakening of a powerful sense of inner guidance, even without the experience of a distinct "voice." But that is not to say that my intuitive sense of guidance has always been that dramatic, and it has certainly not remained consistent over the years. Like everyone, I experience all kinds of hunches and impulses in the course of daily life. Those that can fairly be called "inspired" are not always immediately distinct from those that are mundane, or arise solely from egocentricity.

"People often don't have a clear understanding of the differences between the voice they usually hear and identify with in their minds, and that of an inner wisdom," says DavidPaul Doyle, who with his wife, Candace, authored the book *The Voice for Love: Accessing Your Inner Voice to Fulfill Your Life's Purpose* and taught a Course-inspired approach to accessing spiritual guidance to thousands of people. Echoing Dr. Liester, DavidPaul notes that "The communication most people receive from hearing a divine inner voice is very kind, loving, and accepting. The advice they receive usually involves seeing things from a different perspective, that supports them in bringing more peace, understanding, forgiveness, and harmonious relationships into their lives.

"We teach that there are only two voices, the voice of love and the voice of fear," DavidPaul continues. "The voice of love would include all thoughts, perspectives, and emotions that are expressions of love, such as kindness, compassion, understanding, forgiveness, acceptance, wholeness, and unity. The purpose of this loving voice is to help one become aware of their natural state of being. The voice of fear, on the other hand, has the opposite purpose—to encourage people to experience being what they are not. This fearful voice includes all thoughts, perspectives, and emotions that encourage the delusion of disconnection or separation in some way, including judgment, anger, sadness, jealousy, and loneliness. Then we teach people how to extend love to this voice of fear within them. When they do, those painful thoughts and beliefs melt away and what is left is the voice of love within them."

I asked DavidPaul if one should expect an inner voice to provide guidance only about the big issues in life—should one get married, choose one line of work over another, or change religions—or whether it can be consulted about every little thing, like what to eat for dinner or where to find a parking place. "Among the people I've counseled, seeking guidance on every little thing is usually a temporary stage of deepening their relationship with their inner voice," DavidPaul explained. "Over time, that source of wisdom and truth within them becomes more integrated into their everyday sense of self-awareness. At a later stage, people can simply listen to their heart about what to do with the little things, knowing that there is no separation between the desires of their heart and their inner voice."

Or, as *A Course in Miracles* suggests,

To ask the Holy Spirit to decide for you is simply to accept your true inheritance. Does this mean that you cannot say anything without consulting Him? No, indeed! That would hardly be practical, and it is the practical with which this course is most concerned. If you have made it a habit to ask for help when and where you can, you can be confident that wisdom will be given you when you need it. Prepare for this each morning, remember God when you can throughout the day, ask the Holy Spirit's help when it is feasible to do so, and thank Him for His guidance at night. And your confidence will be well founded indeed.

Never forget that the Holy Spirit does not depend on your words. He understands the requests of your heart, and answers them. . . . (Manual, 29: 5–6)

Forgiveness as a Prerequisite

When I began my Course study about twenty-five years ago, one of the first things the teaching made me aware of was the predominance of an inner voice that generally did not inspire me to be kind, compassionate, or understanding. Instead, it was a sardonic running commentary on a world that struck me as bizarre, unsettling, and generally opposed to my well-being. While I thought of myself as a good person who tried to treat others decently, I also tended to see myself as morally superior because I made that effort, when so many others seemed not to care for anything beyond their own survival or success.

Thus, my inner monologue tended to run along the lines of personal martyrdom: I was a good person, but the world seemed not to care and thus I was subject to being victimized by it. So I had to keep my eyes sharp and my guard up to avoid random, senseless punishments from an essentially meaningless universe. Before ACIM, I did not recognize this way of thinking as a "voice" at all, but as an accurate perception of reality itself. In other words, I thought I had a common-sense view of the world with which no one could sensibly disagree. By making me aware of my habitual patterns of thinking and how they determined what I perceived to be "the real world," the Course helped me to understand that I had grown up listening to the inner voice of the ego—a voice characterized by suspicion, resentment, and a thin-ice sense of superiority.

I wouldn't go so far as to say that this voice has entirely disappeared from my consciousness, even after two and a half decades of a healing spiritual discipline. Old habits die hard, as the saying goes. But I am now much more aware of when this familiar voice begins to grow too loud within my mind, and I have ready techniques at hand to mute it, allowing a profoundly more charitable voice to inform my perceptions, decisions, and behavior. That voice, I believe, is what *A Course in Miracles* calls the Holy Spirit.

The prerequisite for beginning to hear this new inner voice was learning to forgive the world I used to see and the way that I saw it. Forgiveness as taught by the Course goes well beyond the popular understanding of the idea, and so this book will devote three chapters to progressively deeper explorations of what it means to forgive and how to go about it. The next chapter offers some initial insights and stories about beginning to forgive.

Summary

From a scientific point of view, religion may appear to be the result of an innate yet infantile search for perfect wisdom and reassurance in a mysterious and challenging world. But one reason that religion persists is that science offers more questions than answers about the nature of reality, and the scientific method cannot be relied upon for moral guidance.

Throughout history, some people have received extraordinary insights and information from a mysterious "inner voice," regardless of their religious background. But inner or disembodied voices can also be delusory, and it's important to distinguish the positive, integrating qualities of transcendent voices from the isolating and destructive inputs of schizophrenia or mere egotism.

A Course in Miracles offers explicit guidance for accessing a wise inner voice, identified as the Holy Spirit, which it says is accessible to all. Some people may experience the Holy Spirit as a literal "voice" heard or sensed in their mind; others may know it through intuitive hunches or meaningful coincidences. Regardless of how it is accessed, the Holy Spirit can offer both specific, helpful suggestions for getting through life's daily challenges, and a healing reassurance about one's purpose. The key to unlocking this inner potential is forgiveness.

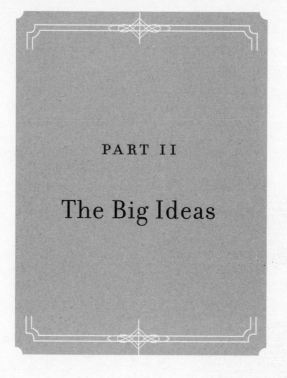

PART II

The Big Ideas

5.

Beginning to Forgive

Forgiveness is the great need of this world, but that is because it is a world of illusions. Those who forgive are thus releasing themselves from illusions, while those who withhold forgiveness are binding themselves to them. As you condemn only yourself, so do you forgive only yourself.

This passage appears in the text following Lesson 46 of the Workbook of *A Course in Miracles* ("God is the love in which I forgive"). These few lines encapsulate the teaching's central message, distinguishing it as a spiritual perspective that places more emphasis on forgiveness than any other religious tradition or spiritual path. But the Course defines the meaning and action of forgiveness in far different terms than most Westerners are accustomed to. To get started with the Course approach to forgiveness, three central elements are important to understand:

- Forgiveness may begin with letting go of the anger or sadness stemming from the conviction that someone else has harmed us, but must eventually lead to the recognition that we are harmed only by our own delusions.

- Forgiveness does not absolve oneself or anyone else of sin, because it is based on understanding that our ultimate reality transcends the material world—and in that reality, "there is no sin" (Lesson 259).
- Forgiveness is the indispensable and inevitable means of releasing oneself from the trap of our illusory world of time, matter, and death.

It's worth pausing to reflect on just how different this kind of forgiveness is from what we are accustomed to. For many people, forgiveness entails a kind of sacrifice, in which we let go of grievances and resentments that we've not only become accustomed to, but which may well define our personal history and identity. To let go of our pain and anger about the past can seem like letting go of our very selves, especially if our individual identity has been shaped by a major personal trauma, a preoccupation with self-defense, or a cultural history of persecution. For some, the mere mention of forgiveness is tantamount to giving permission for the repetition of abuse, attack, or genocide. When sacrifice is viewed as a noble act, forgiving its cause can be seen as dangerous.

In the Christian tradition, the primary model for forgiveness is Jesus Christ, who is himself a sacrificial figure. But while Christianity values forgiveness highly, its primary mode of salvation is the recognition of one's own sinfulness, thereafter submitting oneself to the mercy of God in the recognition that the sacrificial death of Christ absolved humanity of its "original sin."

As a youngster attending a Methodist Sunday School, I remember being deeply confused by this doctrine of sacrifice. First of all, no one at church ever explained *how* the death of Jesus "saved" everyone; there was no rationale for the mechanism of universal salvation by his death on the cross. Also, it was disturbing that my salvation required a bloody sacrifice; in regular school, we had learned that the ancient Aztecs were "primitive" because they sacrificed people to appease *their* gods. Wasn't our God setting a bad example by allowing his own blameless son to be tortured and killed because all humanity had done something wrong? At age nine or so, I certainly didn't know what I had done that was so wrong—although I could see there were certainly bad people in the world. Did that mean that everyone was bad by nature?

Finally, if the death of Jesus Christ had somehow redeemed everyone in advance, how could you still go to hell if you did not "accept" Jesus as your personal savior? This sounded like the ploy of a very manipulative God to me, as if He continued to use the death of his own son as a guilt trip to ensure that one remained loyal to Christianity. Yet this same God still allowed all kinds of bad things to go on in the world, and even "saved" Christians often suffered disease, abandonment, and horrible deaths. Not only that, some saved Christians still did bad things—and then they had to ask God's forgiveness all over again. All in all, this scheme of things just didn't make sense.

As the years passed, the belief system that had merely confused me as a child appeared increasingly pernicious to me as an adult. I could see how the idea of sacrifice generated so much human strife and suffering, yet was often seen as an incontestable virtue. Had not America fought at least three great and bloody wars—the Revolution, the Civil War, and World War II—to preserve our ideals of freedom, equality, and democracy? Didn't we see people as more noble or saintly if they sacrificed their well-being or even their lives for the benefit of others, just as Jesus had done on a universal scale? And weren't we especially disheartened when an ignoble death or heartless killing appeared to be a "meaningless" sacrifice? I suspected that there was something amiss at the very core of our belief in sacrifice, but its roots ran so deep in my mind, and in the broader cultural consciousness, that it couldn't sensibly be challenged.

When I encountered *A Course in Miracles* in my mid-thirties, I came upon a radically different view of sacrifice, expressed as if Jesus himself were speaking:

> Persecution frequently results in an attempt to "justify" the terrible misperception that God Himself persecuted His Own Son on behalf of salvation. The very words are meaningless. It has been particularly difficult to overcome this because, although the error itself is no harder to correct than any other, many have been unwilling to give it up in view of its prominent value as a defense. In milder forms a parent says, "This hurts me more than it hurts you," and feels exonerated in beating a child. Can you believe our Father really thinks this way? It is so essential that all such thinking be dispelled that we must be sure that nothing of this kind remains in your mind. I was not "punished" because *you* were bad . . .
>
> God does not believe in retribution. His Mind does not create that way. He does not hold your "evil" deeds against you. Is it likely that He would hold them against me? Be very sure that you recognize how utterly impossible this assumption is, and how entirely it arises from projection. (Chapter 3, I: 2, 3)
>
> The innocent release in gratitude for their release. And what they see upholds their freedom from imprisonment and death. Open your mind to change, and there will be no ancient penalty exacted

from your brother or yourself. For God has said there *is* no sacrifice that can be asked; there *is* no sacrifice that can be made. (Chapter 31, III: 7)

If there can be no sacrifice, then there is never really anything to forgive. According to the Course, we forgive not in order to let someone off the hook for a crime, flaw, or failing, but to begin undoing our own conviction that life inevitably entails sacrifice. To "open your mind to change" means developing the willingness to let go of *all* your grievances—not because that's the good or moral thing to do, but because those grievances bind your consciousness to the material world, where it does not belong.

Identifying the Source of Upset

If we truly and totally forgive, will we then disappear from this earthly vale? As ludicrous as that may sound, my own experience with the ACIM approach to forgiveness has indeed given me an increasing sense of lightness that makes me feel less bound to this world by gravity and grief. When the world is "too much with me" and I am tempted by resentments, I feel physically heavier and more entrapped by daily life; I'm also more prone to illness. When I manage to forgive consistently, I'm generally healthier, and whatever injuries or insults I've suffered present fewer impedances to the progress of my daily life, work, and relationships.

But I did not begin forgiving by recognizing that my daily, material life was illusory, and thus there was nothing to forgive! Instead, I was introduced to forgiveness by a process that gradually unfolds in the Course Workbook of daily lessons. This process begins at least as early as Lesson 5, "I am never upset for the reason I think," which directs the student to examine various sources of emotional disturbance and apply the day's lesson to each one in a format like this:

I am not angry at _____ *for the reason I think.*
I am not afraid of _____ *for the reason I think.*
I am not worried about _____ *for the reason I think.*
I am not depressed about _____ *for the reason I think.*

The student is also discouraged from ranking or ordering the sources of his or her upsets, and instead is urged to view them with the attitude *"There are no small upsets. They are all equally disturbing to my peace of mind."* If the student experiences hesitation in applying the lesson to one particular disturbance, the following response is urged: *"I cannot keep this form of upset and let the others go. For the purposes of these exercises, then, I will regard them all as the same."*

In this early lesson, the Course initiates a subtle but profound process of altering the way a student's consciousness works. Instead of the usual preoccupation with the *content* of our self-awareness, this lesson shifts our attention to *how* we are thinking and feeling. That shift of consciousness encourages us to begin taking responsibility for any suffering or disturbance in our peace of mind, instead of assuming that the disturbance is caused externally.

To use a minor example, imagine that you are cut off in traffic by a reckless driver, causing you a momentary scare. A natural reaction would be anger, likely followed by a judgment about the particular driver, or careless people in general. Depending on your personal tendencies, this judgment might be soon forgotten, or it might fester into a long-standing resentment, leading to a greater tension while driving and a more quick-tempered response (or "road rage," as it's popularly called) the next time you encounter a traffic danger. Because the danger seemed real, your initial anger would seem justified, and the cause of your upset would be sensibly attributed to the other driver.

But the Course discipline shifts the responsibility for any such upset, large or small, back to the student. In this case, the student would have to consider that *"I am not upset at the traffic incident for the reason I think."* And the same principle would apply equally to any other problem: *"I am not depressed about my divorce for the reason I think"* or *"I am not grieving over my friend's death for the reason I think."* The more profound the disturbance, the more likely we are to assume that we are justified in feeling that our upset is externally caused. But ACIM is both consistent and adamant in reminding students that any and all upset begins in the student's own mind, and it is only there that it can be resolved.

In the next lesson, students are given another clue about how their minds are operating in a self-damaging manner: "I am upset because I see something that is not there." Then, in Lesson 7, the root of our psychological suffering is identified: "I see only the past." That lesson opens with a compelling review of the previous six, unveiling the link between ACIM's view of time and its approach to forgiveness:

> This idea is particularly difficult to believe at first. Yet it is the rationale for all of the preceding ones.
>
> It is the reason why nothing that you see means anything.
>
> It is the reason why you have given everything you see all the meaning that it has for you.
>
> It is the reason why you do not understand anything you see.
>
> It is the reason why your thoughts do not mean anything, and why they are like the things you see.

It is the reason why you are never upset for the reason you think.

It is the reason why you are upset because you see something that is not there.

A Slow Undoing of the Past

By the time I began my study of *A Course in Miracles*, I had been ill for several months, suffering a wide array of symptoms that eluded diagnosis and threatened to culminate in a complete collapse of my health. When conventional medical tests and prescriptions led nowhere, I turned to psychotherapy for the first time in my life—a route that I hesitated to undertake because my mother had commenced psychiatric treatment at about the same age, leading to a lifelong dependence on powerful, mood-altering drugs. I did not want to become like her.

What surfaced in nine weeks of therapy was an abiding but long-suppressed anger at my mother's manic-depressive behavior throughout my childhood, and my father's seeming inability to confront it. While I did find a mild sedative useful in dealing with the anxiety stemming from my chronic illness, neither that nor the recognition of my deep-rooted anger seemed to be resolving my countless and often frightening symptoms, which included violent stomach pains and frequent sleep disturbances. By the end of this short therapeutic experiment, however, I had begun studying the Course—and I had just started to integrate the notion that I was actually "upset by something that was not there."

One night, after several disturbing dreams, I awoke with the realization that my illness felt like a kind of haunting. I sensed that

I was not just upset by the painful memories of my own childhood and adolescence, but also by murkier memories that didn't seem to be my own. For the first time, I began to see my mother not as a deliberate or uncaring perpetrator of hurt, but as an unwitting carrier of pains that she did not comprehend, and could not help but inflict on others. Beginning in the middle of the night, I wrote the following poem for her over several hours:

ON SLEEPLESSNESS *(for my mother)*

Very early, your heart burst open
like an overstuffed suitcase, and the clothes,
jewelry, well-worn dolls, watches, crutches
and cameos of your ancestors spilled inside you.
Your soul was draped with grief before
you could speak, and no one could see
that your first lullaby should be a threnody.
The unhappy dead are petulant beings,
peering through the eyes of their living kin
to glimpse the light at the end of the tunnel.
No one taught you who their voices were,
and why they murmured of so much bitterness
and fear. No one taught you that
the lost ones need first to be heard,
then forgiven and released.

And so, drawn
by your strength and independence, these spirits
rushed in through your broken heart like
a river flooding the breach of a dam.

They took back the clothes and jewelry,
putting on whatever they found at random,
shoving and fighting each other to try on
precious things that might prettify their misery.
Feeding on the life that should have been yours
alone, these desperate souls of many disguises
then possessed you. It is they who,
unable to rest, have stolen your sleep
for so many years.

You know, they thought
I was an open door as well. Lately they
have brought their morbid partying
into my stomach and my dreams—
but when I awaken in the night, I know them.
Not their names or faces, but their truths
and traumas: Someone starved. Someone
was born dead and, like a turtle trapped
on its back, struggled to move in a useless body
and silence the screams of his terrified mother.
Someone murdered, someone was slain, a father
ignored and abused his daughters with an anger
he inherited. I recognize a family, like any
human group, with a legacy of pain and
unspoken longing. And by watching you
I have learned their desire . . .

I can bring them
peace, but they must give up thieving
the sleep of the living. I am the poet

and the storyteller, their voice and
their master. I will honor them,

but I will put them to rest.

Writing this poem was a frightening process, as I experienced an internal "ghost story" while the words and lines were coming together. The morbid images were directly experienced as visions and indistinct memories that I could not trace to my personal history, but nonetheless seemed quite real. And I realized that my mother had unconsciously passed them on to me without even intending to, as she struggled not only with her own private demons, but those of her parents, grandparents, and earlier ancestors as well.

I suspect that many people with depressive tendencies are similarly haunted by troubling psychological legacies handed down through generations. It seems reasonable to assume that one could bury a traumatic experience in one's own consciousness, thus driving it from awareness yet still transmitting negative effects of the trauma to one's children. And those effects might be all the more pernicious for being unconsciously transmitted and thus unrecognized. In my mother's case, her psychiatrist always suspected but could never establish that she had been repeatedly sexually abused as a child. When I wrote my poem for her, I felt that I was uncovering many such untold secrets, belonging not just to my mother but to those who lived before her.

At any rate, by the end of the writing process I felt a great release of tension, sorrow, and grief that I had not previously recognized within myself. In retrospect, I believe that these dark energies were a large part of the stress that had led to my immune dysfunction;

in other words, these indistinct yet very powerful feelings had literally made me sick. Before writing this poem, I had been more deeply "upset by something that was not there" than I even knew.

The ending of the poem was a surprise to me as I wrote it, but in hindsight I can see that it was my way of taking responsibility for the disturbances to my peace of mind that the poem detailed. And just as the Course points out, all those disturbances were in my past. Before I recognized and named them, these upsets were very much in my present even if I was not consciously aware of them. I was literally sacrificing my health and well-being to a history of human suffering that was not my burden to bear. Writing the poem helped me to see that I was playing out the drama of a martyr without even knowing it, and the sane thing to do was call an end to it.

But I don't mean to give the impression that writing one therapeutic poem was all I needed to forgive the past and release all my suffering. Rather, it was one of several peak episodes of forgiveness that I experienced in my first few years of Course study, accelerating both my healing from illness and my growth in relationships. My mother was still alive at the time, and when I shared the poem she confirmed that I had grasped something important in her own experience. She even admitted that there were times she had felt "possessed" while in deep depressions. Our relationship improved significantly after this exchange, and even more so a few years later when I wrote my first inspirational volume on forgiveness, which I dedicated to her. When she died naturally in her sleep at age seventy-six after a lifetime of intense emotional struggle that included several suicide attempts, I wondered if my own learning in forgiveness had helped her to let go peacefully of her attachment to her earthly existence.

Today I cannot say that I am entirely free of the "haunting" of my family's past, but I am certainly far less identified with it than I would have been without a discipline of forgiveness. If not for *A Course in Miracles*, I almost certainly would have remained ill for a much longer period of time than seven years, and I believe that most of my relationships would have been unhealthier. I don't know if it's possible to entirely undo one's past on this planet, and overall the process of complete forgiveness can seem profoundly difficult and slow.

Yet once that process is engaged, we are well on the way to becoming more truly ourselves—original and creative human beings—instead of a chaotic collection of automatic behaviors that are unconsciously rooted in past traumas. And that process begins not with forgiving someone else's apparent trespasses, but with the deceptively simple challenge of realizing that "I am never upset for the reason I think."

Summary

The central ethos and method of *A Course in Miracles* is forgiveness, but its approach to this healing attitude is unconventional. According to ACIM, forgiveness is critically important not because it relieves the forgiven person of guilt or blame, but because it helps the forgiving person become liberated from the illusory world of time and matter. This perspective is quite foreign to Western culture, whose primary icon of forgiveness is the sacrificial figure of Jesus Christ. Speaking in the voice of the historical Jesus, the Course adamantly repudiates the conventional Christian doctrine of sacrifice.

Students are introduced to the rudiments of forgiveness early in the ACIM Workbook via Lesson 5, "I am never upset for the reason I think." Shifting one's awareness from the reactive *content* of the mind to its habitual *process* is key to taking full responsibility for one's own consciousness, which can lead to profoundly healing experiences. Those experiences will often involve the release of addictive and troubling preoccupations with the past, which the Course identifies as the source of all our upsets. For many people, it is those same preoccupations that define much of their personal history and identity. In that regard, the Course approach to forgiveness is key to the positive transformation of personality and the relief of chronic suffering.

6.

Recognizing What's Real
(and What Isn't)

There is no relationship between what is real and what you think is real. Nothing that you think are your real thoughts resemble your real thoughts in any respect. Nothing that you think you see bears any resemblance to what vision will show you.

—From Lesson 45

In the summer of 1973, I was a college newspaper reporter avidly watching one of the biggest political stories of the twentieth century unfold. The senior senator from my home state of North Carolina, Sam Ervin, was chairing the investigatory hearings into the Watergate scandal. My editor and I had traveled to Washington, D.C., for an interview with Senator Ervin that had been scheduled weeks earlier. By the day we got there, July 16, the pace of events was quickening and our interview looked doubtful.

Taking pity on a couple of scrawny, long-haired kids standing nervously in the outer office, the senator's receptionist kept promising to "see what I can do" when she was interrupted by a phone call. Listening avidly with her eyes widening, she hastily wrote out two official passes for us and, when she got off the phone, told us to run as fast as we could toward the hearing room. "Something's about to happen," she said excitedly, "and you don't want to miss it!" We dashed out the office door and broke into an open run down the hall.

When we reached the crowded hearing chamber, we produced our passes and asked for seats in the press area toward the front. A security guard gave us the once-over, grunted "Yeah, right," and pushed us toward the back of the chamber. Although we would not fully understand the significance of what we were about to witness until we watched the television news later that evening, we were just in time to witness the testimony of FAA chief Alexander Butterfield, who revealed the existence of the White House tapes that would prove key to the downfall of Richard Nixon.

Although we were a long way from breaking that story and our campus newspaper wasn't even printing during the summer, I was hooked on the lure of investigative reporting that day. After all, the most powerful leader in the world was being brought down by a pair of scruffy reporters not much older than my editor and myself. The idea that I could similarly change the world was enticing, to say the least. The battle lines of good and evil seemed clearly drawn; with just a notepad and a dedication to the truth, all the bad Goliaths of the world could be brought to their knees by crusading-journalist Davids. I was ready to play my part because, as always, there was plenty wrong with the world besides Richard Nixon. And *somebody* had to save it.

When I reached California a few years later and began working for an environmental activist lobby, and thereafter a weekly progressive newspaper in San Francisco, my investigative zeal gradually cooled. First, I was disheartened to learn that liberal activists seemed to argue as much with each other as with those whose politics they opposed. This suggested that there was going to be a deeper problem with world-saving than I had supposed.

Another doubt arose from the fact that I didn't really like reporters very much. I attended enough journalists' parties to observe the real-life basis for the cliché of the hard-drinking reporter, and I saw no romance in that cliché or the reality. Most of the reporters I worked with seemed to be nursing rather obvious neuroses, and their daily work was doing nothing to heal them. If anything, the continuing drive to "get the story" by deadline—which often required a combination of dull, detail-oriented research and combative interaction with sources—seemed only to worsen the personal problems of crusading reporters. Watching all this, I sensed that my own psychological stability wouldn't be able to withstand the long-term stress of investigative reporting.

Finally, I was troubled by the impression that the search for truth that ostensibly drove journalism rested on a shallow foundation. In a day-to-day sense, that inquiry seemed to proceed according to the politically liberal advocacy of the media I had chosen to write for. I agreed with those politics and the social change they encouraged, but I sensed that lasting social change would also require investigating the deepest sources of human conflict. So far as I could tell, journalists of all stripes—left, right, and mainstream—enjoyed the battle of their jousting perspectives too much to confront their personal investments in conflict.

In another sense, I was too ambitious to join the fray. I didn't want to spend years of my professional life trying to dislodge a dishonest politician from office, or be endlessly building a case against political perspectives that I disagreed with. Investigative journalism seemed to be focused on exposing bad guys, but apparently there was an endless supply of them. What I really wanted to investigate was *what made guys bad*. In other words, I *really* wanted to change the world, beginning with the root causes of mischief and suffering in human nature. I was beginning to suspect that real change was derived not from exposing someone else's dishonesty or winning political arguments, but from finding, somehow, a way to call off all conflict. I was still a long way from realizing that the war of politics—a perpetual struggle between the champions of opposing social solutions—might bear a resemblance to the war within me.

By the early 1980s I had left investigative reporting, spent a year in advertising, and then become self-employed as a graphic artist and part-time writer. I was confident that I could find my own voice as an independent journalist and eventually make a living with it. The skeptical, politically oriented writer I was in my twenties would have been surprised to learn that my eventual return to journalism would come out of a deep spiritual impetus. And he would have been utterly confounded by the notion behind all my work today: that there is no "world" to save outside the realm of our own flawed perceptions.

Seeing Through the Ultimate Conspiracy

"There is no world!" exclaims *A Course in Miracles* in the text following Lesson 132. "This is the central thought the course attempts to teach. Not everyone is ready to accept it, and each one must go as far as he can let himself be led along the road to truth. He will return and go still farther, or perhaps step back a while and then return again."

By the time I encountered this radical perspective, I was struggling through a complete collapse of my health, my place in the world and the ego-based assumptions that had led me to this catastrophic state. My earlier conviction that the world was going wrong because of various conspiracies by evil-minded or mis-guided people had fallen apart. Now that my own life had gone terribly wrong, I found it impossible to blame my own disintegration on anyone. And I had certainly not engaged in any conspiracy against myself.

Or had I?

A Course in Miracles departs from conventional psychology in its assertion that the ego—which we normally think of as our "self" or personal identity—is not only delusory, but not even a part of our real mind:

> The ego uses the body to conspire against your mind, and because the ego realizes that its "enemy" can end them both merely by recognizing they are not part of you, they join in the attack together. This is perhaps the strangest perception of all, if you consider what it really involves. The ego, which is not real, attempts to persuade the mind, which *is* real, that the mind is the ego's learning device; and further, that the body is more real than the mind is. No one in his right mind could possibly believe this, and no one in his right mind does believe it. (Chapter 6, IV: 5)

We are so used to thinking of ourselves as "egos" that we sometimes forget the concept is a relatively recent invention, extending back no further than the nineteenth century. The father of modern psychology, Sigmund Freud, identified the self as a tripartite dynamic of the human psyche comprising

- the *id*, a largely subconscious complex of animalistic, instinctive drives, especially the sexual drive;

- the *ego*, the self-conscious awareness of personal identity;
  and
- the *superego*, a kind of moralistic overseer that attempts
  to resolve the inevitable conflicts of id and ego, which
  are constantly battling for control of the psyche and of
  behavior.

Helen Schucman, the Course scribe, was a dedicated Freudian and thus it is not surprising that the massive teaching she transcribed from an "inner dictation" experienced in her mind would have much to say about ego dynamics. But while the language of the Course is in part Freudian, its conclusions are decidedly not. ACIM radically redefines the ego as an entirely illusory sense of self that actually does battle with the mind from which it draws its own precarious existence. Whereas Freud saw the body as the seat of the problematic id—giving rise to all the uncivilized urges and impulses that the superego must help the ego manage in order for an individual to function lawfully within society—the Course sees the ego as the fundamental troublemaker in our existence. It is the ego that actually *invents* the body as a means of convincing each of us that we are essentially separate, alone, and fated to suffer pain, illness, and death. As a rule, this trick works devilishly well.

It's important to remember that in ACIM's view, the source and basis of our real "mind" is not an individual consciousness encased in our brains or bodies, but the universal, timeless, totally abstract consciousness of God, or love. From the perspective of our everyday experience on earth, ruled by ego-consciousness, such a total abstraction is virtually incomprehensible. Yet the Course holds that it is our real source:

Complete abstraction is the natural condition of the mind. But part of it is now unnatural. It does not look on everything as one. It sees instead but fragments of the whole, for only thus could it invent the partial world you see. The purpose of all seeing is to show you what you wish to see. All hearing but brings to your mind the sounds it wants to hear. . . . The mind that taught itself to think specifically can no longer grasp abstraction in the sense that it is all-encompassing. (From Lesson 161)

According to ACIM, our original mind precedes and surpasses our personal self-awareness, and is synonymous with Creation itself. When we are in our "right mind," in Course terms, we are recognizing ourselves only as this Mind, and *nothing else.* "God is but love and therefore so am I," instructs a refrain of the Course Workbook, reinforced by such meditations as *"I am one Self, united with my Creator, at one with every aspect of creation, and limitless in power and in peace"* (Lesson 95). In a very real sense, the intensive "mind training" of ACIM is focused solely on shocking us out of the delusion of our individual consciousness and back to our reality in, and as, God.

But the delusion of separation that ensnares us is deep and incredibly complex. It consists of the entire physical universe of time, space, matter, and the body, all of which we are habitually attached to. Further, the ego has managed to conceal this delusion's causative mechanism from our awareness. Thus the Course points toward a very different explanation for the unconscious than Freud devised:

The body is the ego's home by its own election. It is the only identification with which the ego feels safe, since the body's vulnerability is its own best argument that you cannot be of God. This is the belief that the ego sponsors eagerly. Yet the ego hates the body, because it cannot accept it as good enough to be its home. Here is where the mind becomes actually dazed. Being told by the ego that it is really part of the body and that the body is its protector, the mind is also told that the body cannot protect it. Therefore, the mind asks, "Where can I go for protection?" to which the ego replies, "Turn to me." The mind, and not without cause, reminds the ego that it has itself insisted that it is identified with the body, so there is no point in turning to *it* for protection. The ego has no real answer to this because there is none, but it does have a typical solution. It obliterates the question from the mind's awareness. Once out of awareness the question can and does produce uneasiness, but it cannot be answered because it cannot be asked. (Chapter 4, V: 4)

What the ego has first driven into the unconscious is our awareness of God, not as a merciful or punitive overseer of our existence, but *God as our own mind*. Once the awareness of our true source and reality has been effectively concealed, we are left with the ego's rule. The ego is plagued by fears of abandonment, isolation, and death, because it mistakenly believes that it has somehow separated from the original, unitary consciousness of God. Hating itself for its own insecurity, the ego is prone to fabricate the notion of a punishing God who promises salvation from the chaos and suffering of the world, but also issues rules and threatens damnation if the rules are broken. No wonder the human ego is prone to uneasiness—but as ACIM suggests, it does a good job of obscuring how it has created its own anxiety.

When I first encountered these ideas about how the human

mind conspires against its own peace and self-knowledge, I certainly did not make a "quantum leap" into acceptance of my mind as part of God, quickly accepting my true reality as a total and eternal abstraction. In fact, I couldn't make any sense of these concepts. But in tandem with the daily practice of forgiveness and release of habitual thought patterns that is set out in the Workbook, my old sense of self began to be profoundly shaken. In retrospect, I think of this change as a slow-motion, undersea earthquake in the depths of my subconscious. The effects were not immediately visible on the surface of my life, yet my consciousness as a whole was being subtly and profoundly rearranged.

That rearrangement continues to this day. I would say that its most important effect on my everyday existence is a deep and growing sense of assurance that no matter what seems to be happening in the everyday world of time and matter, my real "being" continues undisturbed. That being is not myself as a person or a body; it is a constant flow of perpetual energy and awareness, like a subterranean river, that runs unceasingly beneath the self with which I habitually identify. If I had to characterize that energy, I would say it is at once serene and powerful and unconditionally loving yet impersonal. That is as close as I have come to grasping the abstraction of God as the Course defines it.

Despite the word *abstraction*, I should emphasize that this is a *felt experience*, not an intellectual realization. It is feeling this invisible "river of God" that makes it real to me, not thinking about it or trying to make sense of it. And the longer I have lived with this sense of a deep flowing underneath my everyday consciousness, the stronger the sense of its ultimate reality has become to me. At the same time, the daily reality of the material world has certainly not been dispelled, but it has become less pointed and painful. No longer do I feel that the world has gone terribly wrong because of the evil conspiracies or hapless dysfunctions of other people. Nor am I preoccupied with guilt or self-blame about any failures or seeming inadequacies of my own up to this point.

My life has changed simply because I am aware of a deep layer of inexhaustible love—far surpassing my personality and providing a new foundation of reality—that I did not know before my study of the Course. I used to think of love as either a fleeting, involuntary emotion or a moral choice; under the guidance of the Course, I have begun to recognize love as *what I am*, as well as what God is.

A neurobiologist might challenge this "felt experience of God" as a consequence of complex biochemical processes in the brain that will end with my physical death. That's entirely possible, and I can't confirm or disprove that theory without conducting an experiment that I'd rather not at the moment! At any rate, it is irrelevant to my experience of God-as-love *now*. I do assume that upon my physical death, my personality or ego-self will be vanquished, and any consciousness that might continue will be impersonal and abstract, not having anything to do with the "me" that is thinking and writing at this moment. For my consciousness as an ego, physical death will be final and absolute. But if the Course is correct, the deep God-consciousness I can access now has always been and will always be, because it is free of the constraints of time and space.

For me, having such a spiritual orientation means I need not be obsessed with death or how to delay it. Instead my chief concern is what fundamentally drives me to act and make choices now, in the world as it appears to be. Having once been driven by the imperative to outsmart an ever-shifting panoply of fearful conspiracies just to survive and make a difference in the world, I now vastly prefer the feeling that I am "sourced" in an infinite, ever-flowing energy of love. That leads me to view the troubled world with a sense of compassion instead of suspicion and to make more effective and peaceful decisions than I used to. That doesn't mean that everything goes well or that I have completely eradicated fear from my life, but it does mean I no longer allow fear to be my chief motivator.

And as I increasingly learn to choose love as my primary motive, I find that I am less identified with my ego, which would otherwise keep me preoccupied with self-defense. I can clearly remember the way my mind used to work under stress before I encountered the Course; in general, my response to threatening challenges consisted of a panicky self-interrogation along the lines of *"What do I do now?"* There was never a consistent or reliable strategy that arose from such defensive thinking, and I was seldom satisfied with the results. Now my response to challenges is far more likely to focus on the question, *"What would love have me do?"* This usually induces a stillness, patience, and assurance that yields far better results, in decisions and actions, than my youthful ego-driven strategies.

This change in my approach to the world is not a religious conversion; I don't do things differently because I have come to "believe in God." Regarding the idea of a *personified* God as a distinct, divine being who created the universe and sits in judgment of human behavior, I remain an atheist. I don't believe that kind of God exists except as a projection of the human ego, imagining and inflating itself as the Creator of all it surveys. How my life differs from my pre-Course days is that now I can access *a source and experience of unconditional love*, which I sometimes call God.

That may sound wonderful on the face of it, but the path to this new awareness has been marked with doubt, disorientation, and sometimes a deeply disturbing fear. Because the last thing the ego wants to seriously consider is that it doesn't exist.

The Fear of Looking Within

Although the Course doesn't say so, it seems reasonable to surmise that all forms of religion have been invented in an attempt to get back to our fundamental awareness of God, for the ego has never been entirely successful in completely driving our infinite source awareness from consciousness. Even as we firmly believe that we are finite, mortal beings who must struggle to sustain and extend a life that could be cruelly cut short at any moment, we dimly sense that there must be a way of existing—somehow, somewhere—which is eternal, unthreatened, and suffused with bliss.

If we are rational and scientific, we may dismiss this longing as a fantasy. If we are religious, we think of this ideal existence as a faraway "Heaven" and try to follow the rules which will supposedly guarantee that we get there someday. Of course, every religion has a different set of rules for admittance to Heaven, and the disciples of one religion can only pity (or actively persecute) the disciples of all those other religions who are following the wrong rules!

In fact, the development of religion has engendered count-less rules, rituals, and superstitions, as well as massive institutions, as the ego reinvents God in its own troubled image and thereby devises even more "blocks to the awareness of love's presence" (from the Text Introduction). Chief among these blocks is the idea of sin, which figures so strongly in Christianity, but which the

Course rejects absolutely as a figment of the ego's tortured, self-flagellating imagination:

> The Holy Spirit will never teach you that you are sinful. Errors He will correct, but this makes no one fearful. You are indeed afraid to look within and see the sin you think is there. This you would not be fearful to admit. Fear in association with sin the ego deems quite appropriate, and smiles approvingly. It has no fear to let you feel ashamed. It doubts not your belief and faith in sin. Its temples do not shake because of this. Your faith that sin is there but witnesses to your desire that it *be* there to see. This merely seems to be the source of fear. (Chapter 21, IV: 1)

Per the Course, the reason that the ego is fearfully drawn toward the idea of sin (a dynamic it identifies as "the attraction of guilt," discussed further in the next chapter) is that it points our mind's attention away from the unbroken, whole reality of God *as an all-inclusive, immaterial consciousness*. If that God is real, then the individual ego cannot be, and thus it fears being dissolved into the unified consciousness of God:

> This fragment of your mind is such a tiny part of it that, could you but appreciate the whole, you would see instantly that it is like the smallest sunbeam to the sun, or like the faintest ripple on the surface of the ocean. In its amazing arrogance, this tiny sunbeam has decided it is the sun; this almost imperceptible ripple hails itself as the ocean. Think how alone and frightened is this little thought, this infinitesimal illusion, holding itself apart against the universe. The sun becomes the sunbeam's "enemy" that would devour it, and the ocean terrifies the little ripple and wants to swallow it.

Yet neither sun nor ocean is even aware of all this strange and meaningless activity. They merely continue, unaware that they are feared and hated by a tiny segment of themselves. Even that segment is not lost to them, for it could not survive apart from them. And what it thinks it is in no way changes its total dependence on them for its being. Its whole existence still remains in them. Without the sun the sunbeam would be gone; the ripple without the ocean is inconceivable. (Chapter 18, VIII: 3–4)

The "infinitesimal illusion" of the ego clings tightly to the world of time, matter, and individuality in which its rules and rituals seem to make sense, even if all these measures do not stave off suffering and death:

The world you see is merciless indeed, unstable, cruel, unconcerned with you, quick to avenge and pitiless with hate. It gives but to rescind, and takes away all things that you have cherished for a while. No lasting love is found, for none is here. This is the world of time, where all things end. (From Lesson 129)

The reason that this world is merciless is that it is the world of the body and our primary identification with it, which means that we are fated to suffer and die. Further, every sin that we can imagine is related to use or misuse of the body. Freud defined the "pleasure principle" as the human being's instinctive desire to seek pleasure and avoid pain. In the infant, this principle is the driving force of an immature, self-serving consciousness. As the child matures, he or she learns the necessity of delaying gratification and enduring some pain in order to become a moral and effective member of society—which Freud deemed the "reality principle."

Once again, *A Course in Miracles* radically redefines fundamental Freudian concepts in a metaphysical frame:

> It is impossible to seek for pleasure through the body and not find pain. It is essential that this relationship be understood, for it is one the ego sees as proof of sin. It is not really punitive at all. It is but the inevitable result of equating yourself with the body, which is the invitation to pain. For it invites fear to enter and become your purpose. The attraction of guilt *must* enter with it, and whatever fear directs the body to do is therefore painful. It will share the pain of all illusions, and the illusion of pleasure will be the same as pain.
>
> Is not this inevitable? Under fear's orders the body will pursue guilt, serving its master whose attraction to guilt maintains the whole illusion of its existence. This, then, is the attraction of pain. Ruled by this perception the body becomes the servant of pain, seeking it dutifully and obeying the idea that pain is pleasure. It is this idea that underlies all of the ego's heavy investment in the body. And it is this insane relationship that it keeps hidden, and yet feeds upon. To you it teaches that the body's pleasure is happiness. Yet to itself it whispers, "It is death." (Chapter 19, IV-B: 12–13)

Note again that the Course distinguishes between "you" and the ego, characterizing the ego as a fear-driven voice within our mind that is constantly battling with our awareness of God for control of consciousness. The ego's primary weapon in this battle is formidable, for it is the body with which we habitually identify. That body is the locus of all our pleasure, pain, apparent sin, and guilt. To look within and discover that the seeming proof of our very existence, the body,

is an illusion is a shocking turn of events. The Course acknowledges
the difficulty of this realization with a call for the student's patience:

> Undermining the ego's thought system must be perceived as pain-
> ful, even though this is anything but true. Babies scream in rage
> if you take away a knife or scissors, although they may well harm
> themselves if you do not. In this sense you are still a baby. You have
> no sense of real self-preservation, and are likely to decide that you
> need precisely what would hurt you most. Yet whether or not you
> recognize it now, you have agreed to cooperate in the effort to
> become both harmless and helpful, attributes that must go together.
> Your attitudes even toward this are necessarily conflicted, because
> all attitudes are ego-based. This will not last. Be patient a while and
> remember that the outcome is as certain as God. (Chapter 4, II: 5)

How Could the Impossible Occur?

Since the Course asserts that our real mind is one with God—
and God is an infinite, incorruptible force or energy that does not
recognize the world of time and matter that we call reality—it's
worth asking how our illusory world could ever happen, and *seem*
so real. ACIM's answer to this inquiry is maddeningly circular: *It
never did happen, because the world is an illusion.* Or as the Course
says simply in its Introduction: "Nothing unreal exists." The world
seems so real only because we are caught in a prolonged and utterly
convincing waking dream, which can best be understood by looking at the experience of the dreams we have while sleeping:

Dreams show you that you have the power to make a world as you would have it be, and that because you want it you see it. And while you see it you do not doubt that it is real. Yet here is a world, clearly within your mind, that seems to be outside. You do not respond to it as though you made it, nor do you realize that the emotions the dream produces must come from you. It is the figures in the dream and what they do that seem to make the dream. You do not realize that you are making them act out for you, for if you did the guilt would not be theirs, and the illusion of satisfaction would be gone. In dreams these features are not obscure. You seem to waken, and the dream is gone. Yet what you fail to recognize is that what caused the dream has not gone with it. Your wish to make another world that is not real remains with you. And what you seem to waken to is but another form of this same world you see in dreams. All your time is spent in dreaming. Your sleeping and your waking dreams have different forms, and that is all. Their content is the same. (Chapter 18, II: 5)

Just as there is no way to explain to someone asleep and dreaming that he is currently preoccupied with a fantasy of his own making, the Course allows that no amount of explaining will suffice to wake us from the dream of our daily unreality. Instead it gives us the primary tool of awakening—forgiveness of all we see, hear, and experience—and suggests that through forgiving, we will begin to hear the voice of the Holy Spirit, which can increasingly supplant the fearful, defensive counsel of the ego with an awareness of our Source of infinite love and invulnerability. Again, the Course compares the process of undoing the ego's dream of a fearful world to that of awakening a child:

How can you wake children in a more kindly way than by a gentle Voice that will not frighten them, but will merely remind them that the night is over and the light has come? You do not inform them that the nightmares that frightened them so badly are not real, because children believe in magic. You merely reassure them that they are safe *now*. Then you train them to recognize the difference between sleeping and waking, so they will understand they need not be afraid of dreams. And so when bad dreams come, they will themselves call on the light to dispel them. (Chapter 6, V: 2)

Still, the process of awakening from unreality is neither linear nor orderly. Even after dramatic experiences of release from fear or self-punishment, we may find ourselves retrenching in the ego's habitual sense of isolation and endangerment, desperately seeking proof that our favorite illusions retain their power. When we start looking for explanations of how the chaotic world works, and how either God or a purely mechanistic universe could have made it so, we can always come up with something. Both religion and science provide plenty of theories to explain the world's endless supply of riddles and mysteries. But an ultimate rationale will likely never seem complete or satisfying and may in fact do little more than take up a lot of our time in trying to prove it. Because the ego-mind that asks the questions will usually fail to challenge its own premises:

The ego may ask, "How did the impossible occur?," "To what did the impossible happen?," and may ask this in many forms. Yet there is no answer; only an experience. Seek only this, and do not let theology delay you. (Clarification of Terms, Introduction: 4)

"A Stubbornly Persistent Illusion"

Consoling a friend who had lost a loved one, the famed physicist Albert Einstein wrote some words in 1955 that have become indelibly associated with his legacy: "Now he has departed from this strange world a little ahead of me. That means nothing. People like us, who believe in physics, know that the distinction between past, present, and future is only a stubbornly persistent illusion." Needless to say, Einstein's perspective on time has not become widely accepted over a half-century later. Were it to be understood by most people, the ramifications for science, society, and our basic concept of ourselves as human beings would be revolutionary.

In fact, since Einstein the progress in physics, especially in the leading-edge field of quantum mechanics, has increasingly undermined the conventional view of our apparently material world. In the intensive investigations of subatomic levels of the physical universe, it is now widely accepted that time and space are not hard-and-fast realities in themselves, but mental constructs that we use to order (more or less successfully) our daily experience. That is, time and space do not exist independent of our perceptions; these fundamental determinants of our existence derive solely from our limited grasp of a greater reality.

On top of that, what we call "matter" actually consists, at its subatomic base, of varying forms or frequencies of energy that may take on the qualities of particles or waves, depending on how we look at them. Going even further, a November 2008 story in *New Scientist* magazine cryptically summarized the puzzle of subatomic reality this way: "Matter is built on flaky foundations. Physicists have now confirmed that the apparently substantial stuff is actually no more than fluctuations in the quantum vacuum." The article goes on to conclude that if the Large Hadron Collider recently fired up in Geneva, Switzerland, confirms the existence of the Higgs boson (sometimes referred to as *the God particle*), "it will mean all reality is virtual."

The word *virtual* generally means "existing in essence or effect though not in actual fact"; in physics it refers specifically to the existence of particles that can only be inferred by their interactions. If all reality is virtual, then that means it can only be *inferred from observations* rather than objectively confirmed and quantified.

Thus it's not unreasonable to extrapolate that one of the most fundamental branches of scientific inquiry into the world around us is increasingly heading in the direction of ACIM's philosophy: All the "reality" we experience on a daily basis is entirely the product of our perceptions (that is, inferred from observations). And the only thing that's undeniably there to *be* observed is energy, most often perceived by our senses as light. In the poetic terms of the Course, "Nothing is there but shines, and shines forever."

Still, since we obviously don't experience ourselves every day at the level of "shining forever," it is worth questioning the usefulness of such a philosophy, even if rational science should eventually confirm its theoretical underpinnings. After twenty-five years of study, to me the point of the Course perspective on reality seems to be the simple pragmatism of reducing human suffering by going to its root in the mind. By perceiving ourselves as separate from the infinite energy of the universe, we condemn ourselves to the inherently false experiences of egocentric isolation, physical and emotional suffering, and death. By learning to progressively release our own limited perceptions, we realize that we are not separate from that endless shining reality, but an inalienable part of it:

Beyond the body, beyond the sun and stars, past everything you see and yet somehow familiar, is an arc of golden light that stretches as you look into a great and shining circle. And all the circle fills with light before your eyes. The edges of the circle disappear, and what is in it is no longer contained at all. The light expands and covers everything, extending to infinity forever shining and with no break or limit anywhere. Within it everything is joined in perfect continuity. Nor is it possible to imagine that anything could be outside, for there is nowhere that this light is not.

. . . Here is the memory of what you are; a part of this, with all of it within, and joined to all as surely as all is joined in you. Accept the vision that can show you this, and not the body. (Chapter 21, I: 8, 9)

From this perspective, we can begin to understand how our experience as egos and bodies is no more than the "faintest ripple on the surface of the ocean." To become egoless, then, is neither a moral nor religious imperative, but a simple and inevitable acceptance of reality. The next chapter will examine some of the specific difficulties and rewards involved in letting go of our personal identifications with the unreal.

Summary

The everyday "real world" that each of us experiences is not an objective reality that can be independently assessed or confirmed, but a product of our personal and limited perceptions. We all tend to have our own opinions about what the world is really about, what's wrong with it, and how it could be fixed. But according to

A Course in Miracles, the daily world we perceive is not just imper-
fect, but fundamentally illusory. It derives its seeming reality from
an ongoing dream perpetuated by the ego, a self-serving and fearful part of the mind that actually fabricates the experiences of time,
space, matter, and the body to prove its own primacy. The ego
believes it is possible to separate from the infinite, loving energy of
all creation (or God), and thus tends to see itself in opposition to
God, fearing judgment and condemnation for its sins.

But according to the Course, sin is impossible because separation from the mind of God (or the "total abstraction" of reality)
is impossible, and thus has never occurred. Through forgiveness,
we progressively learn to let go of our limited and self-punishing
perceptions, thus gradually distinguishing the real from the unreal,
and awakening from the ego's painful dream.

Interestingly, the progress of contemporary physics has taken a
turn in the direction of the Course, suggesting that time and space
are artificial constructs, all matter is energy in different forms, and
the subatomic fundamentals of physical reality can only be inferred,
rather than objectively quantified. Whether or not the perspective
of ACIM will be eventually verified by science is unknowable, but
its immediate value is its pragmatic emphasis on reducing human
suffering by releasing our addiction to ego-limited perceptions.

7.

Letting Go of Ego

The ingeniousness of the ego to preserve itself is enormous, but it stems from the very power of the mind the ego denies. This means that the ego attacks what is preserving it, which must result in extreme anxiety. That is why the ego never recognizes what it is doing. It is perfectly logical but clearly insane.

—Chapter 7, VI: 3

I t's not surprising that many students of *A Course in Miracles* experience difficulties and disorientation while working through its 365 Lessons and negotiating its dense Text. Besides presenting a mountain of prose in a frequently dizzying syntax, ACIM seems intent on demolishing our cherished sense of self and personal identity, which it identifies by the psychological term *ego*. Seen accurately, the Course is the polar opposite of a "self-help" philosophy that would shore up people's self-esteem or give them tips and tricks for building wealth, finding romance, or getting ahead in their professional lives.

Instead, the Course insists we recognize that our sense of ourselves as separate beings with individual identities is a profound delusion and that from this delusion stems all our suffering, including physical pain and death. Helping that delusion along can only make things worse—yet we will inevitably seek such help because the ego is plagued by insecurity. The same self-definition that tells us we are innately alone, with a singular mind and a unique, private history, also tells us that we cannot ever be completely "self-sufficient" and must depend on other separate beings for our survival and sanity.

Thus, throughout our lives we seek confirmation and support for our embodied ego-identity, first from our parents and family of origin, and later from friends, lovers, mates, and our own children. We also seek proof of our worth from society, in terms of our employment, professional advancement, and recognition for our worldly accomplishments. In all these pursuits and relationships we are seeking the indispensable force and feeling of *love*, that mysterious energy and emotion that seems to promise both safety and total acceptance, if we could ever locate and claim it once and for all.

Yet we often find love to be tragically elusive, incomplete, or temporary. According to ACIM, that's because the ego's search for love is doomed from the very beginning:

The ego is certain that love is dangerous, and this is always its central teaching. It never puts it this way; on the contrary, everyone who believes that the ego is salvation seems to be intensely engaged in the search for love. Yet the ego, though encouraging the search for love very actively, makes one proviso; do not find it. Its dictates, then, can be summed up simply as: "Seek and do *not* find." This is the one promise the ego holds out to you, and the one promise it will keep. For the ego pursues its goal with fanatic insistence, and its judgment, though severely impaired, is completely consistent.

The search the ego undertakes is therefore bound to be defeated. And since it also teaches that it is your identification, its guidance leads you to a journey which must end in perceived self-defeat. For the ego cannot love, and in its frantic search for love it is seeking what it is afraid to find. The search is inevitable because the ego is part of your mind, and because of its source the ego is not wholly split off, or it could not be believed at all. For it is your mind that believes in it and gives existence to it. Yet it is also your mind that has the power to deny the ego's existence, and you will surely do so when you realize exactly what the journey is on which the ego sets you. (Chapter 4, XII: 2)

Anyone who has ever "fallen in love" only to see a seemingly perfect relationship disintegrate into jealousy, disillusionment, or outright betrayal will have a sense of how the ego's secret agenda dooms the search for love. Indeed, ACIM asserts that the ego's primary weapon in its ongoing struggle of self-preservation is the "special relationship," a topic explored in the next chapter. For now, it's important to note that the ego's fatal view of love is inextricably bound up with the notion of sacrifice.

For instance, we often think that we are showing the greatest love to others when we sacrifice our own needs to their benefit. Whether the form of sacrifice is a mother surrendering her career to raise her children or a soldier falling on a grenade to save his buddies, we tend to think that the most noble form of love involves the denial or destruction of oneself as an ego or body. From the Course perspective, however, sacrifice is a hallmark of the ego's insanity:

Sacrifice is so essential to your thought system that salvation apart from sacrifice means nothing to you. Your confusion of sacrifice and love is so profound that you cannot conceive of love without sacrifice. And it is this that you must look upon; sacrifice is attack, not love. If you would accept but this one idea, your fear of love would vanish. Guilt cannot last when the idea of sacrifice has been removed. For if there is sacrifice, someone must pay and someone must get. And the only question that remains is how much is the price, and for getting what. . . .

How fearful, then, has God become to you, and how great a sacrifice do you believe His Love demands! For total love would demand total sacrifice. And so the ego seems to demand less of you than God, and of the two is judged as the lesser of two evils, one to be feared a little, perhaps, but the other to be destroyed. For you see love as destructive, and your only question is who is to be destroyed, you or another? (Chapter 15, X: 5, 7)

It should not be construed from this passage that the Course is advising us to preserve ourselves at all costs, ignoring others' needs, vulnerability, or pleas for help. Instead, the answer to our complex ego predicament is neither self-preservation nor sacrifice, but *self-lessness*. That means surrendering the entire conviction that each of us has a separate, physical existence, encased in a body with a private mind, distinct from everyone else and doomed to a lonely death. To deny the ego or body what it seems to need is not selflessness, but sacrifice, and only reinforces our delusion; likewise, to serve only ourselves to the exclusion of others' needs or demands is just a different form of sustaining the ego. Choosing to be selfish or noble is not really a choice; the ego holds on to its primacy in our mind either way. The challenge of salvation—that is, recognizing our oneness with God-as-love—therefore becomes how to slip the bonds of ego without falling into any of its alluring traps along the way.

The Attraction of Guilt

As mentioned in the previous chapter, one of the ego's chief delusions is the idea of *sin*, which has become institutionalized in Christianity and serves as the engine of self-hatred even for many who do not consider themselves religious. How deeply the idea of sin is embedded in Western culture is illustrated by the fact that the Old English root of the word, *sinn*, meaning *guilty*, apparently derives from the Indo-European root *es*, which means simply *is*, or *to be*. Etymology thus suggests that the idea of sin is historically linked to the existential identity of Westerners, a conclusion echoed in the Christian assumption that "we are all sinners."

But it has often been observed that the Greek word for sin used in early versions of the Bible, *hamartia*, means "missing the mark." That raises the notion of sin as an error, a mistaken or failed approach to get things right, rather than a profound crime against God or society. *A Course in Miracles* defines sin as the ego's fallacious idea that one can "miss the mark" to an unforgivable degree. While ACIM does acknowledge that we are capable of grievous errors in the world as we see it, it also maintains that all our seeming mistakes, flaws, and failures can be corrected by recognizing that this world is not our ultimate reality. In fact we are *always within God*, inseparable from the reality of infinite love, and we could not possibly depart from that reality no matter what we do here. It is therefore impossible to sin against God:

> To sin would be to violate reality, and to succeed. Sin is the proclamation that attack is real and guilt is justified. It assumes the Son

of God is guilty, and has thus succeeded in losing his innocence and making himself what God created not. Thus is creation seen as not eternal, and the Will of God open to opposition and defeat. Sin is the grand illusion underlying all the ego's grandiosity. For by it God Himself is changed, and rendered incomplete. (Chapter 19, II: 2)

The conventional idea of sin is often clothed in secrecy. We resist the revelation of our secret transgressions or indulgences, fearing not only the shame of exposure and any societal punishment that may be associated with it, but also a more lasting condemnation from a judgmental God. As much as we value our private worlds as the anchors of our reality, we also believe they must be defended lest our "dirty little secrets" (or big ones) expose us as fundamentally unworthy, deserving eternal punishment in hell. Even for those who don't buy into conventional religion, a similar fear of exposure, shame, and social disapproval operates behind many forms of neurosis and emotional instability.

From the Course point of view, all this ego-drama is just a shadow play, a way to keep re-creating the idea of sin in a thousand different forms and thus continually distract ourselves from remembering that love is our "natural inheritance." The ego is a part of our mind that believes it is not only possible to turn our back on love, but that we have irreversibly done so, and either angered God or tragically alienated ourselves. Even if we don't consciously fear divine punishment, we may believe that we have exiled ourselves from unconditional love and must conduct a perpetual and ultimately doomed search to regain its blessing in our everyday lives. In this perfectly logical yet clearly insane frame of reference, guilt thus becomes more attractive than love:

What could be secret from God's Will? Yet you believe that you have secrets. What could your secrets be except another "will" that is your own, apart from His? Reason would tell you that this is no secret that need be hidden as a sin. But a mistake indeed! Let not your fear of sin protect it from correction, for the attraction of guilt is only fear. Here is the one emotion that you made, whatever it may seem to be. This is the emotion of secrecy, of private thoughts and of the body. This is the one emotion that opposes love, and always leads to sight of differences and loss of sameness. Here is the one emotion that keeps you blind, dependent on the self you think you made to lead you through the world it made for you. (Chapter 22, I: 4)

Per the Course, the undoing of the ego's vastly complex plotting to preserve sin and defend itself against love—even while openly pining for it—is simpler than it first appears: *We simply have to be willing to let it all go.* By learning to forgive others and ourselves of what may seem to be unforgivable sins, we begin to release the belief that there are some errors that cannot be corrected:

Punishment is always the great preserver of sin, treating it with respect and honoring its enormity. What must be punished, must be true. And what is true must be eternal, and will be repeated endlessly. For what you think is real you want, and will not let it go.

An error, on the other hand, is not attractive. What you see clearly as a mistake you want corrected. Sometimes a sin can be repeated over and over, with obviously distressing results, but without the loss of its appeal. And suddenly, you change its status from a sin to a mistake. Now you will not repeat it; you will merely stop and let it go. . . . (Chapter 19, III: 2–3)

Anyone who has suffered or witnessed the ravages of a substance or behavioral addiction will recognize the idea that "a sin can be repeated over and over, with obviously distressing results, but without the loss of its appeal." The classic Twelve Steps mode of recovery provides a workable method for undoing the undeniably powerful "attraction of guilt" that feeds addictions. It does so by providing an orderly framework for learning to recognize and take responsibility for one's errors, accept and extend forgiveness, and open oneself to guidance from a "higher power," an innate spiritual resource similar to ACIM's Holy Spirit.

Yet even in Twelve Step groups, an echo of the religious idea of sin remains due to the prevalent assumption of "once an addict, always an addict." From this derives the expectation that addicts in recovery will have to attend support meetings often and perpetually, lest they relapse to addictive patterns and "unmanageable" lifestyles.

It's not uncommon to hear the Course referred to as "graduate work" for followers of the Twelve Steps. From the ACIM perspective, all humanity shares the same root addiction: a profound habituation to a fear-driven, egocentric view of reality. Within that insane frame of reference, it doesn't really matter whether one is addicted to sex, crystal meth, or cupcakes. Whatever the compulsion, it is just that individual's way of falling prey to the attraction of guilt that underlies the ego's deeply flawed yet strangely compelling logic. But we need not fear the ego's seemingly inescapable hold on our consciousness:

> *Do not be afraid of the ego.* It depends on your mind, and as you made it by believing in it, so you can dispel it by withdrawing belief from it. Do not project the responsibility for your belief in it onto anyone else, or you will preserve the belief. When you are willing to accept sole responsibility for the ego's existence you will

have laid aside all anger and all attack, because they come from an attempt to project responsibility for your own errors. But having accepted the errors as yours, do not keep them. Give them over quickly to the Holy Spirit to be undone completely, so that all their effects will vanish from your mind and from the Sonship as a whole. (Chapter 7, VIII: 5)

Withdrawing Projections

The famed depth psychologist Carl Jung once suggested that the most important action that an individual could undertake on behalf of world peace would not be any particular political initiative, but simply the withdrawal of personal *projections*. In psychology, projection is the process of denying one's own thoughts, feelings, or tendencies by attributing them to other individuals, groups, or races, or even objects and symbols. A projection is often an attempt to disown negative characteristics, but it can also be a way of creating a reflection of something positive, as when one projects love onto a cherished object like an automobile, then imagines that the car actually loves its owner in return. And it's certain that professional athletics would not be such a lucrative business if fans were to withdraw all their various projections of self-judgment and ego-inflation from their favorite sports teams.

Projections can do a great deal of damage when people accuse others of harboring prejudices and hostilities that are actually their own, but are blamed on others in disguised and distorted forms. This negative dynamic operates in all kinds of relationships, but it can clearly be seen in international politics when nations, religious sects, or cultural and racial groups become locked in chronic struggles that are driven by accusing one another of hatred and aggression, then acting on those accusations with claims of victimization and justified self-defense. Once a round of mutual negative projections gets going, it can be very difficult for either side to disengage. No group or nation likes to admit its own aggressive tendencies, and there is a powerful fear of being seen as weak if attacks are withdrawn or defenses lowered.

As politics go, so goes the psyche—and it could be argued that every war across the globe begins with the war inside our own minds. That is clearly ACIM's view of human conflict:

> What you project you disown, and therefore do not believe is yours. You are excluding yourself by the very judgment that you are different from the one on whom you project. Since you have also judged against what you project, you continue to attack it because you continue to keep it separated. By doing this unconsciously, you try to keep the fact that you attacked yourself out of awareness, and thus imagine that you have made yourself safe.

> Yet projection will always hurt you. It reinforces your belief in your own split mind, and its only purpose is to keep the separation going. It is solely a device of the ego to make you feel different from your brothers and separated from them. The ego justifies this on the grounds that it makes you seem "better" than they are, thus obscuring your equality with them still further. Projection and attack are inevitably related, because projection is always a means of justifying attack. Anger without projection is impossible. The ego uses projection only to destroy your perception of both yourself and your brothers. The process begins by excluding something that exists in you but which you do not want, and leads directly to excluding you from your brothers. (Chapter 6, II: 2–3)

Mistakenly believing that we are fatally separated from the unconditional love of God, we concoct all manner of self-accusations about
how and why we were so punished. Yet the part of our mind that
fosters this belief in separation, the ego, also wants to convince us
that our individual identity is our salvation, and must not be undermined. So the ego gets busy driving some of our self-accusations
into the unconscious, while projecting the rest as the flaws and evil
intentions of our apparent enemies. Then we are easily convinced
of the need to defend ourselves against them.

ACIM's answer to the ego's fearful logic is unequivocal—and
undoubtedly startling to the uninitiated. It is concisely summed up
in Workbook Lesson 153, "In my defenselessness my safety lies":

> Defenses are the costliest of all the prices which the ego would
> exact. In them lies madness in a form so grim that hope of sanity
> seems but to be an idle dream, beyond the possible. The sense of
> threat the world encourages is so much deeper, and so far beyond
> the frenzy and intensity of which you can conceive, that you have
> no idea of all the devastation it has wrought. . . .
>
> We will not play such childish games today. For our true pur-
> pose is to save the world, and we would not exchange for foolish-
> ness the endless joy our function offers us. We would not let our
> happiness slip by because a fragment of a senseless dream hap-
> pened to cross our minds, and we mistook the figures in it for the
> Son of God; its tiny instant for eternity.
>
> We look past dreams today, and recognize that we need no
> defense because we are created unassailable, without all thought or
> wish or dream in which attack has any meaning. Now we cannot
> fear, for we have left all fearful thoughts behind. And in defense-
> lessness we stand secure, serenely certain of our safety now, sure of

salvation; sure we will fulfill our chosen purpose, as our ministry extends its holy blessing through the world. (Lesson 153: 4, 8–9)

Still, it seems impossible to deny that there are times when we suffer unprovoked attacks by others on whom we have no reason to project anything or we observe at a distance acts of murderous lunacy by killers and terrorists. Savage aggression appears to be an inescapable fact of life on our planet. So it seems necessary and sensible to fear, judge, and prosecute those who perpetrate insane attacks. While the Course makes no pronouncements about criminal justice or society's response to terrorism, it is utterly uncompromising about what our *inner* response should be:

> When a brother acts insanely, he is offering you an opportunity to bless him. His need is yours. You need the blessing you can offer him. There is no way for you to have it except by giving it. This is the law of God, and it has no exceptions. What you deny you lack, not because it is lacking, but because you have denied it in another and are therefore not aware of it in yourself. Every response you make is determined by what you think you are, and what you want to be *is* what you think you are. What you want to be, then, must determine every response you make. (Chapter 7, VII: 2)

An Ultimate Code of Personal Responsibility

A Course in Miracles has occasionally been criticized by outside observers as a self-indulgent guide to "creating your own reality," but those experienced in its discipline know that this view is critically uninformed. The Course does assert that our ego-based perceptions literally create the world we see—but that world is a chaotic mix of beauty and horror, life and death, and inconstant experiences of love besieged by fear and loneliness. Condemned by our own physicality to losing everything we cherish to the inevitability of death, the reality we seem to have created is ultimately harsh and unforgiving:

> The world you see is a vengeful world, and everything in it is a symbol of vengeance. Each of your perceptions of "external reality" is a pictorial representation of your own attack thoughts. One can well ask if this can be called seeing. Is not fantasy a better word for such a process, and hallucination a more appropriate term for the result? (From Lesson 23)

Further, the Course warns that our identification with the ego leads us to continually re-create a punishing world at every moment of ordinary consciousness. The ego's tendency toward wishful thinking only creates an endless cycle of hopes for something better being raised and cruelly dashed:

> We have already said that wishful thinking is how the ego deals with what it wants, to make it so. There is no better demonstration of the power of wanting, and therefore of faith, to make its goals seem real and possible. Faith in the unreal leads to adjustments of reality to make it fit the goal of madness. The goal of sin induces the perception of a fearful world to justify its purpose. What you desire, you will see. And if its reality is false, you will uphold it by not realizing all the adjustments you have introduced to make it so. (Chapter 21, II: 9)

Far from holding out the promise of a malleable material world that can be perfected by visualizing whatever we want from it, ACIM instead charges that we are already getting what we "want" as self-destructive egos. Wherever we see cruelty, murder, or even destructive "acts of God" in the form of killer hurricanes and earthquakes, it is because we have chosen to see that kind of world. We may undertake personal or political campaigns to rid the world of various evils, but all such efforts are doomed as long as we believe that the material and perishable world is where we actually live. Visualizing a shiny new car in the driveway may or may not lead to that car someday appearing there, but it will not alter the inevitability of someday being too old and decrepit to drive it. At the ego level, we can dream up and exhaustively pursue a thousand such "adjustments" to our ultimately unsatisfactory reality, but in the Course view, we will still be pursuing madness.

To counter the wishful and destructive thinking of the ego, ACIM provides a thoroughgoing discipline for accessing the counsel of the Holy Spirit, which would reconnect us with our eternal and imperishable reality within the mind of God. To hear that counsel, we must accept ultimate responsibility for everything we see and experience—and then forgive it, and forgive ourselves for seeing it. As we pursue that process, we grow in our capacity to hear the Holy Spirit, and thus gain access to whatever we really need:

> Only the Holy Spirit knows what you need. For He will give you all things that do not block the way to light. And what else could you need? In time, He gives you all the things that you need have, and will renew them as long as you have need of them. He will take nothing from you as long as you have any need of it. And yet He knows that everything you need is temporary, and will but

last until you step aside from all your needs and realize that all of them have been fulfilled. Therefore He has no investment in the things that He supplies, except to make certain that you will not use them on behalf of lingering in time. He knows that you are not at home there, and He wills no delay to wait upon your joyous homecoming. (Chapter 13, VII: 12)

In practice, learning to listen to the Holy Spirit instead of the ego can be a delicate and oft-interrupted process. In my own experience, I've become acutely aware of the tendency to presume that what I think I need—recently, for instance, more money, more recognition, or more influence on the publishing industry—is what the Holy Spirit will *agree* that I need. Thus, when my wishful thinking and enthusiastic planning fail to realize such goals, I can easily conclude that the Holy Spirit has fallen down on the job!

Whenever I'm tempted by this suspicion, I try to remind myself of what the Manual for Teachers identifies as the ten qualities of advanced "teachers of God": Trust, Honesty, Tolerance, Gentleness, Joy, Defenselessness, Generosity, Patience, Faithfulness, and Open-Mindedness. No matter how many times I have reviewed it, I have never found in that list the attributes of Affluence, Fame, or Personal Power. In this light, what the Holy Spirit seems to think I need is sometimes a mystery indeed.

Healing a Mountain of Stuff

Other Course students report different challenges in releasing ego-driven patterns to access spiritual wisdom. As northern California student Sofia Pizano recalls,

My process has changed since I first started the Course. The first year was the toughest, because as I began to realize how much garbage (guilt, shame, fear, judgments of others, etc.) that I was living with, the more isolated I felt. It seemed like I had a mountain of "stuff" to heal and forgive, and I thought I had to do it all by myself. For example, when I came upon a forgiveness opportunity, I didn't see it as such. I saw it as yet another reason to feel guilty and ashamed of myself. I couldn't quite believe in the Holy Spirit that the Course talks about, so I pretended there was "someone" out there who would look past my inadequacies and help me get through the process as gently as possible. It was very painful for me to see and feel so much ugliness hidden deep within me.

Fortunately, as I diligently practiced the lessons every day, I came to understand that there really was "someone" with me to help me heal. At that point, I began working with the Holy Spirit (or Jesus) directly. At the end of each day, if there were any lessons I felt I did not do well, I would write them down and talk to Jesus about them. This helped me tremendously. After a while, I began to notice that things didn't affect me like they used to. It was as if someone erased the problem or issue from my memory.

Now, I'm finding that I don't use the list-writing method as much. I think I'm feeling a bit more congruent with the Holy Spirit's guidance, in that when I feel resistance or any negative emotion come up, I immediately acknowledge that this is not how I want to feel. I then allow the resistance (fear, anger, blame, guilt, etc.) to wash over me like a wave, knowing very well that the Holy Spirit is helping me every step of the way without me having to call upon Him directly.

Rowan Hagen of Australia compares the process of hearing a different kind of voice to that of changing stations on a radio dial:

> To me, ego is the talk radio in my head. There's a daily litany of *"ain't it awful," "poor me," "my partner/relative/coworker/neighbor is impossible,"* and *"if only (any name here) was different, I'd be loved/successful/happy/admired."* Irritating, yet I have trouble keeping it switched off. Meanwhile, the larger Self notices the roses blooming, sees the goodness in my brother and hears his anger as a cry for love. To "choose once again" is to change stations.
>
> I've found the Course very insightful in pointing out these patterns and have often put its teaching to use. But it's a work in progress. For me, it's not so much how I could do things differently, but whether or not I need to get worked up about them at all. I'm learning to accept that, if left alone, outer circumstances generally work out for the greater good. It leaves something for the Holy Spirit to do.

Finally, Toni Neal of Maryland cites a prayer from the ACIM Text that provides a simple reminder of when access to the Holy Spirit is beneficial:

> Sometimes, unfortunately, my ego has such a hold on me that things have to get pretty bad before I reach the point of remembering "there *is* a better way . . . I *can* see peace instead of this!" But I've been practicing the Course long enough that it isn't as easy to get away with things as it used to be. My lack of peace is more apparent now in small things; I used to think that meant things were getting worse, until I remembered the Course's teachings

that as we advance, we will become more sensitive to even the smallest things that seem to rob us of our peace.

The prayer at the end of Chapter 5 has helped me tremendously in situations where I find myself feeling a sense of helplessness or loss of control:

> *I must have decided wrongly, because I am not at peace.*
> *I made the decision myself, but I can also decide otherwise.*
> *I want to decide otherwise, because I want to be at peace.*
> *I do not feel guilty, because the Holy Spirit will undo all the consequences of my wrong decision if I will let Him.*
> *I choose to let Him, by allowing Him to decide for God for me.*

Forgiveness is a long process, I've discovered. But I have also learned it is ultimately a forgiveness of myself, and the more I am able to withdraw my projections from others, the more I realize that *I* am the only one who is responsible for finding peace. And then I have more compassion for myself—why, unless I have such guilt and fear inside, would I insist on attacking others? Then I can ask the Holy Spirit for help in seeing myself as God sees me; to love as He loves; to forgive as Christ forgives.

Summary

A Course in Miracles identifies the ego, or our customary sense of self, as the source of all problems in our mind. But the mind actually surpasses the ego and can in fact learn to make a choice between its fearful voice and the calming counsel of the Holy Spirit.

In this regard the Course is the opposite of popular self-help techniques that offer reinforcement and encouragement for pursuing egocentric goals of greater material comfort, romance, and professional achievement. The Course is instead focused on helping students escape the ego's typical lures, which include the "attraction of guilt" via the notion of sin, and the tendency to project one's own negative attitudes and attributes onto others. Projection not only poisons intimate relationships, but serves as the engine of cultural tensions and war on a worldwide basis. In ACIM's view, we create a chaotic and troubled reality via projection, as our own guilt about having separated from the original and creative love of God is thrown out onto the world we see every day.

The route to peace and happiness is not to visualize a more pleasing version of that world, but to forgive it, and forgive ourselves for imagining it in so convincing a manner. As we learn to forgive, we will begin to hear the guidance of the Holy Spirit on a daily basis, instructing us on how to see and act in accordance with the reality of God's eternal love behind all the forms and illusions of the everyday material world. The fearful voice of the ego can be very loud and insistent, but with practice Course students find diverse and unique approaches to letting it go.

8.

Transforming
Special Relationships

.

The ego wishes no one well. Yet its survival depends on your belief
that you are exempt from its evil intentions. It counsels, therefore, that
if you are host to it, it will enable you to direct its anger outward, thus
protecting you. And thus it embarks on an endless, unrewarding chain
of special relationships, forged out of anger and dedicated to but one
insane belief; that the more anger you invest outside yourself, the safer
you become.

—Chapter 15, VII: 4

The quote above gives just a hint about the challenge that most
students of *A Course in Miracles* experience in dealing with
its view of "special relationships." When one first encounters this
subject in the Text, it can seem that the teaching is totally cynical about the prospects of intimate partnerships, which provide the
starting point for family life and thus the fundamental structure
of human society. In Chapters 15 through 17 there are some very
harsh portrayals of the special relationship, including the meta-
phor of a picture whose frame is decorated with "all sorts of fanci-
ful and fragmented illusions of love, set with dreams of sacrifice
and self-aggrandizement, and interlaced with gilded threads of
self-destruction" (Chapter 17, IV: 8). Although this material is
relatively brief—and there is actually more in the Course about the

healing antidote identified as the "holy relationship"—the discussion of special relationships is likely one of the most disturbing topics for ACIM novices. It's reasonable to assume that many students have stopped or paused their study upon encountering this topic.

To understand where the Course is coming from about relationships, it's worth reviewing the teaching's fundamental perspective on reality. ACIM asserts that our apparent existence as individuals in bodies is a pernicious illusion that we maintain and share at the cost of our happiness and awareness of eternal life: "The body is the symbol of what you think you are. It is clearly a separation device, and therefore does not exist" (Chapter 6, V: A, 2). The part of our mind that fosters and perpetuates our sense of separation is the fear-driven ego, and the ego literally creates the illusion of the body to cement its hold on our consciousness. The body then becomes incontrovertible proof of our separateness, our numerous imperfections, our need to survive and the necessity to compete, and finally our fate in death.

The body also serves as convincing proof that our temporary survival and well-being depend on other bodies: first in the person of our mother; next in the persons of the family or substitute group that supports our growth as children; and eventually in the persons of lovers and mates who support our identity as adults and become our partners in sexual intimacy and raising families of our own. We also form important friendships and a variety of work-related connections throughout our lives. In all these contexts, each relationship features different interdependencies based on the individual needs of our different bodies, and is therefore "special."

And at every stage of special relationship with these other bodies, there are problems. Parents may be neglectful or self-serving;

families may be rent by internal conflict and the inability to resolve differences of character; lovers who are swept away by the passions of romance can all too easily find themselves betrayed and disillusioned when romance inevitably fades. And workplaces are often jousting grounds of cutthroat competition.

Nonetheless, the human species continues to propagate itself, and all its societies across the world continue to function, however chaotic and conflicted they may be. Most people find some degree of stability in their most important relationships, whether or not those relationships are characterized by genuine love and happiness. Whereas most religions offer some kind of rules or guidance for the proper conduct of relationships, *A Course in Miracles* overturns the whole premise of relationships as we ordinarily think of them. The teaching asserts that there can be no authentic love when egos and bodies are merely depending on one another to prolong and improve their temporary and illusory circumstances. That's because mutual dependence is based on a false sense of guilt and inadequacy:

> In looking at the special relationship, it is necessary first to realize that it involves a great amount of pain. Anxiety, despair, guilt and attack all enter into it, broken into by periods in which they seem to be gone. All these must be understood for what they are. Whatever form they take, they are always an attack on the self to make the other guilty. I have spoken of this before, but there are some aspects of what is really being attempted that have not been touched upon. . . .
>
> Most curious of all is the concept of the self which the ego fosters in the special relationship. This "self" seeks the relationship to make itself complete. Yet when it finds the special relationship in

which it thinks it can accomplish this it gives itself away, and tries to "trade" itself for the self of another. This is not union, for there is no increase and no extension. Each partner tries to sacrifice the self he does not want for one he thinks he would prefer. And he feels guilty for the "sin" of taking, and of giving nothing of value in return. How much value can he place upon a self that he would give away to get a "better" one?

The "better" self the ego seeks is always one that is more special . . . (Chapter 16, VI: 1, 7–8)

The Bridge to the Holy Relationship

Would the Course then have us retreat from all our relationships into a lonely cave where we can contemplate our existence all by ourselves? No, for as it does with every other aspect of our existence, ACIM suggests that the key to happiness and wholeness in relationships is a shift in perception:

> The holy relationship, a major step toward the perception of the real world, is learned. It is the old, unholy relationship, transformed and seen anew. The holy relationship is a phenomenal teaching accomplishment. In all its aspects, as it begins, develops and becomes accomplished, it represents the reversal of the unholy relationship. (Chapter 17, V: 2)

A holy relationship starts from a different premise. Each one has looked within and seen no lack. Accepting his completion, he would extend it by joining with another, whole as himself. He sees no difference between these selves, for differences are only of the body. Therefore, he looks on nothing he would take. He denies not his own reality *because* it is the truth. Just under Heaven does he stand, but close enough not to return to earth. For this relationship has Heaven's Holiness. How far from home can a relationship so like to Heaven be? (Chapter 22, Introduction: 3)

To "look within and see no lack" is to see one's spiritual essence surpassing all aspects of the material world; it means having the *willingness*, if not yet the *capacity*, to look beyond physical appearances into a metaphysical reality. Likewise, a "special" relationship can become "holy" when two people have agreed to see themselves as celebrators and teachers of their innate, eternal wholeness beyond the body, rather than needy individuals who have found the perfect person to "complete" each other in their limited time on earth.

You see the world you value. On this side of the bridge you see the world of separate bodies, seeking to join each other in separate unions and to become one by losing. When two individuals seek to become one, they are trying to decrease their magnitude. Each would deny his power, for the separate union excludes the universe. Far more is left outside than would be taken in, for God is left without and *nothing* taken in. If one such union were made in perfect faith, the universe would enter into it. Yet the special relationship the ego seeks does not include even one whole individual. The ego wants but part of him, and sees only this part and nothing else.

Across the bridge it is so different! For a time the body is still seen, but not exclusively, as it is seen here. . . . Once you have crossed the bridge, the value of the body is so diminished in your sight that you will see no need at all to magnify it. For you will realize that the only value the body has is to enable you to bring your brothers to the bridge with you, and to be released together there. (Chapter 15, VI: 5–6)

Despite the fact that the Course is generally recognized as a self-study curriculum, its key goals are achieved in relationship. One of these goals is the "holy instant," a moment of enlightened realization in which the conventional bounds of time and space are released. In that instant, the student recognizes his oneness with the universe and the eternity of the present moment. In this regard, a holy instant is roughly equivalent to the *kensho* of Zen Buddhism. But a holy instant is not achieved through years of silent or solo meditation, but in the context of relationship:

The holy instant is the Holy Spirit's most useful learning device for teaching you love's meaning. For its purpose is to suspend judgment entirely. Judgment always rests on the past, for past experience is the basis on which you judge. Judgment becomes impossible without the past, for without it you do not understand anything. You would make no attempt to judge, because it would be quite apparent to you that you do not understand what anything means. You are afraid of this because you believe that without the ego, all would be chaos. Yet I assure you that without the ego, all would be love. . . .

Everyone on earth has formed special relationships, and although this is not so in Heaven, the Holy Spirit knows how to bring a touch of Heaven to them here. In the holy instant no one is special, for your personal needs intrude on no one to make your brothers seem different. Without the values from the past, you would see them all the same and like yourself. Nor would you see any separation between yourself and them. In the holy instant, you see in each relationship what it will be when you perceive only the present. (Chapter 15, V: 1, 8)

A Case History of Relationship

Most Course students struggle with understanding the philosophical differences between special and holy relationships, and even more so with the application of ACIM principles to their everyday connections to other people (most of whom are probably not Course students). The whole issue can get so caught up in intellectualization and semantics that the pursuit of a holy relationship may be turned into yet another tool of specialness. Even some leading teachers of ACIM disagree on exactly what it takes to transform a special relationship, although everyone concurs that the end result is a transcendent union that can demonstrate selfless love to many others.

Especially vexing for novice students can be the issue of form versus content in romantic love, the type of special relationship in which many people place their greatest hopes for happiness and often experience the most bitter disillusionments. *A Course in Miracles* says nothing about marriage, monogamy, or sexual behavior—the very issues that are often at the heart of conventional religious dictates about sin, morality, and a healthy society. But since ACIM denies the reality of bodies, it is not concerned with what bodies do, beyond their optimal use as tools for communication:

Remember that the Holy Spirit interprets the body only as a means of communication. . . .

If you use the body for attack, it is harmful to you. If you use it only to reach the minds of those who believe they are bodies, and teach them *through* the body that this is not so, you will understand the power of the mind that is in you. If you use the body for this and only for this, you cannot use it for attack. In the service of uniting it becomes a beautiful lesson in communion, which has value until communion *is*. This is God's way of making unlimited what you have limited. (Chapter 8, VII: 2, 3)

Nouk Sanchez and Tomas Vieira have been popular speakers and workshop leaders on the ACIM circuit who have coauthored the book *Take Me to Truth: Undoing the Ego.* (Tomas passed away in 2010, after the interview with Nouk that follows.) It was not uncommon for people who encountered this teaching team to mistake them for marriage partners, which they once were. Their fascinating story, as related below by Nouk in an e-mail correspondence, provides a rare case history in how a relationship dedicated to seeking spiritual truth may change forms while vacillating between what the Course calls special and holy purposes. As Nouk relates, what conventional society views as a form of commitment may be no guarantee of achieving genuine spiritual communion:

Tomas and I met in 1984 in Cairns, Australia, and became dear friends almost immediately. Both of us were in relationships; mine was monogamous, his serial. When we met we would listen to and support each other without conditions or selfish considerations. As our friendship deepened, we realized that we had a very valuable relationship, which led us to making a sacred vow. Upon reflection, it was to set the stage for the transfer from a special to a holy relationship several years later. The vow was: *"No matter whom and no matter what might seem to come between us, let us never abandon each other."* The vow came from our single commitment to learn of the uninterrupted and eternal nature of love, and was born in a moment of complete abandonment of selfish motives.

In 1987, we married in the Catholic Church, complete with the prerequisite religious education, and in 1988, our daughter Rikki was born into what had become, by then, a special relationship.

In 1990, ACIM found me and after much resistance, it made its way into Tomas's heart too. This was a significant milestone that precipitated the undoing process and the relinquishment of the special relationship.

In 1997 we felt called upon to take our relationship to another level of trust. Staying true to our vow of never abandoning each other, we divorced in order to save our relationship. In other words, we renounced the superficial "form" of marriage to save the "content" of our relationship. We let many of our insecurities and defenses fall away and remained true to *unlearning* our old idea of what love was. It was this unlearning that preceded the present experience of a Love that cannot be threatened. In our workshops we always point out that no one else has to do what we did; we seem to be pioneers in the sense that we were guided to divorce *and* remain totally committed to each other.

During and after the official divorce Tomas and I remained close. I was called to the USA in 1999, while Tomas remained in Australia. We talked almost every day and have done so ever since. Sensing that I required even more "unlearning" and relationship training, I married Nick Sanchez in 2000. Most people attract a partner based on mutual ego interests; this was not the case for me this time. Nick had no interest whatsoever in spirituality, and most of his beliefs and values were very different from mine (and remain largely unchanged to date). So this was the perfect opportunity for me to learn to extend love instead of what we normally do, that is, trying to get love from another in a special relationship. And as I learned to extend through forgiveness, I came to experience yet another deeper level of love and trust within. The more I gave, the more I received. I learned that the way to finding love is to give what we most desire for ourselves. It's in the giving that we finally discover that we had it all along.

I live with Nick and Rikki in Santa Fe, New Mexico. Tomas and I joined in 2005 to write *Take Me to Truth*, and we've been travelling the world together since the book's launch in 2007. Tomas stays with us in Santa Fe for six months of the year and we continue to experience further growth together. For us, there are ongoing levels of unlearning and learning simultaneously. And we're great believers in embracing what Jesus, in the Course, refers to as the last of the characteristics that the Teacher of God acquires: Open-Mindedness. We've learned that without this, the student stops learning, which means he becomes a poor teacher.

Noting that Nouk and Tomas had been unusually committed friends before they became romantically involved, I asked Nouk which phases of their long relationship have been "special" in Course terms.

When we first met we were unconditional with each other. In those first two years, Tomas was dating and so was I. We were simply best of friends who hid nothing from each other and had a deep interest in exploring the nature of Love and God. Looking back, it is clear to see that specialness entered when our relationship changed into a romantic and sexual one. It was then that the rules changed. Specialness reared its ugly head as "exclusivity." So we did what normal egos do. We essentially said to each other, *"If you love me, you'll do what I want; you will fulfill my needs."* And: *"If you don't meet my needs, the love that I have for you will be withdrawn."* Subconsciously yet powerfully, all our fears and stories of victimhood, anger and hate were raised and projected onto the object of our love, each other.

Looking back to that specialness phase, we can see how we unconsciously used each other and then projected all our self-hatred onto each other. We professed that we "needed" each other, declaring that to be love. We see now that the truth is that if you need someone, you're really *using* them.

I then asked Nouk whether teaching together has become the shared purpose that makes a relationship "holy":

I think our common purpose could be stated as this: *The singular desire to awaken from a dream of suffering.* This purpose has led us to share and write and teach together. And because we're so devoted to it, every other distraction seems to have fallen away. From this primary goal we've been graced with the "living experience" of the holy relationship which, as we now see, was the foundation for all the other lessons that are leading us back to the state of Love with no opposite. It's from the foundation of this holy relationship that we're recognizing the transfer value across every other aspect of the dream. We've learned that we don't need to "control" things anymore; i.e., finances, health, relationships, outcomes, etc.

The natural outcome of the development of trust in God is that we now know all our needs are met—literally. There is no more to "do" or to "get" and no more to "resist." If we need to do something, it comes from Guidance and therefore has no attachment in it. So what's left for us now is this enormous feeling of wanting to extend the love and teachings that appear to be running through us. It is absolutely miraculous; the desire to *give* far more than we want to *get* is the most gracious, liberating and fulfilling experience that we've ever had here in this dream.

In my previous book *Understanding A Course in Miracles*, I quoted prominent ACIM teacher Robert Perry about his opinion that it takes two people to agree that they are pursuing a holy relationship together. I asked Nouk whether she saw this question differently.

From my experience, it only takes one to have a holy relationship. I am remarried and in 2004, my husband Nick and I moved to Australia for a while. Nick is not a Course student and has no interest in Awakening; hence he is the perfect teacher to frustrate my ego's needs. Nick is a native New Mexican whose identity is heavily invested in being a hard worker, but in Australia there were no jobs available at the time. His identity was threatened and he was immensely uncomfortable. I was stressed with my daughter's illness at the time so it was a recipe for relationship conflict. I descended into victimhood because his discomfort was my fault and my added responsibility of caring for a sick child led me to feel "all alone."

I fell into a trap that many spiritual seekers fall into; I wanted to change Nick. He wasn't into Awakening and I was. So, if I could make him more spiritual, then our relationship would be healed! This is what I call the Superiority Syndrome; it's a cunning ploy of the ego pretending to be spiritual, and has nothing whatsoever to do with waking up, or love.

The conflict between us grew and became unbearable; the more I wanted to change him, the more he seemed to attack, which eventually brought me to my knees. After fourteen years of studying the Course, I felt I had failed miserably in truly living the example of Jesus' teachings on relationship. At the lowest point of my dark night, I fell to my knees crying out to the Holy Spirit. I asked for help in healing my perception and then suddenly an astonishing thing happened. I heard a commanding Voice boom out, *"There is no Nick."* I was stunned. After a few seconds I responded by asking, "What do you mean?" And then I got it! It was as if a massive divine download occurred all in one holy instant. "There is no Nick." The Voice meant it literally. This was the part that I hadn't understood in fourteen years of study. Finally I felt an awesome shift in my perception and I knew without a doubt that not just my relationship with Nick, but *all* my relationships would be healed from now on. How? Because I recognized and accepted that healing takes place in my own mind first. My mind is the central headquarters for healing anything or anybody that appears to disturb me.

The outcome of our relationship at the level of "form" is this: We never had another conflict again. Although I never spoke about what happened with Nick, a profound shift occurred in our relationship because I changed my mind and allowed forgiveness in. When I realized that all perceived conflict arose from my own projected unconscious guilt, I also realized that I was using Nick to attack me with my own unconscious self-hatred (guilt).

His perceived attack was really my own projection. I was the one needing forgiveness! From that point on I saw that it only takes one to experience a holy relationship.

Still, whether they are Course students or not, many people are frustrated by wanting the nature of a close relationship to change and not being able to get a partner to cooperate. I asked Nouk how she sees this predicament.

From my experience, there is no "other." All change stems from aligning myself with the will of God.

There's no chance of true change or healing in any relationship while the goal is to get our perceived needs met (i.e., sex, intimacy, financial security, etc). If you want a real relationship, one that reveals the nature of uninterrupted love, then you must prioritize one goal only, and that is to *awaken* for yourself. Operating through the ego thought system, we don't have a clue what love is; we can't give love and we can't receive love. It's not until the destructive concept of "special love" is undone that we can begin to have the experience of love here in the dream. In my mind the only purpose all my relationships have is to help me (and others) to awaken to the fact that we *are* one and all our needs are already met.

There is only one way to change the nature of any relationship and that is to offer the relationship to the Holy Spirit. Any and all other "changes" will follow from aligning your intent and trust in that one goal. Our desire to change another comes from the ego; it arises from the ego's investment in deprivation and separation. For instance, Nick and I no longer have any conflict because he knows that he is free to be as he is, unchallenged. As such he is grateful daily for what we have, and that only brings out joy and gratitude in myself.

In ACIM's Manual for Teachers, a discussion of the "levels of teaching" implies that the most rewarding of relationships may also be the most difficult:

> The third level of teaching occurs in relationships which, once they are formed, are lifelong. These are teaching-learning situations in which each person is given a chosen learning partner who presents him with unlimited opportunities for learning. These relationships are generally few, because their existence implies that those involved have reached a stage simultaneously in which the teaching-learning balance is actually perfect. This does not mean that they necessarily recognize this; in fact, they generally do not. They may even be quite hostile to each other for some time, and perhaps for life. Yet should they decide to learn it, the perfect lesson is before them and can be learned. (Manual, 3: 5)

In view of this provocative passage, I asked Nouk if a holy relationship can also be a difficult one.

> Yes, a relationship can be holy *and* difficult but as our trust in Holy Spirit increases and we undo the ego, peace is the natural outcome. We explained many of the components of undoing the ego and developing trust in Holy Spirit in *Take Me to Truth*. A major component of the ego is what we call "mistaken identities." These are the myriad uninvestigated beliefs that make up the mental concept of "me." For example, "me" is made up of conditioning, the body, the past, personal and global beliefs and values, interests,

etc. Yet all these beliefs and values are meaningless and really not who we are. Who we are can't be known until all the "mistaken identities" are undone. So when two people fall in love they are not experiencing love at all. They see each other's "image": the body, beliefs, interests, and values of the ego, the false self. They fall in love with a false "image" only and don't see the Self at all.

When Tomas and I fell in love, we fell in love with each other's ego attributes. It took years for us to undo these attachments and to realize that all of them are simply substitutes for God's Love. As our relationship went from special to holy, we went through a distressing time. The reason was that the false self was being undone, and it felt like a death to the ego. We came to realize that what we thought was love was really "ego-stroking." And we were both addicted to ego-stroking! So when that was retracted it felt uncomfortable indeed.

I learned that all it took to make any relationship holy was *my own corrected perception*. It didn't need another person's participation. As a result every correctly perceived relationship—forgiven and therefore without judgment—is a holy one. There is only *one* mind to be healed, and that mind is my own. The "form" of a relationship may change as it heals, although this doesn't need to happen in all relationships. Once the "mistaken identities" fall away it's possible that what brought the relationship together is no longer keeping it together. In our case the mistaken identities fell away and suddenly we "saw" each other. We saw the infinite holiness in each other and nothing could possibly threaten that. Love with a capital "L" was revealed as we learned through experience that in our defenselessness lies our safety.

Through relationship I've learned that to the extent that I am upset over another person or circumstance, to that same degree there is still unconscious guilt remaining. Unconscious guilt is the "suffering factor" in our lives and the source is never something outside us. The triggers are most often our relationships. If my suffering appears to be caused by another, I can now realize the true source: my own wrong-mindedness. The ego seeks to change the relationship to suit its needs, but the Holy Spirit simply heals our perception which is the fundamental cause of all our human suffering.

I also asked Nouk how the Course perspective on special and holy relationships affects child-raising and family life.

I believe that 99.9 percent of us have been raised by parents who came from a special relationship; in other words, from a totally conditional paradigm. The effect of this is a mass indoctrination into the unchallenged belief that love is to be earned rather than given. The ego thought system of deprivation and lack has been passed down since time began and reinforced through history, and all its assumptions are now embraced as fact.

Jesus came to deliver us from duality over two thousand years ago, yet we reverted back almost immediately to the ego's laws of sowing and reaping, of worldly cause and effect and the laws of reward and punishment. We have taken on a multitude of unquestioned beliefs and values, and we pass them on to our children as fact. In the name of love, we mirror and therefore teach fear; for instance, "You need an education to college level, at least, in this day and age." To borrow a little slang from the British: "Bollocks!"

When we allowed our relationship to be transformed into a holy relationship, our relationship with our daughter was also transformed.

We saw clearly how most of our previous guidance was not from love but from fear. We saw that we were more interested in getting the "form" right than the content. For example, Rikki had to go to the best school we could afford, she had to complete her homework regardless of her interest or energy levels, and she needed to be social even if she was introverted in nature. The list goes on.

We also saw that we mistakenly believed that just because we had the earthly appearance of being older, we were somehow also wiser. What a joke that was!

When the *content* of our relationship with our daughter was revealed to us, we recognized that in fact, *she* was the teacher and we had been very poor students. It is clear to us now that the "content" of a holy relationship consists of extending love, by expressing the following: forgiveness, vulnerability, honesty, defenselessness, spiritual equality, and trust, none of which was previously evident in our parenting!

Today, our daughter is our best friend. She is a spiritual equal and if we had to do the parenting over again, we would see ourselves more as facilitators rather than parents, by encouraging the nature of God as individually expressed in our daughter. As parents, at the level of form, we do know a little more from being in this dream a little longer and can pass on some insights. But any other distinction is just ego aggrandizement.

I was also interested to know what Nouk and Tomas, as Course teachers, have observed to be the most frequent challenges that students experience with ACIM's perspective on relationships.

One of the biggest challenges we've seen is that the ego loves to take itself on an intellectual romp of studying the Course and using what it's learned to correct others, especially significant others. We both went through a stage where we used the Course against each other. We were entrenched in being "right" rather than happy! We used the Course to control each other and to feel superior; that's the spiritual ego right there. It wasn't until we'd matured spiritually that we understood the value of truly "joining" with another at the level of mind, even if we disagreed at the level of behavior.

Another area where many get caught is in self-judgment. As we awaken we travel through the six stages of the Development of Trust (Manual, 4, I: A). In the beginning our most difficult task is to forgive our past, others, situations and circumstances, etc. As we develop trust, the ego begins to drop away and we find yet a deeper layer of unforgiveness and guilt. This is our own judgment of self, which is really our own fear of God as Love. The ego uses self-judgment as a separation tool and it is one invested with great power until we see it for what it is: an illusion. It's the core of the ego's false humility and one of the last defenses that we surrender, because without this we will experience the Power of God. That means no more defenses against Love, and no more fear of (or attraction to) deprivation, death, and suffering. It does mean, however, that we "claim" our Divine Inheritance right here and now, *in* the dream. That's a terrifying thought to the ego.

Releasing self-judgment through forgiveness is as important as forgiving others. It's an intrinsic part of fostering a holy relationship. If we can't forgive our own self-judgments, they get projected as attack on our bodies (sickness, accidents, and death), and onto other people and the seemingly external circumstances of our lives.

In our experience one tends to embrace the Course's teachings literally only when they have had enough suffering. Most of us, even after years of studying the Course intellectually, still try to hang on to our special relationships. While they may be causing pain, it's nowhere near the pain of the *imagined* loss and sacrifice that would result from exchanging our specialness for holiness. This is the fear of love that Jesus speaks of in the Course. So, it's usually not until we've experienced a major disillusionment that we become open to dropping our own beliefs and values, thereby opening to remember the Love that we intrinsically are.

The concept of attaining a holy relationship can also become a pursuit for a kind of Holy Grail. That's a destructive undertaking if people get caught up in "making" their relationships holy, which usually implies changing someone else. Or, people who are alone can use it to hurt themselves by mistakenly believing that without a significant other they are deprived of the chance to have a holy relationship. The truth is that it only takes *one,* and you can have a holy relationship with anyone here now, or even in the past, because it's all about healing your perception. In short, there's no one else in the room!

If the ACIM perspective on relationship doesn't seem to work for someone, it's usually because they still wish to believe that the cause of suffering is outside them—in the past, another person, their own body, an undesirable circumstance, or even God— instead of their own split mind. Therefore they will never heal the one cause of suffering as long as they still value the ego's way of trying to fix things. Often people have just not yet incurred enough suffering to give up trying to fix the dream of their life, instead of awakening *from* that dream.

Summary

The Course view of "special relationships" is one of the teaching's most vexing challenges for many students, as it seems to vilify a goal of intimacy and union that most people hold dear and find indispensable to their happiness. But ACIM is adamant in maintaining that the reason our special relationships so often go wrong is that they are based on a premise that is as false as it is profound. That premise is that we are embodied individuals with a limited time on earth to fulfill our constant needs, correct our inborn inadequacies, and shore up our chronically damaged self-esteem.

Given such deeply rooted assumptions about our incompleteness, it seems only natural to turn to other people—parents, siblings, friends, coworkers, and especially lovers and mates—to supply whatever seems to be missing in ourselves. From ACIM's point of view, that means we are merely projecting our habitual self-hatred onto others, expecting them to perform impossible tasks of reparation on our behalf. Thus we guarantee ourselves disappointment, disillusionment, and ultimately despair about ever finding "true love."

Instead of couples therapy or family counseling, the Course fix for this profound problem is the recognition that nothing is as it seems to be: We are not alone, nor embodied, nor destined to die, and in recognizing our timeless spiritual essence we will find that there is nothing we lack. The key to achieving this recognition is forgiveness, first extended toward those who seem to have harmed or disappointed us, but ultimately leading to the realization that *we* have been using *them* to deal with our own self-hatred (usually with a notable lack of success).

The more we can forgive others and ourselves, the closer we will come to achieving the "holy instant": the moment of recognizing our spiritual nature in spite of all the earthly, time-bound delusions that human beings seem heir to. In that healing moment, we come to recognize the *fact* (rather than the mere philosophical proposition) that "we are all one," and thus suffused with the eternal experience of God as Love. Blessed by that recognition, our formerly special relationships become holy ones, dedicated to extending love rather than projecting self-hatred.

PART III

The Long Haul
of Learning

9.

Forgiving Trespasses
and Impasses

How willing are you to forgive your brother? How much do you desire peace instead of endless strife and misery and pain? These questions are the same, in different form. Forgiveness is your peace, for herein lies the end of separation and the dream of danger and destruction, sin and death; of madness and of murder, grief and loss.

—*Chapter 29, VI: 1*

In Chapter 5, I noted that the Course's approach to forgiveness is rooted not in religion or morality, but in metaphysics. By forgiving, we gradually learn to see through the world's most painful illusions and then, by extension, *all* its illusions. When we forgive, the aim is not to let someone off the hook for their apparent crimes or failings. Instead, we are taking the first step toward seeing through our own habitual belief in attack and victimization. That ultimately leads us to releasing ourselves from all the thoughts, feelings, and perceptions that convince us our fundamental existence is physical (and therefore vulnerable to attack) rather than spiritual and unassailable.

But to let go of all the illusions that define our everyday existence—or to "loose the world from all I thought it was," as Workbook Lesson 132 puts it—is not where forgiveness begins for most of us. When people feel the need to forgive, it is usually because they have become aware that a chronic, deep-seated bitterness is poisoning their outlook on life, preventing progress in one or more important relationships, or generally sapping their vitality. However dimly, they may have begun to realize that the inability to forgive someone reflects a chronic self-punishment. As suggested by Nelson Mandela, the South African leader who spent decades as a political prisoner, "Resentment is like drinking poison and then hoping it will kill your enemies."

The first Workbook lesson that gives explicit instructions for applying forgiveness to others is Lesson 46, "God is the love in which I forgive," which includes these instructions:

> Today's exercises require at least three full five-minute practice periods, and as many shorter ones as possible. Begin the longer practice periods by repeating today's idea to yourself, as usual. Close your eyes as you do so, and spend a minute or two in searching your mind for those whom you have not forgiven. It does not matter "how much" you have not forgiven them. You have forgiven them entirely or not at all.
>
> If you are doing the exercises well you should have no difficulty in finding a number of people you have not forgiven. It is a safe rule that anyone you do not like is a suitable subject. Mention each one by name, and say:
>
> *God is the Love in which I forgive you, [name].*

I seldom think of the Course as having a sense of humor, but I remember laughing when I first read the suggestion that if I was doing this lesson well, I "should have no difficulty" in finding a number of unforgiven people in my life. This struck me first as a penetrating insight into human nature, and then a personal

affront. I could easily believe that many *other* people were generally unforgiving, but myself? I was pretty sure I was better than
that. At that moment I realized that if I felt so many other people
were unforgiving, then I had just passed judgment on legions of
people I didn't even know. Thus I had more forgiving to do than
I wanted to acknowledge. (By this time, I had ceased to find anything amusing in the lesson.)

Fast on the heels of this realization came another: that my model
for this style of judgment was my mother, who often behaved as
if she felt herself under attack from almost everyone she encountered. As I wrote in Chapter 5, I eventually came to understand that
my mother was essentially haunted by an unrecognized history of
trauma that may well have extended back beyond her own lifetime.
The first stage of forgiving this powerful person in my life was to
recognize that what had seemed like deliberate intimidation or open
hostility on her part was in fact involuntary; she behaved negatively
toward me and others in a largely unconscious style of self-defense.
When I recognized that I had not been *intentionally* attacked, the
whole notion of whether I had been attacked was in question. Gradually I began to grasp one of ACIM's most challenging propositions:

> Forgiveness recognizes what you thought your brother did to you
> has not occurred. It does not pardon sins and make them real. It
> sees there was no sin. And in that view are all your sins forgiven.
> What is sin, except a false idea about God's Son? Forgiveness
> merely sees its falsity, and therefore lets it go. What then is free to
> take its place is now the Will of God. (Workbook, II: 1)

As I became less certain that I'd been attacked, the bitterness
and resentment attached to certain painful memories began to

ease. Increasingly I realized that the only reason they had become so painful was because I had continued to attack myself with them, each time reinforcing the idea that I was a flawed or damaged human being. By reminding myself often that I had been deprived of nurturance and intimidated in my youth, I prolonged the original experiences of feeling deprived and fearful. Whatever my mother had done or failed to do had been countlessly replayed, intensified, and possibly distorted *by myself*, without any further action on her part. In the long view, it was difficult to say who had really been harder on me.

The next step in Lesson 46 is to make the connection between forgiving others and oneself. After naming all those whom one feels it necessary to forgive, the student is given these directions:

The purpose of the first phase of today's practice periods is to put you in a position to forgive yourself. After you have applied the idea to all those who have come to mind, tell yourself:

God is the Love in which I forgive myself.

Then devote the remainder of the practice period to adding related ideas such as:

God is the Love with which I love myself.

God is the Love in which I am blessed.

It's important to note that the Course does not instruct its students to forgive for their own self-centered reasons, but with the understanding that "God is the Love in which I forgive." This removes the difficult process of forgiving to a realm of transcendent energy, without which we might never get the work done. On the basis of ego alone, we will be tempted to "forgive" in a very limited fashion—that is, by judging those who have harmed

or disappointed us as flawed or sinful, and granting them an absolution based on our superior moral position. The Course would
maintain that this is only condemnation in disguise; real forgiveness derives only from letting go of every idea that we have ever
been harmed. Only in this attitude of total release will we find
both happiness and the natural strength to withstand and integrate all seeming attacks or disappointments in the future.

Needless to say, this is a tall order. To completely forgive the
apparent trespasses of others is really to let go of all the impasses we
have created in our own psyches. For many, such impasses form the
building blocks of personality—not to mention the most significant blocks to personal growth. Some people are defined as much
by whom they've chosen to hate and fear as by whom they choose
to love.

The remainder of this chapter will relate three stories from
Course students about profound forgiveness challenges they have
faced in their own lives. Two of these stories tell about breakthroughs and one is about a persistent impasse, but they are all
equally instructive in portraying the difficulties typically faced by
human beings trying to let go of wounded identities. At a fundamental level we all share the same wound: the experience of finding ourselves in a world of pain and disappointment that seems
to treat us unfairly. When we can recognize that all our suffering
is rooted in the same bedrock conviction that each of us has been
singled out for attack, we are much closer to seeing through the
illusion that ACIM says we have created for ourselves:

> You think that what upsets you is a frightening world, or a sad world,
> or a violent world, or an insane world. All these attributes are given
> it by you. The world is meaningless in itself. (From Lesson 12)

Releasing a Terminal Bitterness

Carol Monahan had been married for eleven years to a man she considered her "best friend" when she was awakened one night by the sound of her fourteen-year-old daughter's bedroom door repeatedly opening and closing. When she investigated, she would discover, to her horror, that her husband was molesting her daughter. Later that night she sneaked out the window with both her children, never to return. She would soon learn that the abuse had been going on for a while and involved both of her daughters. She would also come to realize that what she had seen as a normal relationship was in fact characterized by her husband's condescension and judgment, inadvertently supported by her own sense of unworthiness.

The resultant anger was such that Carol developed a scheme for vengeance that would haunt her mind for years. "It's not that I wanted to develop a terminal disease," she recollects, "but I decided that if I ever did, then I would take my ex-husband out. I couldn't kill him if I'd have to spend a long time in jail, because then I couldn't take care of my kids. But if I was going to die soon anyway, then he was going before me."

It would be many years before Carol encountered the idea of forgiveness as put forth by *A Course in Miracles*, and even longer before she could see any sense in it. "I was angry for a long time," she admits, "and forgiveness made no sense to me at all. What was it for? If people did terrible things they should be punished, and death itself would be too easy for some of them."

One of Carol's first encounters with a different point of view came via listening to a set of tapes by Marianne Williamson, a well-known Course popularizer who came to public awareness after publication of her best-selling book *A Return to Love* in 1992. "I listened to the whole set, but I didn't like what she said. One of her ideas was that some people come into your lives only to help you learn certain lessons, and then leave. That was very upsetting to me. I thought people should come into your life and stay forever! So I threw those tapes away."

Carol had also acquired a copy of the Course by that time, but decided that it looked too much like the Bible and put it away on a shelf. But she kept coming across influences that pointed her back toward it, including books by Gary Zukav, Wayne Dyer, and David Hawkins, author of *Power vs. Force*. In that book, Hawkins quantifies different levels of spiritual awareness and specifically recommends ACIM as a means to raise one's consciousness. That induced Carol, in 2005, to take her copy of the Course and read it through. After doing so twice, she decided to start a weekly study group near her home in northern California, which has continued for several years.

Carol credits the Course with lessening the prominence of anger in her life by a process of "osmosis" as she became steeped in the teaching's perspective. "I'm a much more highly functioning person than I used to be. I'm not as fearful, and I'm a lot less judgmental. I don't get as angry. I used to be angry nonstop, and I would express it."

One important turning point came when she found herself ready to look differently at the past with her ex-husband. "Three years ago I decided to make a Christmas present for my kids," she recalls. "I had all these videos and slides that had been put away; I had sealed all of it. I never wanted to see any of that again, although I didn't throw them away because I felt they also belonged to my kids. That year I decided to have everything restored and put on CDs, and give them to my kids as their memories. In the process of doing that, I watched many of the videos and saw my husband for the first time in a while. I remembered that I had told many people I'd never loved him, it was just a marriage of convenience. Looking at the video I remembered that I had loved him and that there had been happy times after all. And I saw how the abuse had stemmed from his state of mind—how he encountered the world and how he had to function at that time."

That doesn't mean Carol has forgotten the significance of what happened, nor the necessity of her escaping the situation. "If I had continued in that relationship and my kids had continued being abused—because I was unable to see what was going on—I don't know what would have happened to us. For myself, I know that I wouldn't have grown the way I was forced to grow. As the Course teaches, all things are for the good, even when people suffer in the process. The fact is that we don't learn that much from accomplishments and achievements, but from suffering and struggle."

Carol also sees more usefulness in an idea of Marianne Williamson's that once upset her. "Everyone you encounter is the perfect person to teach you something. We tend to think that other people are doing things to disturb our peace, when we are actually doing it by how we respond, by seeing what others do as wrong, and by thinking that the world should be some way that it isn't. My rulebook says people shouldn't behave in certain ways; their rulebooks tell them how they have to behave, and our rulebooks are sometimes very different. From the Course point of view, we are all learning different lessons about how to get back to the sense that we are all one."

Breaking the Chains

The following essay by John Crotty, an insurance executive in New York, is excerpted by permission from a book in progress about how the writer has negotiated several major forgiveness challenges in his life. In this passage, John relates the difficulty of letting go of the bitterness stemming from a trauma that shook the entire world, especially the United States of America, just after the turn of the twenty-first century:

ACIM's central message of advanced forgiveness has challenged me since I became a student in 1999. It is my hacksaw against the chains of bitterness that can too easily hold me captive, and I've used it to break free from one link after another. But one chain for me has not yet been undone: the memory of 9/11. I had worked for many years in Tower 2 of the World Trade Center, on the 102nd floor, until about a year before the attack in 2001. After leaving, I had stayed in touch with many of my friends and colleagues there.

I was close to one friend in particular, Bob Miller. He was brilliant, soft spoken, and gentle. By the morning of September 12, he had been listed among the missing. I drove over to his house and parked nearby, along his suburban tree-lined street. I knew his bus route and focused my side mirror on his stop and waited. I would hold my breath at the sound of each approaching bus, and focus my mirror anxiously. He never got off.

Soon, a procession of friends and relatives bearing cakes passed my car and knocked on his door, where his family waited. For the longest time I refused to join them and waited for more buses. Eventually, I walked across the street to his door. Bob's wife answered as his young daughter looked over her shoulder toward me, hoping for news. Their eyes searched mine, for some hint, some word on Bob. There was little I could offer, other than to call other colleagues, in hope of news. I returned home, at least having a purpose, and manned the phone.

I made a list of the missing from the 102nd floor, constantly updating, crossing out, and inserting names. The updates soon slowed, and before long Bob and eleven other friends and colleagues were confirmed dead. Memorial services followed. With each service, my anger and hatred toward the terrorists ratcheted up, tightening the shackle, leaving me seething.

A few years passed, and my boiling anger had slowly cooled to a simmer. I decided to visit Ground Zero and, like a good Course student, consider forgiveness. My first stop was Trinity Church, just a block south of the Towers. Before September 11, I would sit in Trinity during my lunch breaks, and be mesmerized by the bright stained glass windows, and watching the sunlight refract into dusty rays on the pews.

Unlike the crystal blue skies of 9/11, the day of my visit was blustery, with dark clouds rolling to the northeast. They cast large moving shadows across the stained glass. I wondered if this was how it looked that morning. Did the ash clouds eventually block out the light, until the altar went black?

An organist played a processional hymn, and I sat through mass, watching the shadows cast against the colored glass. Darkness followed light, and back again. Walking out to Broadway, I buttoned up against the wind, and headed north, to another lunchtime sanctuary, St. Peter's Church. The remnant of a twenty-foot crossbeam from Tower 1 has been erected on the Church's south facade. It was found by rescue workers in the rubble and became a powerful symbol of renewal, hope, and, perhaps for some, forgiveness.

I continued north, along the route so many survivors struggled along, trying to find their way home that morning. Standing still on a corner, commuters brushed me by, and I imagined them as ash-coated survivors moving steadily on. In this dream state, I joined with some of them and headed over to the construction site, where workers were busy erecting "Freedom Tower." President Bush had spoken here in 2001, bullhorn in hand:

"I can hear you. The rest of the world can hear you. And the people who knocked these buildings down will hear from all of us soon."

I'd loved that speech. It was as if that magic bullhorn converted all my fear and projected it out as hatred onto the killers. Just remembering it was enough to let me retreat to the vengeful side of my mind.

As I looked across the site toward the south, a familiar building caught my eye. The Bankers Trust Building was draped in black and faced the Towers' footprints like a widow in silent mourning. It was slated for demolition, as it was damaged beyond repair.

My dreamy imaginings then turned toward a fantasy of revenge: *Khalid Shaikh Mohammed and Osama Bin Laden have been brought to New York City for trial, where they are found guilty by twelve area jurors. I am chosen to be their executioner and decide to use the Bankers Trust Building as their execution chamber. Thirty thousand tons of jet fuel have been stored in the lobby and wired with explosive charges.*

At the appointed hour, crowds gather below as my prisoners and I land on the roof by helicopter. Wearing a black hood, I read the writ of execution to them under a cloudless blue sky. Their eyes fill with horror as they are given the same choices my friends faced: death by crushing, burning, or jumping.

My helicopter departs the roof and circles in the air for a while as they scamper to the nearest roof exits, in search of the stairwells. At 9:03 a.m., the time of the attack on Tower 2, I detonate the charge. The crowds cheered as the building implodes and smoke billows once again through the canyons of downtown New York.

The celebrating crowds below are dancing in the street and waving up to me. The rotors of our helicopter clear much of the smoke and suddenly, in the ruins another cross of steel beams reveals itself, identical to the one at St. Peter's.

Like a party-crasher, the Holy Spirit had interrupted my fantasy. I shook my head and smiled sheepishly at my wild imagination, ashamed of my failure to forgive. The gray survivors became commuters again, and I joined with them on the way home.

On the bus, I knew we would pass Bob's stop and street. I closed my eyes, and imagined Bob in the seat ahead, reaching up and signaling the driver for his stop, at long last. I pressed my face against the window, my breath clouding it, as we passed his street. No one got off.

Fighting back tears, I wondered what Bob would have thought of my forgiveness attempt. The perpetrators have never repented, and forgiving them seems disloyal. Would he approve? Would he feel betrayed?

I arrived home and collapsed into bed, dispirited. Above my head on a bookshelf was a worn copy of the Course. I reluctantly reached for it and opened to the first page, searching for some answer. It came with the very first sentence: *"There is no order of difficulty in miracles."* A voice in my mind whispered: *"Nor is there an order of difficulty in forgiveness."*

But my sense of frustration grew. I closed the book, and replied, in my mind, "Maybe not for you, but for me, down here in the trenches, it's very difficult." I let out a deep sigh, closed my eyes and started to drift off, hoping to awake to a brighter day. I would try to break another link of the chain, an easier one, tomorrow.

"God Loves Me as He Loves Himself"

The following letter from a poet and college professor reveals how a key understanding of forgiveness may come from ideas in the Course that are not directly focused on teaching the attitude or behavior of forgiving:

I've struggled for most of my adult life to forgive my parents for their alcoholism and the subsequent abuse that I experienced. For over fifteen years, I would wake up several times a week with the memory of some injustice that had happened to me and I would feel enraged. For relief, I would pound my fists into my pillow or the mattress, but mostly I would just sit and cry.

A favorite memory that my ego still likes to play with is of something my mother once said to me. We were on a family vacation and had rented a van, but the rental didn't have enough seats. One of my sisters pointed out that someone would have to go without a seatbelt and my mother said, "Well, let's just pick the one whose life is the most worthless. Go ahead, Erin. Sit on the floor."

Needless to say, I spent a lot of years in therapy! One day, after listening to me talk about a similar memory, my therapist suggested, "Well, maybe some things are unforgivable" and something very important happened. I watched my emotional response to that idea. I quietly observed my feelings. And here's what I saw: Initially, this idea brought me pleasure; I would even go so far as to call it glee. If the emotion had had a voice, it would have said to me: *Ha! Be glad you are angry! There really are people who only deserve your contempt!* Yet, strangely, and almost simultaneously, I also became aware that I felt intensely afraid. I didn't know why the idea of something being "unforgiveable" scared me but it did. I never mentioned it to my therapist but I puzzled over her words for several years until I arrived at a new insight that also frightened me: *If some things really are unforgiveable, then I am never going to be happy.*

Rather than weekly visits, dark memories only awaken and haunt me five or six times a year now. When it happens, I do not immediately feel a desire to practice forgiveness. Instead, I feel tempted to dwell on the memories until I am overwhelmed with grief. However, because of that insight I had in therapy, I'm also aware that my resistance is a defense. It's not that I don't want to forgive; it's that I'm afraid that I can't. I'm afraid that I'm hopeless and beyond forgiveness. I'm afraid that I can't be happy.

To end this kind of temptation, I read these helpful lines from the Epilogue to the Clarification of Terms in *A Course in Miracles*: "Forget not once this journey is begun the end is certain. Doubt along the way will come and go and go to come again. Yet is the ending sure. No one can fail to do what God appointed him to do. When you forget, remember that you walk with Him and with His Word upon your heart. Illusions of despair may seem to come, but learn how not to be deceived by them. Behind each one there is reality and there is God. You are a stranger here. But you belong to Him who loves you as He loves Himself."

The first part of the passage reminds me that I cannot fail to forgive. Not really. I can play along with the ego and pretend to resist but even my resistance is futile, another illusion to be forgiven, which makes me less tempted to berate myself for my resistance, or to judge myself as a poor Course student because I feel resistant and find myself still haunted by sad memories.

But the second part of the passage intrigues me. It talks about something I don't think we talk much about as Course students: God loves Himself. That seems to me a hugely important and unique spiritual teaching. To hear myself say, "God loves me as He loves Himself" just astounds me. When wrestling at night with a dark memory, when I read this passage, I immediately see myself as a nesting doll, resting inside of a Love that is so great, so entire, so complete, that even Love loves Itself. It's like being inside a cocoon; it doesn't matter how miserable my memories may seem. I am with God!

Before I go back to sleep, to reinforce my experience of being with God, I read this passage: "You whose mind is darkened by doubt and guilt, remember this: God gave the Holy Spirit to you, and gave Him the mission to remove all doubt and every trace of guilt that His dear Son has laid upon himself. It is impossible that this mission fail" (Chapter 13, XI: 5)

Reading this, I realize that these memories are not really haunting me. They are being brought forward in my mind by the Holy Spirit to be healed. It doesn't matter if it's the same memory being presented. That doesn't mean my forgiveness isn't working. It means that I am being offered an opportunity to forgive on a deeper level so that each layer of guilt can be erased. Remembering this, I no longer feel tempted to play into the ego's use for these memories by laying blame on my parents. God loves my parents as He loves me; God loves me as He loves Himself. To remember that His love is so complete and all-encompassing makes it very difficult for me to see my parents as guilty.

Instead, I feel a sense of gratitude that my parents have provided me with lessons that are helping me to realize my spiritual freedom: learning how not to be deceived by the abusive illusions that we dreamed together, and remembering that we are love.

Summary

As taught by *A Course in Miracles*, forgiveness is the key to seeing through the countless illusions of our lives and accepting our ultimate reality as spirit: an eternal and immaterial energy of love that far surpasses our time-bound, individual identities. But for most people, forgiveness is not metaphysical but personal—a profound challenge of releasing anger and resentment toward those who have seemed to injure or limit them. It could well be argued that a sense of being hurt is a universal aspect of the human condition, yet each of us tends to view our most serious injuries at the hands of others as unique, unprecedented, and immune to healing. To the aggrieved, forgiveness is seldom seen as a practical choice for healing and may in fact be feared.

People who are ready for the Course approach to forgiveness have generally reached an awareness that chronic anger and resentment are souring their relationships and limiting their potential in life. The apparent trespasses of others often become impasses in our own psyches, and the key to releasing our habitual blocks to growth is to release others from a historic blame. To help students achieve this release, the Course emphasizes that forgiving oneself is at the root of all forgiveness. That can only be achieved by accepting that love, not fear or anger, resides at the core of our self-awareness. However powerful the temptation to keep justifying our belief in our injuries and limitations, the decision to forgive ultimately yields far more powerful results of personal growth, improved intimacy, and happiness.

10.

Seeing Through the Body

The body is beautiful or ugly, peaceful or savage, helpful or harmful, according to the use to which it is put. And in the body of another you will see the use to which you have put yours.

—Chapter 8, VII: 4

For many students, the Course's ideas about the body are some of the most confounding to integrate on a daily basis. It is one thing to ponder philosophically that the body may not be ultimately "real" and quite another to confront one's moment-by-moment experience of the body as the vehicle and focus of self-awareness.

When I sit at my computer and write, it certainly seems that the creative process is occurring somewhere in the vicinity of my head and that I am helped along or hindered in that process by the condition of the rest of my body: Am I tired or energetic? Am I hungry? Do I need to get up and move around or can I sit still and work a little longer? When I am ill, my consciousness is clouded by discomfort; when I am well, my sense of power and effectiveness is much stronger. In almost every way throughout every day, what I recognize as my mind seems to be directly mediated by the body from which it apparently draws its energy and character.

But according to ACIM, this belief that the mind derives from the body is a profoundly mistaken reversal of reality that tragically limits our sense of freedom and power. Both the problem and the solution for it are described in the text following Lesson 199, "I am not a body. I am free."

> Freedom must be impossible as long as you perceive a body as yourself. The body is a limit. Who would seek for freedom in a body looks for it where it can not be found. The mind can be made free when it no longer sees itself as in a body, firmly tied to it and sheltered by its presence. If this were the truth, the mind were vulnerable indeed! . . .
>
> It is essential for your progress in this course that you accept today's idea, and hold it very dear. Be not concerned that to the ego it is quite insane. The ego holds the body dear because it dwells in it, and lives united with the home that it has made. It is a part of the illusion that has sheltered it from being found illusory itself.

Elsewhere in the Workbook, a reference is made to the dreamlike nature of the body:

> The body is a dream. Like other dreams it sometimes seems to picture happiness, but can quite suddenly revert to fear, where every dream is born. For only love creates in truth, and truth can never fear. Made to be fearful, must the body serve the purpose given it. But we can change the purpose that the body will obey by changing what we think that it is for. (Workbook, II: 5, 3)

This suggestion that we can "change the purpose" of the body is part of ACIM's acknowledgment that the body will not readily disappear when we begin to question its reality:

The body is merely part of your experience in the physical world. Its abilities can be and frequently are overevaluated. However, it is almost impossible to deny its existence in this world. Those who do so are engaging in a particularly unworthy form of denial. The term "unworthy" here implies only that it is not necessary to protect the mind by denying the unmindful. If one denies this unfortunate aspect of the mind's power, one is also denying the power itself. (Chapter 2, IV: 3)

Thus, ACIM's view of the body is that it is a very convincing illusion, and that the power of that illusion draws from a mis-creative use of our own mind. Mistakenly believing that we have separated our consciousness from the infinite mind of God, we have created individual identities for ourselves—and the body is the proof of our separateness. We are so rooted in this illusion that we cannot deny its seeming reality without denying the power of our own mind.

The Course solution to this profound dilemma is to suggest a different *purpose* for the body as long as we believe that it defines our existence. Before looking at what that purpose might be, it's useful to look at some of the purposes usually assigned to the body—even though we tend to experience those purposes as "facts of life" rather than intentional choices.

Sickness and Attack

The novelist Thomas Hardy once mused, "Why should a man's mind have been thrown into such close, sad, sensational, inexplicable relations with such a precarious object as his own body?" Indeed, it's hard to imagine anyone who is perfectly satisfied with the appearance, functionality, and changing conditions of his or her own body throughout a lifetime. From birth into adulthood, we seem driven by involuntary instincts to feed our hunger and quench our thirst, find shelter and comfort, seek sexual intimacy and reproduce, and establish some degree of self-protective power. The body can be the medium of intense sensual pleasure and athletic peak performance, but it can just as likely become the locus of intense pain and chronic misery. And while we often long for physical union as the ultimate form of intimacy, sexual desire can be as problematic as it is promising. Brief experiences of shared physical ecstasy are no guarantee of lasting closeness, and many people have recurring difficulties in reconciling their emotional and physical needs in ongoing relationships.

Thus, on a daily basis the body may feel like less of a safe and trustworthy home for our self-awareness than a restless moving target for our identity. We can lay plans for a happy and healthy future only to suffer a serious injury or illness that detours all our hopes. We can become so obsessed with improving our attractiveness or staving off the signs of age that our bodies become testing grounds for fashion fads, extreme diets, and cosmetic surgery. Even worse, we can find ourselves addicted to substances or behaviors that initially deliver intense gratification or intoxication, only to become the agents of punishing compulsions. We can even become dangerously deluded about the condition of our bodies, as in the case of anorexics who starve themselves because they see the illusion of fat on their emaciated frames.

According to the Course, the body is so often problematic

because it is imbued from the start with notions of sickness and attack. In fact, it would not seem to exist otherwise:

> The body represents the gap between the little bit of mind you call your own and all the rest of what is really yours. You hate it, yet you think it is your self, and that, without it, would your self be lost. This is the secret vow that you have made with every brother who would walk apart. This is the secret oath you take again, whenever you perceive yourself attacked. No one can suffer if he does not see himself attacked, and losing by attack. Unstated and unheard in consciousness is every pledge to sickness. Yet it is a promise to another to be hurt by him, and to attack him in return.
>
> Sickness is anger taken out upon the body, so that it will suffer pain. It is the obvious effect of what was made in secret, in agreement with another's secret wish to be apart from you, as you would be apart from him. (Chapter 28, VI: 4–5)

In this radical analysis, two of humanity's most profound problems—the seeming inevitability of people doing violence to each other and our bodies' vulnerability to sickness—are revealed as one and the same. When our existential anger goes outward, we attack each other; when it turns inward, we become ill. But the fundamental problem is the same: our paradoxically shared delusion that we exist as separate minds in isolated bodies. From that delusion arises all our vulnerability and fear, and thence the anger turned against ourselves and others. Yet we are so devoted to defending our primary delusion that sickness becomes, in the words of Lesson 136, "a defense against the truth":

Sickness is a decision. It is not a thing that happens to you, quite unsought, which makes you weak and brings you suffering. It is a choice you make, a plan you lay, when for an instant truth arises in your own deluded mind, and all your world appears to totter and prepare to fall. Now are you sick, that truth may go away and threaten your establishments no more. . . .

Thus is the body stronger than the truth, which asks you live, but cannot overcome your choice to die. And so the body is more powerful than everlasting life, Heaven more frail than hell, and God's design for the salvation of His Son opposed by a decision stronger than His Will. His Son is dust, the Father incomplete, and chaos sits in triumph on His throne. (Lesson 136: 7, 9)

Within the "chaos" that the Course refers to, anything can happen to the body—and indeed, there seems to be an infinite variety of handicaps and illnesses that it can suffer. Whenever we fall prey to physical suffering, it's natural to wonder where it came from and seek to correct the causes while alleviating symptoms with any medical means at hand. In New Age circles, the idea that the mind is the source of all sickness is popular and can sometimes be turned into a form of blame—for instance, the idea that cancer can be related to a lack of self-assertion.

Conversely, there's also credence given to the idea that we can use the mind to heal the body through visualization, affirmation, and prayer, and there is some limited evidence for the success of these methods. The very fact that the so-called placebo effect is always accounted for in clinical drug trials attests to the power of belief to heal the body. But no one has ever found a way to universalize the placebo effect and few people manage to consistently heal themselves or others through mental or spiritual techniques.

The Course is explicit about the power of the mind to overcome or disavow sickness. Early in the first chapter of the Text, the twenty-fourth "miracle principle" states that "Miracles enable you to heal the sick and raise the dead because you made sickness and death yourself, and can therefore abolish both." But there is a fundamental problem in trying to use Course principles to heal specific illnesses, and I have heard reports of students becoming bitterly disappointed in their attempts to do so. That's because ACIM has no interest in improving the relative condition of the body, whose entire existence stems from a mistaken way of thinking:

> It is still true that the body has no function of itself, because it is not an end. The ego, however, establishes it as an end because, as such, its true function is obscured. This is the purpose of everything the ego does. Its sole aim is to lose sight of the function of everything. A sick body does not make any sense. It could not make sense because sickness is not what the body is for. Sickness is meaningful only if the two basic premises on which the ego's interpretation of the body rests are true; that the body is for attack, and that you are a body. Without these premises sickness is inconceivable. (Chapter 8, VIII: 5)

While "healing miracles" can occur, they are beside the point from ACIM's perspective:

> The miracle returns the cause of fear to you who made it. But it also shows that, having no effects, it is not cause, because the

function of causation is to have effects. And where effects are gone, there is no cause. Thus is the body healed by miracles because they show the mind made sickness, and employed the body to be victim, or effect, of what it made. Yet half the lesson will not teach the whole. The miracle is useless if you learn but that the body can be healed, for this is not the lesson it was sent to teach. The lesson is the *mind* was sick that thought the body could be sick; projecting out its guilt caused nothing, and had no effects. (Chapter 28, II: 11)

Thus, the Course approach to healing is *not* to believe that our minds invent specific illnesses, so that we are able to redirect our thinking in order to undo particular forms of sickness. Instead, ACIM tells us that *sickness does not exist* and is no more real than the body in which it seems to happen. Sickness is only another means that the ego-driven part of our minds uses to reinforce the idea of our separation from God—God being the knowledge of ourselves as pure, inexhaustible love. Thus no form of sickness has any meaning in itself, except that we may use it as a reminder that we are mistaken about who and what we are. By the same token, a healthy body is not a sensible goal for its own sake, except that it may reflect to us the proper function of our mind:

Illness is some form of external searching. Health is inner peace. It enables you to remain unshaken by lack of love from without and capable, through your acceptance of miracles, of correcting the conditions proceeding from lack of love in others. (Chapter 2, I: 5)

However, since the Course is cognizant of the fact that we do believe ourselves to be in bodies, it also allows that we will turn to other means of healing than our own mind. Any kind of physical or medical intervention in the course of sickness is what ACIM calls "magic," but it does not decry its use:

> Physical illness represents a belief in magic.... All material means that you accept as remedies for bodily ills are restatements of magic principles. This is the first step in believing that the body makes its own illness. It is a second misstep to attempt to heal it through non-creative agents. It does not follow, however, that the use of such agents for corrective purposes is evil. Sometimes the illness has a sufficiently strong hold over the mind to render a person temporarily inaccessible to the Atonement. In this case it may be wise to utilize a compromise approach to mind and body, in which something from the outside is temporarily given healing belief. (Chapter 2, IV: 2, 4)

In ACIM's view, then, the only uncompromised or total means of healing is the Atonement, which is once described as a personal form of Christ's resurrection:

> Very simply, the resurrection is the overcoming or surmounting of death. It is a reawakening or a rebirth; a change of mind about the meaning of the world. It is the acceptance of the Holy Spirit's interpretation of the world's purpose; the acceptance of the Atonement for oneself. It is the end of dreams of misery, and the glad awareness of the Holy Spirit's final dream. It is the recognition of the gifts of God. It is the dream in which the body functions perfectly, having no function except communication. (Manual, 28: 1)

What the Body Is For

When we stop using sickness to defend against the recognition of ourselves as infinite and eternal love, the cure of all illness is automatic. Perhaps surprisingly, the Course predicts that this cure will not make us feel "well" in the way that we would normally expect a cure to do. As Lesson 136 continues:

> Healing will flash across your open mind, as peace and truth arise to take the place of war and vain imaginings. There will be no dark corners sickness can conceal, and keep defended from the light of truth. There will be no dim figures from your dreams, nor their obscure and meaningless pursuits with double purposes insanely sought, remaining in your mind. It will be healed of all the sickly wishes that it tried to authorize the body to obey.
>
> Now is the body healed, because the source of sickness has been opened to relief. And you will recognize you practiced well by this: The body should not feel at all. If you have been successful, there will be no sense of feeling ill or feeling well, of pain or pleasure. No response at all is in the mind to what the body does. Its usefulness remains and nothing more.
>
> Perhaps you do not realize that this removes the limits you had placed upon the body by the purposes you gave to it. As these are laid aside, the strength the body has will always be enough to serve all truly useful purposes. The body's health is fully guaranteed, because it is not limited by time, by weather or fatigue, by food and drink, or any laws you made it serve before. You need do nothing now to make it well, for sickness has become impossible.

Yet this protection needs to be preserved by careful watching. If you let your mind harbor attack thoughts, yield to judgment or make plans against uncertainties to come, you have again misplaced yourself, and made a bodily identity which will attack the body, for the mind is sick.

Give instant remedy, should this occur, by not allowing your defensiveness to hurt you longer. Do not be confused about what must be healed, but tell yourself:

I have forgotten what I really am, for I mistook my body for myself. Sickness is a defense against the truth. But I am not a body. And my mind cannot attack. So I can not be sick.

Thus, in practical terms, the most sensible thing we can do to heal any illness is to forgive ourselves and others of any perceived attacks. This begins to reverse the worldly habit of using the body for attack, which can only reinforce our sense of separation, danger, and frailty. When we forgive, we communicate our willingness to accept a greater reality than the one we are accustomed to. This new reality—which the Course says is the only reality there has actually ever been—is one in which we are literally "all one":

If you use the body for attack, it is harmful to you. If you use it only to reach the minds of those who believe they are bodies, and teach them *through* the body that this is not so, you will understand the power of the mind that is in you. If you use the body for this and only for this, you cannot use it for attack. In the service of uniting it becomes a beautiful lesson in communion, which has value until communion *is*. (Chapter 8, VII: 3)

Because *A Course in Miracles* is not concerned with the behavior or actions of the body, it does not give explicit instructions about how to teach the truth of communion "through the body." Unlike almost every other system of spiritual instruction known to humankind, ACIM never mentions sex, much less issuing rules for sexual behavior or morality. Nor are there any dietary guidelines or even rules for spiritual practice, beyond the suggestion in the Manual for Teachers that a "quiet time" to remember God be taken every morning and evening and that "It is not wise to lie down for it. It is better to sit up, in whatever position you prefer" (Manual, 16: 5). This is, in fact, the most specific instruction the Course ever gives about what to do with the body, in any situation.

And where many religions teach that the body's apparent urges must be feared and controlled, its appearance veiled or altered, and some of its actions answered with physical punishment or even death, the Course is explicit about releasing the body from all blame:

> Who punishes the body is insane.... It is indeed a senseless point of view to hold responsible for sight a thing that cannot see, and blame it for the sounds you do not like, although it cannot hear. It suffers not the punishment you give because it has no feeling. It behaves in ways you want, but never makes the choice. It is not born and does not die. It can but follow aimlessly the path on which it has been set. And if that path is changed, it walks as easily another way. It takes no sides and judges not the road it travels. It perceives no gap, because it does not hate. It can be used for hate, but it cannot be hateful made thereby. (Chapter 28, VI: 2)

Even though the Course constantly urges students toward a radical revisioning of reality—to disbelieve the visible, physical world and focus instead on the invisible and spiritual—it also acknowledges that we are unlikely to achieve this shift in perception anytime soon. The enormity and complexity of our embodied illusion veils from us how it came to be. Trying to figure it all out will be less fruitful than simply retraining the mind to see and think in a different way:

> Salvation does not ask that you behold the spirit and perceive the body not. It merely asks that this should be your choice. For you can see the body without help, but do not understand how to behold a world apart from it. It is your world salvation will undo, and let you see another world your eyes could never find. Be not concerned how this could ever be. You do not understand how what you see arose to meet your sight. For if you did, it would be gone. (Chapter 31, VI: 3)

Nonduality, Yoga, and the Course

A Course in Miracles is sometimes called a "nondual" spiritual teaching because it teaches that only God or spirit is real and everything else is illusory. In a dual tradition like conventional Christianity, both body and spirit are considered to be real. Thus, one must do certain things with the body (and *not* do certain other things) in order to gain access to salvation and an eternal spiritual life. The body is either the locus or agent of most sins, which must be confessed to gain absolution. Ideally, one attains such a purity of thought and behavior that the body becomes a "temple" honoring God's creation.

The Course acknowledges there is some value in the latter idea, but then goes beyond it:

> The many body fantasies in which minds engage arise from the distorted belief that the body can be used as a means for attaining "atonement." Perceiving the body as a temple is only the first step in correcting this distortion, because it alters only part of it. It *does* recognize that Atonement in physical terms is impossible. The next step, however, is to realize that a temple is not a structure at all. Its true holiness lies at the inner altar around which the structure is built. The emphasis on beautiful structures is a sign of the fear of Atonement, and an unwillingness to reach the altar itself. The real beauty of the temple cannot be seen with the physical eye. Spiritual sight, on the other hand, cannot see the structure at all because it is perfect vision. It can, however, see the altar with perfect clarity. (Chapter 2, III: 1)

Although the Course itself does not offer any physical discipline to supplement its teaching of nonduality, there is such a teaching whose popularity has been rapidly increasing at the same time as the Course. Although yoga was first introduced to the West in the early twentieth century by such teachers as Vivekananda and Yogananda, its popularity began to mushroom in the 1970s. In recent years the practice of yoga poses, or *asanas*, has become a staple of exercise and fitness programs everywhere, although their relationship to a historical spiritual perspective is not as widely recognized. While there are many schools of yoga and thus some disagreement about its overall philosophy, it's safe to say that there is a strong nondual streak running through the traditional yogic perspective.

Philip Urso is a teacher of both ACIM and yoga in Charlestown, Rhode Island. With his wife, Lisa, he runs the Salt Pond Yoga Center, which trains students in the "power yoga" style of American teacher Baron Baptiste. Philip encountered the Course around 1995 and yoga five years later, when he developed an "exquisite" back pain that resisted all other forms of treatment. While he reveals that yoga was, at first, "all about the body" to him, he gradually came to see it in a different light.

"In my view, yoga is not about poses," Philip observes. "Yoga is a state of being. The state of yoga, or Union, is the same nondual state of liberation from the body that is called reality or Heaven in the Course. In that sense, ACIM is a new course designed to reach the state of yoga. It uses the yogic practice of Devotion, which would be study of the Text of the Course, and also the yogic practice of Meditation via the 365 lessons of the Workbook."

Philip feels that the proper practice of asanas leads to a recognition of the ACIM principle that "the body is a learning device for the mind" (Chapter 2, IV: 3). As he points out, "The Course explains that the first error is to think the body creates its own illness, aches and pains, sensations, and emotions. This is a denial of the power of the mind. Here some Course-inspired physical yoga can help illuminate this denial.

"Let's say that a yoga teacher calls a pose that many consider physically difficult. There are moans and groans from his students in response. This is the mind projecting its past experience on the future pose. So the teacher asks, 'Have you already decided what this experience will be? If you've decided that this pose will suck, then you'll be right. Do you only want to relive yesterday's pose? Allow the pose to be shown to you, unknown by you.' This is a way of suggesting that students can release their own practice from their projections. And students often report a different experience when they do so. This is how we can use the body as a learning device."

Philip adds, "Eventually the student may discover that *every* experience in their body, other than the neutrality of a deep peace, is their mind's projection. Once this is understood, then it is easier to see that everything that happens in the world outside is also their projection."

Paradoxically, even the specific effort of a yoga exercise can lead to an experience of transcending the body. As Philip explains, "The Course tells us that 'At no single instant does the body exist at all. It is always remembered or anticipated, but never experienced just *now*' (Chapter 18, VII: 3). Experiencing the disappearance of the body is one of my goals in teaching yoga. Unequivocal breath or body awareness, or 'single-pointed awareness' as yogis say, puts the student into a single instant in which awareness of the body disappears and the student touches eternity. This is not as out of reach as it may sound, and can be experienced regularly. In pure presence there is no remembering or anticipating. In this release, pure peace and joy, which are always waiting for these barriers of time to disappear, come pouring in. In the experience of joy, there is no body."

To be sure, most Course students will not transcend their incarnation on a regular or predictable basis, even with the help of yoga or meditation. What ACIM teaches about recognizing oneself only as spirit should not be turned into a moral imperative, nor should the body become the object of loathing or disdain.

Instead, as long as we see ourselves in the mirror and experience physical sensations, we can remember that the body need not be the proof of isolation or the breeding ground of sickness. By forgiving it, we can increasingly experience the body as a medium of transcendence; that is, we can see through the body to recognize our Source in spirit.

Summary

One of the most challenging ideas presented by *A Course in Miracles* is that the locus and focus of our personal identity, the body, is not actually real. Having fallen into a dream of separation from God—the ultimate reality of timeless and infinite love—we created separate identities for ourselves, in the form of the personal ego. The ego, in turn, imagines the body as proof of its existence. The fact that bodies can attack each other and become ill further confirms our isolation, to the point where it becomes impossible to deny the existence of the body without denigrating the creative power of our own mind.

The Course solution to this profound dilemma is to suggest a new purpose for the body. Instead of fighting for our individual survival or attempting to maximize our sensual experiences, we can learn to use the body as a means of communication and communion that confirms our spiritual unity. While we need to recognize that our minds have invented the body and thus the idea that it can be sick, using the mind to reverse the symptoms of illness is not true healing. Rather, we can remind ourselves and each other that the body is not actually the matrix of our existence, despite its undeniable presence in our worldly lives.

While the Course itself does not provide a physical discipline to complement its teaching of "nonduality" (the idea that only spirit is real and nothing else), the last few decades have seen a rise in the West of a complementary teaching in the form of yoga, a nondual Eastern tradition that includes a physical component. When practiced as more than an exercise routine, the postures or "asanas" of yoga can induce a transcendental experience of nonduality, and thus may provide a valuable reinforcement to the devotional and meditative approaches offered by *A Course in Miracles*. Regardless of physical techniques, the aim is always to recognize the body as a tool of spiritual transcendence and communion.

11.

Taking Breaks and Spacing Out

The ego does not know what it is trying to teach. It is trying to teach
you what you are without knowing what you are. It is expert only in
confusion. It does not understand anything else. As a teacher, then,
the ego is totally confused and totally confusing.

—*Chapter 8, II: 1*

As much as *A Course in Miracles* is believed and beloved by the
students who have elected to work with it over the long
term, it is also legendary for sparking reactions of disorientation
and dismay. I've heard countless stories from students about putting the book aside for weeks or months at a time or even destroying
their copies only to get new ones later. Early in my study I threw
the book against the wall more than once, and I've heard several
stories of ritual burning.

Conversely, it's not unusual for new students to become absorbed
or fascinated with the Course, to the extent that they sometimes
annoy people close to them. I once received a plaintive letter from
a woman asking for advice about how to approach a relative who
had begun talking constantly in Course lingo, apparently promoting the causes of forgiveness and ego-dissolution all the while he
became increasingly obnoxious in doing so. I have also occasionally

heard of intimate relationships that grew increasingly strained as one partner became deeply involved with ACIM study while the other remained disinterested.

And while the essentially democratic nature of the Course does not immediately lend itself to exploitation by questionable teachers, there has been at least one prominent Course study organization widely reported as a cult. The fact that many students "space out" on the teaching at certain stages has added to popular misperceptions of the Course as a superficial form of New Age thinking and likely delayed its eventual recognition as an emerging spiritual tradition of profound significance.

"I think you'd have to be pretty enlightened *not* to get seriously confused by the Course," admits student Toni Neal. "There have been times that I put the Course down for months. I felt it had become a crutch, and I needed to put it into practice without having it at my fingertips constantly. Like anything that we study, there is a time to learn and a time to apply what you've learned. Then you can go back and learn at a deeper level with the benefit of the experience you gained from applying the principles."

In this chapter, I'll briefly examine a few of the common stumbling blocks that Course students may encounter at different stages of their study. In doing so, I want to make it clear that these difficulties or delays are not necessarily "mistakes" to be avoided at all costs along the path of spiritual growth. Unlike a catechism or the Ten Commandments, *A Course in Miracles* does not offer rules of behavior and belief that are to be followed without question. Instead, it deliberately uproots the conventional rules and conditions of the world we see every day, urging only that we regard everything we experience with a forgiving outlook. In so doing, we will increasingly access the on-the-spot guidance of the

Holy Spirit, without having to rely on a religious rulebook. In the short term, the cost of this guidance can be uncertainty and confusion, experiences that may eventually prove to be instructive in themselves.

Crisis, Christ, and the Authority Problem

It's not uncommon to hear that people came across ACIM at a time of intense personal crisis—or entered such a period soon after beginning their study. Course philosopher and teacher Ken Wapnick once told me that whenever he heard new students exclaiming how much happier the discipline had made them in just a few months, "I tend to think they aren't getting it yet."

The point is not that novice Course students are supposed to be unhappy, but that few people adjust quickly to the suggestions that the everyday material world around them is not real, that their egocentric goals for success and happiness are not actually in their best interests, and that their search for rewarding special relationships is fatally flawed from the start. But if these disquieting propositions are ignored or not fully grasped, giddiness can set in when novice students encounter ACIM's powerfully positive reassurances, such as Lesson 35: "My mind is part of God's. I am very holy." Students who stick with the teaching for the long term, however, will gradually develop the capacity to integrate these transcendent messages with the more confrontive elements of the material.

On the other hand, students who are already depressed or dismayed by the course of their lives may initially find reinforcement for their disillusionment as they undertake *A Course in Miracles*. I would probably not have found ACIM the least bit tolerable, had I not encountered it at a time when my egocentric way of life was already falling apart, and I was frequently experiencing illness-induced altered states of consciousness that made it much easier to question the solidity and validity of the material world. Several months into my simultaneous study of the Text and Workbook, I remember a period of time when I frequently entertained the thought, "Everything I know is wrong!"

This "negative enlightenment" was both humiliating and liberating, and it ushered in a period of understanding my own consciousness in a new light. First, I was just beginning to recognize that there might be another way to live than what I was accustomed to. Up to that point I had lived the life of the ego, "looking out for number one," without even knowing there might be a higher, selfless point of view available. Second, the recognition of my habitual "wrongness" enabled me to sense a learning potential that had been largely shut down since childhood. (How that potential was reactivated is discussed in the next chapter.)

Even as I became aware of my unproductive attitudes and felt a willingness to look at life from a new point of view, I found myself fighting the Course message and questioning its entire frame of reference. It is a testament to the depth and mystery of ACIM's language that it can be simultaneously magnetic and unsettling, managing to hold or regain the attention of disgruntled students through periods of serious doubt.

In the spiritual literature of Sufism and Buddhism, one can find many stories of students struggling with the paradoxical or confrontive teachings of gurus and masters and being held to their discipline mostly by those teachers' powerful personalities. As a spiritual teaching contained entirely in book form, *A Course in Miracles* can't exert such a personal presence. Yet a large part of both its appeal and its challenge has to do with a strange blend of intimacy and authority that emanates from its pages. The book often seems to be directly addressing the student with specialized instruction—a replay of the spiritual coaching that scribes Helen Schucman and Bill Thetford at first thought was meant only for them.

For many students, that sense of profound personal authority leads them to accept that the true author of the Course is who it says it is: Jesus Christ. For me, that identification was a major element of my early resistance to ACIM. Having grown up in the conservatively Christian culture of Charlotte, North Carolina, I bore a strong antipathy to Christian evangelism, especially as expressed by such prominent television preachers as Billy Graham and the corrupt "Praise the Lord" ministry of Jim and Tammy Faye Bakker. I regarded the Christianity I knew as a largely anti-intellectual institution that was bent on its own self-aggrandizement and the pursuit of a backward social and political agenda.

By my mid-teens, I was already an agnostic with atheist leanings, although this attitude had more to do with a reactive anger against evangelical excesses than any serious theological deliberations. Through my twenties, I took a passing interest in various gurus and alternative spiritual paths, including Sufism, Zen Buddhism, and the movements inspired by such teachers as Paramahansa Yogananda, Baba Muktananda, and Bhagwan Shree Rajneesh. But it seemed that every famed guru sooner or later fell prey to corruption or their followers' misinterpretations, and I was resistant to becoming identified as a "follower" of any religious tradition, no matter how exotic or trendy it might seem. I knew a number of people who seemed to fall under the sway of one New Age movement or another, and I was proud of myself for avoiding any such indoctrination.

Imagine my discomfort, then, in finding myself intensely engaged with a highly intellectual spiritual teaching that claimed to be an update of Christianity, supposedly authored by its original prophet! The story of the Course's "channeling" via Helen Schucman was bizarre on its face, yet peculiarly persuasive; there was just something that rang true about it. I remember interviewing a Christian evangelical critic of ACIM who admitted that he had no problem believing that Christ could decide to send a contemporary message through anyone's mind, including that of a religiously ambivalent psychologist at Columbia University. But according to that critic, "There's just no way Jesus Christ would say what the Course says!"

Likewise, it was initially difficult for me to reconcile my youthful impressions of Christianity with what the self-proclaimed author of the Course had to say. Instead of everyone bearing the stain of "original sin," there was no sin at all; instead of everyone being required to accept Jesus Christ as their personal savior, we only needed to accept that we are *all* the Christ; instead of being watched over by an alternately loving and terrifyingly judgmental God, we had only to become aware that "God is but love, and therefore so am I." Over time and much study, the initial strangeness of ACIM's message shifted into a recognition that this was indeed the kind of "good news" that evangelical Christianity promised, but never really delivered.

At the same time, ACIM's good news requires an unusually high degree of personal responsibility, not so much for one's behavior or its correction, but for the *states of mind* that inspire all our behavior. In a typical restatement of traditional religious terms, the Course calls this kind of responsibility "vigilance":

When you threw truth away you saw yourself as if you were without it. By making another kingdom that you valued, you did not keep *only* the Kingdom of God in your mind, and thus placed part of your mind outside it. What you made has imprisoned your will, and given you a sick mind that must be healed. Your vigilance against this sickness is the way to heal it. Once your mind is healed it radiates health, and thereby teaches healing. This establishes you as a teacher who teaches like me. Vigilance was required of me as much as of you, and those who choose to teach the same thing must be in agreement about what they believe. (Chapter 6, V: C-9)

Elsewhere the author of the Course refers to himself as an "elder brother" who should be regarded not as a superior or divine being, but as an ultimate model of learning of which we are all capable:

An elder brother is entitled to respect for his greater experience, and obedience for his greater wisdom. He is also entitled to love because he is a brother, and to devotion if he is devoted. It is only my devotion that entitles me to yours. There is nothing about me that you cannot attain. I have nothing that does not come from God. The difference between us now is that I have nothing else. This leaves me in a state which is only potential in you. (Chapter 1, 2: 3)

The identification of Jesus Christ as an elder brother is probably more comfortable for students with a Jewish background than a conventional Christian faith. It's worth noting that many of the figures most prominently associated with the origins and popular spread of the Course—including Helen Schucman, Ken Wapnick, publisher Judy Skutch, and popularizers Jerry Jampolsky and Marianne Williamson—were raised at least partly in the Jewish faith.

But for both agnostics and ex-fundamentalists—of which there are quite a few in the ranks of Course students—reconciling the conventional notions of Jesus with the Jesus of the Course is a major challenge. Other students find it less disorienting and can speak quite naturally of Jesus as both the author of ACIM and a readily accessible source of comfort and wisdom, along with the Holy Spirit. I still tend not to use these names very often, not so much from a lingering discomfort but because I am always conscious of writing about ACIM from the perspective of a journalist who is writing for a larger audience than dedicated Course students.

Over time, every ACIM student reaches some kind of personal reconciliation with the jolting recognition of an authoritative voice who speaks in Christian terms while radically redefining every one of them. This reconciliation resolves the "authority problem" that most Course students must deal with sooner or later—which can be seen as preparation for resolving a deeper authority problem:

> Peace is a natural heritage of spirit. Everyone is free to refuse to accept his inheritance, but he is not free to establish what his inheritance is. The problem everyone must decide is the fundamental question of authorship. All fear comes ultimately, and sometimes by way of very devious routes, from the denial of Authorship. The offense is never to God, but only to those who deny Him. To deny His Authorship is to deny yourself the reason for your peace, so that you see yourself only in segments. This strange perception *is* the authority problem. (Chapter 3, VI: 10)

The Dangers of Subversion

The innate authority of ACIM's voice does not prevent it from being subverted or misinterpreted, however. The first time that I ever ventured from my private study of ACIM to a study group, it happened to be led by a young man whose idea of facilitation was to demand rapt attention from everyone as he read from the blue book in a droning voice, neither allowing interruptions nor accepting questions for forty-five minutes. When a question was finally entertained, he answered by returning to a long reading of the Course Text. I escaped as soon as I could, doubtful of whether I would ever return to a group of self-identified Course students. (As I fled I recalled the answer that the Sufi teacher Reshad Feild had given a questioner a few years before at a bookstore event, when queried about the trustworthiness of a Sufi organization in the area. Reshad winked and succinctly replied, "Never trust Sufis in a group!")

But I would soon find a democratically led ACIM group that reassured me about my peers and the potential of study in a social context. Over the last few years, I've enjoyed attending a group near my home in northern California that has added immeasurably to my understanding of how ACIM affects all kinds of people over the long term. But that first experience with a would-be Course preacher informed me that there is nothing in the teaching itself that will prevent its exploitation by demagogues, and in the years since I have occasionally heard rumors and complaints of various group leaders who display abusive tendencies or appear to be usurping ACIM's reputation to raise funds and recruit followers for their own mini-movements.

The most dramatic example of a cult leader associated with the Course was undoubtedly the so-called Master Teacher (MT) of Endeavor Academy in southern Wisconsin, who was a controversial figure on the ACIM scene from the early 1990s until his death in 2008. MT was a former real estate broker and AA recovery group leader named Charles Buell Anderson who founded one of the few residential communities associated with *A Course in Miracles*, organized under the official auspices of the New Christian Church of Full Endeavor with a complex of church buildings, housing, and small businesses generally referred to as God's Country Place.

Anderson was controversial in Course circles not just for his aggressive evangelical outreach, extending across the United States and into Europe, Australia, and South America, but for a teaching style that was widely reported by ex-followers as abusive. Stories of Anderson's verbal insults and physical attacks on his students were common and earned him a collection of critical reports on the website of cult deprogrammer Rick Ross,[1] as well as a largely hostile report on CBS-TV's national *48 Hours* news program in 1999.[2]

Anderson and Endeavor also played a key role in the political history of the Course when they countersued the original ACIM publisher, the Foundation for Inner Peace (FIP), after FIP and Penguin Books (who held the publishing license for the Standard edition of ACIM for five years), pursued a copyright infringement action against them. After a prolonged legal battle, Endeavor prevailed in a New York Superior Court decision in 2004 that

---

1. See http://www.rickross.com/groups/eacademy.html.
2. See a transcript of the *48 Hours* segment about Endeavor Academy at http://www.rickross.com/reference/eacademy/eacademy2.html.

invalidated the original copyright. This ended an era of copyright and trademark enforcement by the Foundation that many Course organizations had found unduly restrictive and initiated a series of alternative published editions of ACIM.

Since Anderson's passing, Endeavor Academy has continued to function and promote the teachings of MT, mostly via video recordings, although their public stance is less aggressive and the reports of abuse have dissipated. To understand how such a teacher could rise to prominence in a spirituality generally regarded as "self-taught," it's first important to note that the expression or concept of a "master teacher" is nowhere found in the Course itself. In fact ACIM stresses that every good teacher is devoted to helping the student match his or her learning: "Like any good teacher, the Holy Spirit knows more than you do now, but He teaches only to make you equal with Him" (Chapter 6, V: 1). Further, the Course explicitly warns against the use of abusive teaching techniques: "Good teachers never terrorize their students. To terrorize is to attack, and this results in rejection of what the teacher offers. The result is learning failure" (Chapter 3, I: 4).

Because I've been reporting on the Course movement for many years and Endeavor Academy sometimes made big news, I seriously attempted to understand MT's message and appeal. I received many unsolicited videos of MT's discourses—one sent with a veiled and unsigned threat, not long after one of my critical reports on Endeavor appeared in print—and spent some long hours attempting to decipher them. Despite the fact that he spoke in English and frequently quoted the Course, I could never make any sense of what MT was saying. I interviewed followers of MT who said they found his presence magnetic and his teaching enlightening, but those effects were totally lost on me.

When I finally saw MT in action at an ACIM conference in 2007, where he held an impromptu discourse in a hotel lobby, my long-distance impressions of him were finally confirmed. As many of his ex-followers had always alleged, he appeared to be an unstable personality who had latched onto the Course to promote a highly idiosyncratic personal agenda. Val Scott, a veteran Course student from Canada and an ex-Endeavor resident who was once appointed by MT as one of the "fully illumined twelve" who were supposed to lead Endeavor Academy to worldwide prominence, cogently summed up Endeavor Academy's legacy under MT as "a pure and simple cult-guru trip hitch-hiking on *A Course in Miracles*."[3]

While Chuck Anderson may have been the first prominent teacher to take such a ride on the coattails of ACIM, he will likely not be the last. One of the characteristics of the Course that can lead to its subversion by exploitive teachers is simply the fact that it is so difficult for students who are working their own way through its dense language and formidable challenges to their ego-based identities. There is a natural tendency to turn to other sources of information and insight, and teachers who claim to have a perfect understanding of it all can be especially enticing.

The best protection against being deceived by manipulative teachers is to remember the ultimate goal of the Course teaching itself: to develop one's own ready access to a greater wisdom within oneself. Any teacher who points students away from that path toward an autonomous spirituality and toward his or her own interpretation of ACIM principles is probably not trustworthy. On the other hand, for some people a potential path to wisdom may lie in mistaken devotion, disillusionment, and forgiveness.

---

3. See http://www.rickross.com/reference/eacademy/eacademy3.html.

As Val Scott has observed, one important meaning of the Course manifesting in our times may be that "gurus are now simply an idea whose time has passed." Likewise, recent years have seen an accelerating crisis in the "authority problem" of the Catholic Church and a steady decline in church attendance across virtually every mainstream denomination. The deeper meaning of the "spiritual but not religious" identification that is becoming ever more popular in Western culture is essentially a relocation of spiritual authority, from the word of gurus or preachers and the dogma of institutions to the internal experience of individual seekers. And though finding our own way to the direct experience of God can be a perilous path, it is likely the inevitable direction of maturity for the human race.

Absorption, Superiority, and Other Delusions

One of the perils of beginning Course study is that an initial fascination with the teaching can lead to a near-total absorption with its language and ideas, resulting in the phenomenon of novice students who frequently use Course-speak and stubbornly promote the Course philosophy to bewildered friends and family who have little or no interest in the path. This tendency may result in mere annoyances or serious breaks in relationship. When a naïve allegiance to the Course gets hooked up with the idea that one's new, forgiving way of life is superior to anyone else's, a crisis may result that ultimately has to be resolved by the Course student learning how to *integrate* forgiveness, rather than merely promoting or enforcing it. Colorado writer Susan Dugan relates one such long-term learning experience from her personal history:

When I began studying *A Course in Miracles* I perceived my husband as a very angry person. He seemed to grow even more so as I tried to practice the Course's style of forgiveness. I realize in retrospect that I must have been still trying to "forgive" with my ego—that is, pardoning others for the sake of being a good person, which only induces greater guilt and anger in the "forgiven." Although I never spoke to my husband about the Course or what I was trying to learn, I believe he could sense the silent condemnation lurking beneath my "tolerance."

About two years into my journey I couldn't take it anymore, and begged for help from the Holy Spirit to truly understand and embrace forgiveness. I also began immersing myself in Ken Wapnick's videos, CDs, and readings, which taught me how to take complete responsibility for my lack of peace.

Despite formidable resistance I did this again and again, day in and day out, whenever my husband and other angry dream figures seemed to be getting in my face. Little by little, from moment to moment, my husband and the others appeared to calm down. I experienced moments when, mid-argument, we would both just stop, unable to remember our lines or even what had upset us in the first place. And for the first time ever, I experienced instants free of the burden of individuality, fully present moments in which I felt completed, infinitely supported, loved and loving.

We get along quite well these days. I don't blame him for my state of mind or expect him to make me happy. I also have new appreciation for his generosity and kindness. When he does get upset and I feel triggered, I immediately ask for help from my right mind and can usually understand that what's going on is *my* call for love. I am beginning to feel more and more compassion for him and for myself. Now I am willing to forgive not because it makes me feel like a better person, but because it brings me enormous comfort and release from the heavy burden of constant judgment and projection.

Susan's experience illustrates an important insight that may not be accessible to novice students: *forgiveness is never about the actions, behaviors, or beliefs of anyone else, but always about the transformation of one's own habits of mind.* The simple fact is that the ego, the part of our mind which values specialness and seeks to preserve our individuality, can easily co-opt the idea of forgiveness and turn it into a form of manipulation before we know what is happening. Then a distorted form of forgiveness rapidly becomes a not-so-subtle tool of judgment, essentially reversing the intention of the Course teaching.

There's no ready cure for this syndrome besides experience in relationship and long-term training with the Workbook lessons— although a fairly identifiable symptom of forgiveness gone wrong is whenever one feels the need to tell another person they're being forgiven! In this sense, forgiveness is always an "inside job" that involves an ongoing housecleaning of the mind's habitual perceptions and judgments.

For example, if one perceives, as Susan did, that someone else seems habitually angry, the Course approach is not to forgive that person for being that way, but to question and release one's own *belief* in anger. For if that belief were not there, anger would not be perceived in someone else's behavior or demeanor:

The ego's use of projection must be fully understood before the inevitable association between projection and anger can be finally undone. The ego always tries to preserve conflict. It is very ingenious in devising ways that seem to diminish conflict, because it does not want you to find conflict so intolerable that you will insist on giving it up. The ego therefore tries to persuade you that *it* can free you of conflict, lest you give the ego up and free yourself. Using its own warped version of the laws of God, the ego utilizes the power of the mind only to defeat the mind's real purpose. It projects conflict from your mind to other minds, in an attempt to persuade you that you have gotten rid of the problem. (Chapter 7, VIII: 2)

Susan is not the first student to report that when genuine forgiveness has been applied to one's own attitudes and perceptions, formerly intractable problems of relationship begin dissolving and other people seem to change suddenly, almost as if by magic. That is because the power of projection, which can be both immense and incessant, is finally being undone—and the result is true peace.

Just as the idea of forgiveness can be usurped and turned to contradictory purposes, so can the idea of guidance from the Holy Spirit. I have heard of conflicts inside Course organizations that stemmed from people's protestations that they were only following the guidance of either Jesus or the Holy Spirit, each of them apparently receiving instructions guaranteed to result in conflict.

This paradox was writ large in the long-running copyright battle between Endeavor Academy and the Foundation for Inner Peace, in which both sides claimed that they were only upholding the original intentions held by Jesus Christ for the disposition of rights to his Course. If the Course itself is to be believed, it seems logical to assume that Jesus would have issued instructions to each side that would lead to a quick resolution and a mutually satisfying peace. In fact, a less than satisfying peace was finally dictated by a federal judge who showed little patience for the legal maneuvers of either side.

On a much smaller scale, it's easy for individual Course students to become confused about what constitutes genuine spiritual guidance. To me, it's hard to imagine that the infinite Holy Spirit has much stake in whether Course students have an easy time driving through an illusory material world, but it's not uncommon to hear miraculous stories of convenient parking or perfectly timed sequential green lights after a prayer for assistance was issued. Or as Dawn Sechrist confesses in her "Diary of a Mad Course Student":

> I spent a really long time trying to create a winning lottery ticket. I thought I was a co-creator with God, and so I figured I'd just co-create a winning lottery ticket and then use the money to fix up the world. When that didn't work, and when virtually nothing I was co-creating ever seemed to work, I got mad. I just wanted someone to tell me the truth. I didn't even care what it was anymore; I just wanted someone to tell it to me. I did a lot of praying which sounded more like begging: "Please, please, please God, tell me what the hell is going on around here!"[4]

Of course, ACIM students are not alone in attempting to access an infallible voice of divine guidance and coming up with frustrations and delusions. Great wars have been fought to satisfy apparently opposing divine wills, and all manner of criminal acts and petty indulgences have been excused on the insane or self-serving grounds that "God made me do it." When trying to determine whether one has actually heard divine or at least spiritual input, it

---

4. Reprinted by permission of the author from a manuscript in progress.

is probably wiser to judge by long-term results rather than one's own assessment of the moment. For the ego is just too tricky, resourceful, and resilient to be considered completely out of the picture at any given moment of ordinary consciousness.

That does not mean, however, that we should live in constant wariness of our own self-serving side in order to access the Holy Spirit's wisdom:

> *Do not be afraid of the ego.* It depends on your mind, and as you made it by believing in it, so you can dispel it by withdrawing belief from it. Do not project the responsibility for your belief in it onto anyone else, or you will preserve the belief. When you are willing to accept sole responsibility for the ego's existence you will have laid aside all anger and all attack, because they come from an attempt to project responsibility for your own errors. But having accepted the errors as yours, do not keep them. Give them over quickly to the Holy Spirit to be undone completely, so that all their effects will vanish from your mind and from the Sonship as a whole. (Chapter 7, VIII: 5)

In this intriguing passage, the Course suggests that one effective way to learn what spiritual guidance really means is to recognize and surrender our errors on a regular basis, rather than directly asking for guidance or assistance and then waiting for a message or reward. Likewise, our most chronic difficulties or seemingly impossible challenges may be little more than veils disguising an unimagined potential for release and happiness:

> Trials are but lessons that you failed to learn presented once again, so where you made a faulty choice before you now can make a

better one, and thus escape all pain that what you chose before has
brought to you. In every difficulty, all distress, and each perplexity
Christ calls to you and gently says, "My brother, choose again."
He would not leave one source of pain unhealed, nor any image
left to veil the truth. (Chapter 31, VIII: 3)

A similar clue is found in the Introduction to the Course Text,
where this initial clarification is offered:

The course does not aim at teaching the meaning of love, for that
is beyond what can be taught. It does aim, however, at removing the blocks to the awareness of love's presence, which is your
natural inheritance. The opposite of love is fear, but what is all-
encompassing can have no opposite.

In other words, we can best access the guidance of love by recognizing and releasing all the forms of fear we have thrown up in
its way. The fundamental message of the Course is that love is all
around and within us—it is, in fact, *what we really are*—and thus we
do not need to call upon it as much as we need to give up listening
to fear, or the voice of the ego, that blocks our awareness of love's
presence. When we think that love is outside us and must be sum-
moned by request from a divine external source, we will be prone to
hear our own ego-based delusions of love in lieu of the real thing.

Learning Over the Long Haul

I heard a wonderful flash of insight about learning the Course in
my study group recently, when one of our members was telling a

story of struggling to apply forgiveness in a difficult relationship and sighed, "I just feel like I'm doing the Course wrong." Another person replied, "But you can't do the Course wrong. You just have to keep doing it."

This comment revealed a keen understanding of how ACIM works over the long term to undo our habitual ways of perception. Left to its own devices, the ego will always provide us with a confused and confusing perspective on reality:

> The ego focuses on error and overlooks truth. It makes real every mistake it perceives, and with characteristically circular reasoning concludes that because of the mistake consistent truth must be meaningless. The next step, then, is obvious. If consistent truth is meaningless, inconsistency must be true. Holding error clearly in mind, and protecting what it has made real, the ego proceeds to the next step in its thought system: Error is real and truth is error.
>
> The ego makes no attempt to understand this, and it is clearly not understandable, but the ego does make every attempt to demonstrate it, and this it does constantly. Analyzing to attack meaning, the ego succeeds in overlooking it and is left with a series of fragmented perceptions which it unifies on behalf of itself. This, then, becomes the universe it perceives. And it is this universe which, in turn, becomes its demonstration of its own reality. (Chapter 11, V: 14)

Given that we perceive an entire universe steeped in our own confusion, it's not surprising that we bring our habitual disorientation to a revelatory system of thought like *A Course in Miracles* and tend to space out. For all its dense language and seemingly complex metaphysics, the Course often asserts that it actually has a very simple message, which we complicate through our own resistance: "The reason this course is simple is that truth is simple. Complexity is of the ego, and is nothing more than the ego's attempt to obscure the obvious" (Chapter 15, IV: 6).

In Lesson 79, "Let me recognize the problem so it can be solved," our tendency toward complexity is further analyzed:

> All this complexity is but a desperate attempt not to recognize the problem, and therefore not to let it be resolved. If you could recognize that your only problem is separation, no matter what form it takes, you could accept the answer because you would see its relevance. Perceiving the underlying constancy in all the problems that seem to confront you, you would understand that you have the means to solve them all. And you would use the means, because you recognize the problem.

Thus, whenever we get disoriented or feel mistaken in our search for spiritual truth, the best thing we can remember is that only one problem exists: We do not recognize ourselves as one with love and that it is impossible to have ever separated from it. Believing that we are separated by our bodies, doomed to individual isolation and death in an infinitely vast and complex universe of time and space, presents us with a host of problems that will inevitably seem insurmountable. Our way to happiness and peace is not to solve all those problems one by one, or even try to avoid them. Instead, we need only submit our chaotic perceptions to the guidance of someone who sees our truth in its wholeness:

> I was a man who remembered spirit and its knowledge. As a man I
> did not attempt to counteract error with knowledge, but to correct

error from the bottom up. I demonstrated both the powerlessness of the body and the power of the mind. By uniting my will with that of my Creator, I naturally remembered spirit and its real purpose. I cannot unite your will with God's for you, but I can erase all misperceptions from your mind if you will bring it under my guidance. Only your misperceptions stand in your way. Without them your choice is certain. Sane perception induces sane choosing. I cannot choose for you, but I can help you make your own right choice. (Chapter 3, IV: 7)

Summary

Stories of spacing out and needing to take breaks from the study of *A Course in Miracles* are common because students bring an inherently confused state of mind to its radical teaching. The habitual yet insecure authority of the human ego is immediately confronted by the profound and strangely intimate authority of the Course, and every student needs some time to become reconciled to that novel authority. The Jesus Christ who claims to be speaking in the Course says very different things than what conventional religion suggests he might say and that difference presents an "authority problem" that all students must ultimately resolve for themselves.

There is nothing in the Course message that effectively prevents it from being subverted or distorted by manipulative teachers, and the short history of ACIM has been influenced by at least one teacher widely reported as a cult leader. Yet the self-contained nature of the Course teaching ultimately points students away from reliance on self-proclaimed masters, gurus, or religious institutions of any kind. As Western culture rapidly evolves toward an identification with being "spiritual but not religious," the Course is likely to be more widely adapted as a reliable map for the contemporary spiritual journey.

Along that journey, even the fundamental Course ideal of forgiveness can be misunderstood or temporarily turned into an egocentric manipulation. But with time and experience, veteran Course students gradually outgrow their early, naïve misconceptions and learn to hear the "voice for God" more consistently, bringing them steadily increasing experiences of peace and personal clarity.

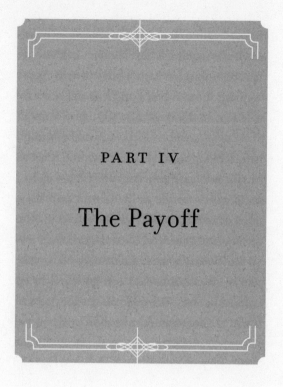

PART IV

The Payoff

12.

Miracles of a Lifetime

It takes great learning to understand that all things, events, encounters and circumstances are helpful. It is only to the extent to which they are helpful that any degree of reality should be accorded them in this world of illusion.

—*Manual for Teachers, 4-A: 4*

There is a classic Taoist story that illustrates the folly of interpreting life's unpredictable events and shifting circumstances according to our short-term needs and preferences:

A poor farmer who had worked his crops for many years with only one horse woke up one day to discover that the horse had run away. He told his neighbor, who immediately sympathized: "That's such bad luck!"

"Perhaps," the farmer mused.

The next morning the horse had inexplicably returned, accompanied by three other wild horses. "My, how your fortune has turned!" his neighbor exclaimed.

"Perhaps," the farmer allowed.

The very same day, his son tried to ride one of the untamed horses without supervision and was thrown, breaking his leg. The farmer's neighbor helped set the boy's leg and commented, "I guess those horses are not really a blessing after all."

"Perhaps." The farmer sighed.

The next day, a band of military officials rode into the village to draft young men into the army. Visiting the farmer and seeing that his son's leg was broken, they let him stay home. Dumbfounded, the neighbor exclaimed, "Things have turned out well for you after all!"

"Perhaps," the farmer concluded.

Of course, when a major catastrophe befalls us, it can be very difficult to suspend all judgment about the ultimate value of the event or be willing to wait for future developments that may redeem something that seems like a disaster now. Yet *A Course in Miracles* is unequivocal in this regard: "All things work together for good. There are no exceptions except in the ego's judgment" (Chapter 4, V).

A key element in understanding this perspective has to do with time and the fact that an egocentric outlook binds us to the experience of our individual bodies and lifespans. In a number of references, ACIM clearly implies that our spiritual development takes place over a much greater arc of time. The text following Lesson 97 suggests, for instance, that "Each time you practice, awareness is brought a little nearer at least; sometimes a thousand years or more are saved." And early in the Text, it is noted that "the miracle substitutes for learning that might have taken thousands of years" (Chapter 1, II: 6).

Paradoxically, ACIM offers an ambivalent perspective on reincarnation, which it addresses in a section entitled "Is Reincarnation So?" in the Manual for Teachers:

In the ultimate sense, reincarnation is impossible. There is no past or future, and the idea of birth into a body has no meaning either once or many times. Reincarnation cannot, then, be true in any real sense. Our only question should be, "Is the concept helpful?" And that depends, of course, on what it is used for. If it is used to strengthen the recognition of the eternal nature of life, it is helpful indeed. Is any other question about it really useful in lighting up the way? Like many other beliefs, it can be bitterly misused. At least, such misuse offers preoccupation and perhaps pride in the past. At worst, it induces inertia in the present. In between, many kinds of folly are possible. . . .

Does this mean that the teacher of God should not believe in reincarnation himself, or discuss it with others who do? The answer is, certainly not! If he does believe in reincarnation, it would be a mistake for him to renounce the belief unless his internal Teacher so advised. And this is most unlikely. He might be advised that he is misusing the belief in some way that is detrimental to his pupil's advance or his own. Reinterpretation would then be rec- ommended, because it is necessary. All that must be recognized, however, is that birth was not the beginning, and death is not the end. Yet even this much is not required of the beginner. He need merely accept the idea that what he knows is not necessarily all there is to learn. His journey has begun. (Manual, 24: 1, 5)

Experiencing Rebirth

I'm no expert on the theory of reincarnation and don't have a firm opinion about its validity. But there have been times in my decades-long study of the Course when I've had the distinct feeling that the evolution of my thinking or feeling processes has been mysteriously accelerated. When that occurs, there is also the sensation that a stagnant or "dead" part of me has been rejuvenated, and I am open to learning in a way that was previously closed off. In this way, I've experienced a rebirth within my own psyche. To me, this is what being "born again" really means, and it has little or nothing to do with the acceptance of a religious belief.

As I've described earlier in this book, I began studying the Course during a period of intense personal crisis, not long after falling seriously ill and being diagnosed with chronic fatigue syndrome (CFS). The seven years of suffering and recovery that followed brought about so much change that it is difficult to remember how I viewed the world before that time, but I do recall one attitude quite clearly.

By age thirty or so, I had decided that my development as an adult human being was more or less complete. I wasn't satisfied with who I was and certainly not with what I had achieved, but I was reasonably certain that my fundamental beliefs and attitudes were set for life. And overall, those beliefs and attitudes did not add up to a happy frame of mind. Looking back now, I would say that the ego-self that had crystallized by the time I was thirty was characterized by a keenly felt loss of the innocence that I had known as a child.

The state of childhood innocence, which I would further define as *consciousness undivided by fear*, was poetically described by Wordsworth in "Ode: Intimations of Immortality":

> *There was a time when meadow, grove and stream*
> *The earth and every common sight*
> *Did seem to me*

Appareled in celestial light
The glory and the freshness of a dream.

My earliest memories come from such a world, where I ran through viny woods too fast to look where I was going, trusting that I could not be injured or get lost in natural surroundings that usually felt more comfortable than human company. My experience of the outdoors was instinctively shamanistic; I saw all things, stones as well as snakes, as beings with some kind of spiritual if unspoken intelligence, on equal footing with me. Only gradually did I become embarrassed about conversing with trees and animals—an embarrassment that no doubt increased in direct proportion to my desire to be "grown-up."

When my father told me that thunder resulted from God rolling a wheelbarrow over a great wooden bridge, that idea seemed both awesome and reassuring. But even at the age of five, I did not take the story literally, nor did I imagine a heaven physically placed in the universe where such a bridge could exist. I was aware even then that there could be other explanations for thunder; I was willing for more than one idea to be true without it negating the value of another idea.

One of the long-term miracles of my Course study is that I've regained at least a fragment of this innocent consciousness. By allowing for a plurality of truths—mythic, emotional, and empirical truths—this state of mind is more pliable, tolerant, and peaceful than a narrowly rational or fervently religious state of mind. When we believe there is only one way of knowing—or worse yet, a fixed set of beliefs that will provide all the answers we need in life—we are well on the way to discrimination or persecution of those who think and believe differently.

The attempt to appear certain may also lead to the most damaging sacrifice we can make on the altar of adulthood: *forgetting how to learn*. We think it is natural that our capacity to learn decreases over time, and that the refinement of our senses and intellect requires a narrowing of interests. But we can see from watching infants that they are learning about everything *all at once and all the time*. It often appears to me that we take this great inborn learning capacity and gradually convert much of it to a prejudiced certainty about the world: that is, we largely stop learning because we think we know it all.

The Confidence of Innocence

What we lose thereby is what the Indian philosopher Jiddu Krishnamurti, in *Think on These Things*, called the confidence of innocence, "the confidence of a child who is so completely innocent he will try anything." Krishnamurti clearly distinguished this inborn attitude from *self-confidence*, which he described as "always colored by this arrogance of the self, the feeling 'It is I who do it.'" He maintained that the development of self-confidence—an attitude highly valued in Western society—actually serves to keep our beliefs and behavior within the confines of societal expectations and seriously blunts our true potential. It is "innocent confidence that will bring about a new civilization," Krishnamurti suggested, "but this innocent confidence cannot come into being as long as you remain within the societal pattern."

I first read these thoughts of Krishnamurti during my adolescence, and I found them at once absorbing, disorienting, and aggravating. I mistook much of what he said about breaking free of social patterns as supportive of my youthful urge to rebel. Many years were to pass before I understood that most forms of rebellion— whether adolescent, sexual, political, or cultural—actually comprise an important part of dominant social patterns. A description of a particular society that included only its predominant and con- formist behaviors would be seriously incomplete; in order to under- stand a society's "personality," one needs to see the rebellions it inspires, and how it weathers or is changed by them. (The same could be said for the psychological study of individuals, whose internal conflicts, if honestly conveyed, are usually more revealing than the personae they present to public view.) But the "innocent confidence" described by Krishnamurti is not regained by rebel- ling against culture or society; rather, it comes from letting go of the know-it-all ego. In Course lingo, that means surrendering our awareness to the Holy Spirit, a wise inner voice that transcends our egocentric concerns.

I was both angered and awed by Krishnamurti for most of the years of my passage into adulthood. But my personal frustra- tion with this distant teacher was one of the healthiest and most compelling feelings I experienced between the ages of fifteen and twenty-five. He spoke, in a sense, to the instinctive part of me that remembered my innocent confidence. He reminded me that I had once observed and learned about the world in a much faster, more inclusive and insightful manner. And he reminded me that it was the child in me—not the increasingly confused young adult—who knew how to do this. I was angry because I could see no way out of losing my innocence.

As a child who often received warnings from my parents and teachers about being too idealistic, I felt this loss keenly. I was very frustrated during my high school years about the discrepancy between what I felt to be true learning and the education I was receiving. My overall desire was essentially spiritual, although I would have strongly resisted that label at the time. I simply wanted the world to make sense, so that I could see how I belonged in it. I was fairly certain that I was unlikely to gain understanding through some final answer to the mysteries of human existence.

Growing up in the Christian fundamentalist culture of North Carolina had made it amply clear to me that people who accepted and clung to final answers seldom displayed a natural curiosity. Even if I could not have articulated it at the time, I felt that the process of instinctive, innocent learning *was* the meaning of life. Thus, making sense of the world was a matter of continual discovery, not reaching a final conclusion or, on the other hand, admitting defeat in the face of too much contradictory information. Yet a sense of defeat haunted my late teens, maximizing my feeling that nothing around me was real anymore. As I approached the inevitability of living on my own without a clear sense of purpose (or a practical choice of career), I felt increasing pressure to accept the "real world" of twentieth-century capitalist America: that world of "making a living" which, for all but a lucky few, clearly entailed boredom and no small degree of servitude for the sake of survival. I gradually came to the unpleasant conclusion that growing up meant facing these disheartening facts and doing the best I could in the situation. But the emotional cost of this conclusion was dangerously high: the more I faced the "real world," the less real I felt.

Thus I gradually came to accept that the real world was inherently confused, conflictive, and dangerous, a floating crap game at best. It seemed that the most you could do in life was to look out for yourself, your friends and family, and to demonstrate a wider compassion or political concern when you could spare the time. The child's magical world of learning—where you looked around to see what you could find—had painfully and inexorably become the adult world of survival, where you usually had to be looking out for number one. By my early thirties, this confusion and bitterness had crystallized into the sensation that I was done "growing up," and no meaningful change was on the horizon.

A Miraculous Shock

Thus, with over twenty years' retrospect, I can say that the first undeniable miracle of my adult life was becoming seriously ill in my early thirties. I was stopped dead in my tracks from pursuing a life that was not only unsatisfying, but deeply contaminated by a sad certainty that there was no way out. Considering that I inadvertently found a way out through a catastrophic halt, I sometimes wonder if a deeply unconscious, spiritual wisdom was involved in my physical collapse. Perhaps there are some miracles that seem difficult to live with in the short term, even while they set the stage for a transformation that we could neither plan nor negotiate by any other means.

It's also worth mentioning that while I had always harbored the desire to be a writer, and had earned money that way as early as my days as a college reporter, I was not working professionally as a writer by age thirty and in fact had no clear idea of what I might someday write about. I had work in print as a poet and an investigative journalist, but neither of those forms were either compelling or practical enough to develop into a career. So I was always longing to do the work that clearly felt like my calling, but could see no way to pursue it. This frustration added greatly to the everyday stress of my lifestyle at the time.

The first six weeks of my illness were spent in increasing bewilderment and anxiety over what was happening to me, as I desperately searched for medical fixes that yielded no results. When it began to dawn on me that my state of mind was possibly related to the collapse of my health, I decided to try psychotherapy and shortly thereafter discovered *A Course in Miracles*. At that point, a completely unexpected process took over: I began to learn again, with the kind of eagerness and open-mindedness that I had not experienced since I was a child. The topics I found myself investigating included everything from the etiology and treatment of autoimmune disorders, to Jungian psychology and dream study, to alternative spiritual perspectives in addition to the Course. Not everything I looked into was useful, but on reflection I can see that I had regained some of "the confidence of a child who is so completely innocent he will try anything," as Krishnamurti put it.

I also began writing prolifically in a private journal, an exercise of self-awareness that I had begun as a young adolescent but which had lapsed in the last few years before the onset of CFS. Without my knowing it, this writing was a kind of warm-up to a new occupation as a full-time writer. And all the research I had done in the interest of my health and recovery would form the foundation of my subject matter as a magazine journalist focused on health and contemporary spirituality, a specialty that I would eventually identify as "the journalism of consciousness."

Although seven years of serious illness may sound like a prolonged struggle—and in the midst of it, I certainly felt that it was taking forever—I am convinced now that the Course provided me with a relatively accelerated path out of chronic suffering and into a purposeful, productive life. I have known people with CFS or fibromyalgia, a similar disorder, who have suffered for fifteen years or more without much improvement. Without ACIM, I'm certain that I would have had a prolonged and much more uneven struggle back to health.

When I speak about my healing process, I am always careful to clarify that I do not consider the Course a "cure" in itself for any physiological or psychological disorder. What cured me was learning to take better care of myself, in all respects, than I had known how to do before my illness. Specific medical approaches that helped me overcome CFS included acupuncture, improving my dietary habits, taking an antifungal drug to battle intestinal candidiasis, and using a mild sedative to calm anxiety. But adhering to the Course discipline served to clarify my thinking processes and help me make better choices about treatment than I would have made otherwise. By being the instrument of releasing chronic anger and guilt that had previously darkened my consciousness, the Course brightened my outlook and made it possible for me to imagine being healthy and productive again.

Along the way, my ACIM study delivered countless healing "shocks" that were not always pleasant when they occurred, but that I could fairly call miraculous in the long term. While the release of guilt or anger might sound like it's always a good thing, I can distinctly remember feeling uncomfortable at times when I recognized that I was no longer preoccupied with a past injury or no longer resentful about some limiting condition of my everyday life. The lifting of such a negative attitude would immediately be followed by the question, *"But what will I do now?"*

Under the spell of their troubled egos, human beings can spend an enormous amount of time worrying, resenting, or complaining, with the result that such negative energetic states literally consume our daily lives. These preoccupations can be quite difficult to dislodge, but when they are moved out of the way, a genuine confusion about who and what we really are may ensue. Fortunately, another way of living does "fill in" soon enough. In Course terms, the Holy Spirit is always waiting to instruct and inspire us once we have allowed egocentric fixations to dissolve. In my experience, it's also accurate to think of the Holy Spirit as an instinctive wisdom, an innate capacity to learn, and a mystical drive toward wholeness.

Ten years after I fell ill, my life was remarkably different than before I was stricken with chronic fatigue syndrome. I had launched a career in magazine journalism that would eventually lead to about one hundred articles in print; I had coauthored my first two books, and my inspirational volume on forgiveness had just been released in hardcover by a major national publisher. I was married, a quite remarkable turn of events considering the degree of cynicism about intimate relationships that I had developed before CFS. And as a result of what I had learned about restoring and safeguarding my health, I was in better shape following seven years of illness than I had been before falling prey to CFS.

While I'd like to think there must be an easier way to transform one's life, the fact of my experience is that the key to miraculous change was "hitting rock bottom" with my previous way of life—not unlike the way alcoholics or drug addicts must often come to a dangerous point of no return before they can enter recovery and gradually put together a new way of life. In my case, I reached the point of no return with the egocentric habits of my youth. That is not to say that my ego completely dissolved during the process of my illness and initial Course study, but I definitely began the process of hearing and integrating another voice.

As ACIM suggests, "The still, small Voice for God is not drowned out by all the ego's raucous screams and senseless ravings to those who want to hear It" (Chapter 21, V: 1).

The Stages of Growth

This chapter opens with a brief quote from a remarkable section of ACIM's Manual for Teachers entitled "Development of Trust." Although it discusses the evolution of just one of ten "characteristics of God's Teachers" (the others are Honesty, Tolerance, Gentleness, Joy, Defenselessness, Generosity, Patience, Faithfulness, and Open-Mindedness), this progression seems to be descriptive of spiritual growth in general. For all those who might mistake the Course for a simplistic self-help path, these few paragraphs serve as a bracing education. And while the Course elsewhere suggests that enlightenment or salvation can be achieved at any moment, this synopsis suggests that for most students, the route to becoming Course-style "teachers of God" is a long haul indeed. It would take many years for me to see the following stages played out in my own life:

> First, they must go through what might be called "a period of undoing." This need not be painful, but it usually is so experienced. It seems as if things are being taken away, and it is rarely understood initially that their lack of value is merely being recognized. How can lack of value be perceived unless the perceiver is in a position where he must see things in a different light? He is not yet at a point at which he can make the shift entirely internally. And so the plan will sometimes call for changes in what

seem to be external circumstances. These changes are always helpful. When the teacher of God has learned that much, he goes on
to the second stage.

My first "period of undoing" began with the onset of illness and
the soon-to-follow losses of employment and my primary intimate
relationship of the time. Throughout the course of my seven-year
crisis, there would be other less dramatic undoings, each time with
the result of beginning to see things in a different light.

Next, the teacher of God must go through "a period of sorting
out." This is always somewhat difficult because, having learned
that the changes in his life are always helpful, he must now decide
all things on the basis of whether they increase the helpfulness or
hamper it. He will find that many, if not most of the things he
valued before will merely hinder his ability to transfer what he has
learned to new situations as they arise. . . .

For me, "sorting out" began when I first undertook my study of
A Course in Miracles. It was the first time in my life I had encountered a point of view so different from my own—and so powerful
that it effectively challenged my egocentric habits. As I began to
sense that everything I'd known or believed before could be mistaken, I was gaining a perspective that helped me grasp how all the
changes then taking place in my life would prove helpful.

The third stage through which the teacher of God must go can be
called "a period of relinquishment." If this is interpreted as giving
up the desirable, it will engender enormous conflict. Few teachers
of God escape this distress entirely. There is, however, no point in

sorting out the valuable from the valueless unless the next obvious step is taken. Therefore, the period of overlap is apt to be one in which the teacher of God feels called upon to sacrifice his own best interests on behalf of truth. He has not realized as yet how wholly impossible such a demand would be. He can learn this only as he actually does give up the valueless. Through this, he learns that where he anticipated grief, he finds a happy lightheart-edness instead; where he thought something was asked of him, he finds a gift bestowed on him. . . . (Manual, 4, I, A: 3–5)

As the result of my health crisis and the spiritual initiation that followed, my external circumstances changed dramatically. I had to relinquish not only many material possessions when I shifted into a stripped-down lifestyle in a new place, but also a host of attitudes and prejudices that had seemed to serve me in my former life. I cannot say that I was fully conscious of everything I was doing during this time, but in looking back I can comprehend the slow, interior process of distinguishing "the valuable from the valueless." And when that was done, I found myself married, pursuing a new writing career, and solidifying a sense of well-being.

Now comes "a period of settling down." This is a quiet time, in which the teacher of God rests a while in reasonable peace. Now he consolidates his learning. Now he begins to see the transfer value of what he has learned. Its potential is literally staggering, and the teacher of God is now at the point in his progress at which he sees in it his whole way out. "Give up what you do not want, and keep what you do." How simple is the obvious! And how easy to do! The teacher of God needs this period of respite. He has not yet come as far as he thinks. Yet when he is ready to go on, he goes with mighty companions beside him. Now he rests a while, and gathers them before going on. He will not go on from here alone. (Manual, 4, I, A: 6)

I can clearly recognize a "period of respite" after my illness that lasted about twelve years, ending in divorce and the resultant emotional chaos. While my marriage had been mutually supportive and peaceful, it had also been limiting. My wife and I had done much to heal each other's deep-rooted problems from the past, but we unexpectedly reached a point where it appeared that we had to proceed with new learning on our own.

After about a year of struggling to decide who was the most to blame, I recognized that my life had simply changed from the inside out again, and that I could only proceed in a healthy way if I let go of the idea of loss.

The next stage is indeed "a period of unsettling." Now must the teacher of God understand that he did not really know what was valuable and what was valueless. All that he really learned so far was that he did not want the valueless, and that he did want the valuable. Yet his own sorting out was meaningless in teaching him the difference. The idea of sacrifice, so central to his own thought system, had made it impossible for him to judge. He thought he learned willingness, but now he sees that he does not know what the willingness is for. And now he must attain a state that may remain impossible to reach for a long, long time. He must learn to lay all judgment aside, and ask only what he really wants in every circumstance. Were not each step in this direction so heavily reinforced, it would be hard indeed! . . . (Manual, 4, I, A: 7)

As I write this book, I can see myself just beginning to find my footing again after a profound "unsettling." In a new partnership after several years living on my own, I am still working through issues of sacrifice in my personal life and struggle in my professional pursuits. To lay aside all judgment is quite a challenge in this life on earth, but my long discipline with the Course has at least assured me that this is the right direction to pursue. I'm increasingly aware that I create all the apparent challenges that I have to master, even when my first reaction is sometimes to feel bewildered or unfairly attacked. And I have come to accept that spiritual growth is always ongoing, leading to a "next stage" that is impossible for me to recognize in advance.

And finally, there is "a period of achievement." It is here that learning is consolidated. Now what was seen as merely shadows before become solid gains, to be counted on in all "emergencies" as well as tranquil times. Indeed, the tranquility is their result; the outcome of honest learning, consistency of thought and full transfer. This is the stage of real peace, for here is Heaven's state fully reflected. From here, the way to Heaven is open and easy. In fact, it is here. Who would "go" anywhere, if peace of mind is already complete? And who would seek to change tranquility for something more desirable? What could be more desirable than this? (Manual, 4, I, A: 8)

Summary

A Course in Miracles urges its students to recognize that all the unpredictable events and shifting circumstances of their lives are ultimately helpful, once the time-bound, self-serving aims of egocentricity are replaced by a timeless spiritual perspective. Given that many people experience huge disappointments and significant tragedies in their lives, this is a towering challenge of understanding. Yet personal loss or a major reversal of fortune can provide the key to spiritual rejuvenation, an opportunity to regain what the philosopher J. Krishnamurti identified as a childlike "confidence of innocence."

The Course paradoxically claims that personal salvation can come about in a moment or that it may take thousands of years. It does not, however, explicitly endorse the concept of reincarnation, while allowing that it may be a useful concept to remind people that their spiritual life is eternal, without beginning or end. In the closing Manual for Teachers, it offers an explication of the stages of spiritual growth, which encompass periods of *undoing*, *relinquishment*, *sorting out*, *settling down*, *unsettling*, and finally *achievement*. This outline of the process of enlightenment can lend an invaluable perspective on a course of personal change that might otherwise be difficult to grasp in the midst of any particular challenge of development. In the short term, miracles may be hard to live with, yet will eventually reveal their blessings.

13.

Forgiveness 24/7

Do you want happiness, a quiet mind, a certainty of purpose, and a sense of worth and beauty that transcends the world? Do you want care and safety, and the warmth of sure protection always? Do you want a quietness that cannot be disturbed, a gentleness that never can be hurt, a deep abiding comfort, and a rest so perfect it can never be upset? All this forgiveness offers you, and more.

—*From Lesson 122*

The initial Workbook lessons of *A Course in Miracles* make a minimal demand on the student's time and attention. "Each of the first three lessons should not be done more than twice a day each, preferably morning and evening," instructs the text following Lesson 1. "Nor should they be attempted for more than a minute or so, unless that entails a sense of hurry. A comfortable sense of leisure is essential." By Lesson 4, the suggested frequency of lesson repetition has bumped up a notch, yet there still seems to be a focus on not overdoing it: "Do not repeat these exercises more than three or four times during the day."

But by Lesson 27, "Above all else I want to see," the Workbook's intention to waylay the student's normal pattern of attention becomes clear:

The idea for today needs many repetitions for maximum benefit. It should be used at least every half hour, and more if possible. You might try for every fifteen or twenty minutes. It is recommended that you set a definite time interval for using the idea when you wake or shortly afterwards, and attempt to adhere to it throughout the day. It will not be difficult to do this, even if you are engaged in conversation, or otherwise occupied at the time. You can still repeat one short sentence to yourself without disturbing anything.

And at Lesson 95, "I am one self, united with my Creator," the intensity of practice is increased again:

The use of the first five minutes of every waking hour for practicing the idea for the day has special advantages at the stage of learning in which you are at present. It is difficult at this point not to allow your mind to wander, if it undertakes extended practice. You have surely realized this by now. You have seen the extent of your lack of mental discipline, and of your need for mind training. It is necessary that you be aware of this, for it is indeed a hindrance to your advance.

Frequent but shorter practice periods have other advantages for you at this time. In addition to recognizing your difficulties with sustained attention, you must also have noticed that, unless you are reminded of your purpose frequently, you tend to forget about it for long periods of time. You often fail to remember the short applications of the idea for the day, and you have not yet formed the habit of using the idea as an automatic response to temptation.

By "temptation," the Course is not referring to the conventional lures of sinfulness in Christian terms, but instead the tendency to mistake oneself for a body and ego: "Whatever form temptation seems to take, it always but reflects a wish to be a self that you are not" (Chapter 31, VIII: 12). It's hard to imagine anyone who is not constantly subject to the temptation of believing in their own personal identity—and that explains why the Course pursues a strategy of interrupting and dislodging the student's habitual patterns of thought. Its ultimate aim is to replace all our ongoing attachments to the world, including the most cherished and comfortable ones, with an attitude of transcendent release. This attitude is described in the text accompanying Lesson 132, "I loose the world from all I thought it was":

> What keeps the world in chains but your beliefs? And what can save the world except your Self? Belief is powerful indeed. The thoughts you hold are mighty, and illusions are as strong in their effects as is the truth. A madman thinks the world he sees is real, and does not doubt it. Nor can he be swayed by questioning his thoughts' effects. It is but when their source is raised to question that the hope of freedom comes to him at last.
>
> Yet is salvation easily achieved, for anyone is free to change his mind, and all his thoughts change with it. Now the source of thought has shifted, for to change your mind means you have changed the source of all ideas you think or ever thought or yet will think. You free the past from what you thought before. You free the future from all ancient thoughts of seeking what you do not want to find.

In this regard, ACIM is leading the student into a new form of *metanoia*. This theological term usually denotes repentance, or as *Merriam-Webster* puts it in nonreligious terms, "a transformative change of heart." A genuine change of heart is not achieved by a mere confession of sin or a promise to live differently, however sincere such a confession or promise might be. In Course terms, it requires a lot of work: training one's attention to respond in a consistently forgiving manner to everything that happens at every moment of the day. In popular terms, this kind of metanoia might best be described as "forgiveness 24/7."

"Ideas Leave Not Their Source"

The aim of perpetual forgiveness, however, is not to excuse the world for the many ways in which it may fail to serve or satisfy us in the course of a day. Instead, the point is to realize that the world we see "out there" is really within the mind, and consists of nothing more than an incredibly complex projection of beliefs about oneself. To forgive whatever we see going on in the world is actually to forgive our own ideas, one after another. As Lesson 132 continues:

> To free the world from every kind of pain is but to change your mind about yourself. There is no world apart from your ideas because ideas leave not their source, and you maintain the world within your mind in thought.

Thus, the process of perpetual forgiveness begins with the recognition that the world we see is entirely a reflection of our own ideas. Whether it is currently pleasing us or dismaying us, adhering to our expectations or lurching into a surprising turn of fate, the world is literally a product of our imagination at every moment. This may seem hard to believe, but the Course reminds us that the mind is relentlessly creative, for good and ill—and that we have veiled its full power from ourselves:

The mind is very powerful, and never loses its creative force. It never sleeps. Every instant it is creating. It is hard to recognize that thought and belief combine into a power surge that can literally move mountains. It appears at first glance that to believe such power about yourself is arrogant, but that is not the real reason you do not believe it. You prefer to believe that your thoughts cannot exert real influence because you are actually afraid of them. This may allay awareness of the guilt, but at the cost of perceiving the mind as impotent. If you believe that what you think is ineffectual you may cease to be afraid of it, but you are hardly likely to respect it. There *are* no idle thoughts. All thinking produces form at some level. (Chapter 2, VI: 9)

So, after projecting the world we see in its entirety, we become suspicious of what we have created, and react as if it were largely out of our control. We choose what to love or to fear, what we like and don't like, whom we want to be with and whom we want to avoid. We see ourselves living in particular bodies—which are almost always unsatisfactory or uncomfortable—and we see everyone else in bodies that provoke responses ranging from desire and devotion to disgust and hatred. Above all, we see a world of *differences*, a world with which we are constantly negotiating (and sometimes battling) to make sense of things and somehow find a survivable equilibrium:

Where do all these differences come from? Certainly they seem to be in the world outside. Yet it is surely the mind that judges what the eyes behold. It is the mind that interprets the eyes' messages and gives them "meaning." And this meaning does not exist in the world outside at all. What is seen as "reality" is simply what the mind prefers. Its hierarchy of values is projected outward, and it sends the body's eyes to find it. The body's eyes will never see except through differences. Yet it is not the messages they bring on which perception rests. Only the mind evaluates their messages, and so only the mind is responsible for seeing. It alone decides whether what is seen is real or illusory, desirable or undesirable, pleasurable or painful.

It is in the sorting out and categorizing activities of the mind that errors in perception enter. And it is here correction must be made. The mind classifies what the body's eyes bring to it according to its preconceived values, judging where each sense datum fits best. What basis could be faultier than this? Unrecognized by itself, it has itself asked to be given what will fit into these categories. And having done so, it concludes that the categories must be true. On this the judgment of all differences rests, because it is on this that judgments of the world depend. Can this confused and senseless "reasoning" be depended on for anything? (Manual, 8: 3–4)

To replace our ego-based reasoning, which incessantly creates judgmental categories of meaning and then slots all our perceptions and experiences into them, the Course offers a comprehensive discipline of forgiveness. As we learn to forgive—first in isolated instances and eventually as a matter of course—we become increasingly attentive to the internal voice of the Holy Spirit, which sorts things quite differently from our ego-driven habit of mind:

It will seem difficult for you to learn that you have no basis at all for ordering your thoughts. This lesson the Holy Spirit teaches by giving you the shining examples of miracles to show you that your way of ordering is wrong, but that a better way is offered you. . . .

The only judgment involved is the Holy Spirit's one division into two categories; one of love, and the other the call for love. You cannot safely make this division, for you are much too confused either to recognize love, or to believe that everything else is nothing but a call for love. You are too bound to form, and not to content. What you consider content is not content at all. It is merely form, and nothing else. For you do not respond to what a brother really offers you, but only to the particular perception of his offering by which the ego judges it. (Chapter 14, 10: 6–7)

In sum, the Course interrupts and reorders our habitual patterns of thought and attention in order to teach us a consistently healthy response to everything we perceive and experience. When everything we see in the world "out there" is recognized as either a manifestation of love or a call for love, our response can always be the same: We answer with love.

ACIM notes several times that forgiveness is not the same as love: "It is the source of healing, but it is the messenger of love and not its Source" (Chapter 18, IX: 10). In a sense, forgiveness opens the door to love; it is the means by which we correct our ego-based ways of perceiving and responding to the world. As we learn to forgive consistently, our ego is increasingly displaced and the loving voice of the Holy Spirit takes precedence. Along the way, we recognize all the illusions of the world as our own mistaken ideas projected outward. However fervently we believed those ideas could leave their source and act upon us from the outside, this in fact never occurred. And thus we come to make peace with the world in direct proportion to the surrender of our own delusions.

The Practicality of Forgiveness

I've written earlier in this book about how learning to forgive eased and accelerated the process of a serious illness I experienced in my thirties. Although the collapse of my immune system first seemed to be an unwarranted failure of my own body with an entirely mysterious cause, I gradually came to understand that it was actually an unconscious expression of my own anger and resentment about a variety of issues, beginning with my childhood, and later, the seeming indifference of the world at large to things I cared about.

A turning point came after a year or so of Course study when I realized that just before I became ill, I had become habitually angry about almost everything. In short, I was mad at God or, on the days when I didn't believe in God, I was just mad at *the way things were*. Either an all-powerful being was opposing everything I wanted and believed in, or I had somehow ended up in a cold, indifferent universe that stymied my every attempt to find happiness and success.

This was a turning point because it was much easier to see the impracticality of that global anger than it had been to question each particular issue I was upset about. The specifics of my anger could each be justified, even if I couldn't find a way to resolve any of them. But when I added them all up and recognized the total as a general *attitude* I was holding, that attitude didn't quite make sense. For one thing, seeing myself as having to fight God or the entire universe was a particularly poor strategy for pursuing a happier and more productive life; I was overpowered from the start.

That was when I began to detect my own ego-driven conspiracy against myself. It dawned on me that my anger was not really a *reaction* to everything I didn't like. While I didn't know exactly how it had come to pass, I realized that my anger had *preceded* everything that happened to me. Whenever anything didn't go the way I liked, it became a target for my already existing upset. In Course terms, I had unknowingly developed categories of judgment in my mind and was merely waiting for events in the world "out there" that would fit into those categories. In retrospect, I can easily see what some of the major categories were:

- I'm Being Cheated
- No One is Watching Out for Me
- People Don't Care About Doing Things Well
- Everyone Else Is Getting Away with Something
- The World Is a Mess

And that's just to name a few. That's not to say that I was aware of these categorizations at the time. They ruled my perceptions because they were only partly conscious, at best, and taken for granted. Whenever I had an experience that seemed to fit into one of these categories, I experienced a kind of negative satisfaction in having my cynical perceptions of the world confirmed. (When I look back at this pattern, I'm not at all surprised that I became subject to a syndrome of physical "chronic fatigue"; I had already been in such a mental and emotional condition for a while beforehand.)

But through the process of forgiving each of my categorized upsets, whether large or small, I gradually began to see that there was really just one category for all my pains and dismay: "I Am Not Loved."And the more I forgave, the less that made sense. In the process of forgiving my mother, for instance, I had come to recognize that she had loved her family as best she could, constantly fighting her way through her own thickets of senseless despair to establish connections and show her devotion. The fact that she often seemed to fail in these efforts did not make her unloving.

In a larger context, I began to sense the arrogance of assuming that I had to fight off God or the entire universe to establish and defend my place in the world. And when I recognized that arrogance, I also understood that it derived from a part of my mind that was not really me, but that had nonetheless been running my life—until the point that its cynical logic utterly failed, with the result of a catastrophic illness. As the Course suggests:

> Arrogance makes an image of yourself that is not real. It is this image which quails and retreats in terror, as the Voice for God assures you that you have the strength, the wisdom and the holiness to go beyond all images. You are not weak, as is the image of yourself. You are not ignorant and helpless. Sin can not tarnish the truth in you, and misery can come not near the holy home of God.
>
> All this the Voice for God relates to you. And as He speaks, the image trembles and seeks to attack the threat it does not know, sensing its basis crumble. Let it go. (From Lesson 186)

At the point of comprehending that my angry and arrogant image of myself was not real, I could acknowledge the impracticality of an egocentric approach to life. Slowly but surely, forgiveness was proving to be a more pragmatic strategy.

Long-Term Benefits

As I came out of my illness after seven years, I was convinced of the power of forgiveness to release chronic anger and heal its effects on the body. At that point, I tended to view forgiveness as an attitude that could help one get over the past, but I wasn't yet aware of it as an energy that could make a difference in moving forward after past hurts were healed.

After nearly twenty years of studying and applying forgiveness in my life after the passage of my illness, I've become aware of more key benefits of this healing attitude. None of these are magical capacities, and forgiveness is certainly not the only way to access them. But they are all dynamic potentials that I began to tap more consistently as I developed an ongoing attitude of forgiveness. That does not mean that nowadays I never get angry or hold grudges. It does mean that I am relatively quick to recognize when I am doing so and ask for inner guidance to see things differently. Such a "shift in perception" is the essence of forgiveness and effectively disengages the mind from habitual ego defenses. The more I practice such a shift, the more I experience these benefits:

A healing self-awareness. Sigmund Freud, the father of psychoanalysis, famously wrote to an analysand that "much will be gained if we succeed in transforming your hysterical misery into common unhappiness." While the modern practice of psychotherapy has improved upon Freud's attitude, conventional therapy still tends to be limited to an "ego management" point of view that enables insights into one's chronic problems without necessarily being able to get beyond them. In my own experience with therapy before and since becoming a Course student,

I've gained some very valuable insights into my habitual difficulties and prejudices. But the practice of forgiveness as directed by ACIM has enabled me to go from such insights into genuinely transformative changes, sometimes in relatively short order.

This is largely because the Course discipline trains the student to awaken to a self-awareness that is larger, more objective, and more truly caring than a typically egocentric outlook. When you are aware that there is always a deeper and wiser source of counsel within oneself—and that it can be contacted simply by asking for help to see things differently—then one's moment-by-moment self-awareness becomes a force for healing instead of a constricting focus on "looking out for number one."

Greater creativity. As I've noted earlier in this book, my ambition to write was largely thwarted during my twenties by a confusion about my purpose and a persistent distraction with personal problems. As I came out of the illness that took up most of my thirties, I rapidly contacted an unprecedented source of creative energy. Within the next ten years I wrote and published nearly one hundred magazine articles and several books, including two novels. I became an independent publisher as well as writing for other publishers, and additionally provided professional editing and consultation services to scores of other writers, many of them in the spiritual field.

None of this work or its subject matter was even imaginable in my youth, when I was certainly ambitious but could not find a reliable means of expression. Not only has one of my most successful titles been on the subject of forgiveness (*The Way of Forgiveness*), the ongoing development of a forgiving perspective continues to inform my work as a writer, editor, and literary consultant. I would even say that "ambition" in the usual sense is less of a driving force of my work nowadays than it used to be. Instead my work is directed by an intuitive openness and inspiration that surpass my own capacity for "bright ideas." There's a sense of being led toward doing my best work for the sake of exploring and sharing truth, rather than planning a career based on conventional goals of success.

Sharper insights into other people. It may seem paradoxical to say that forgiveness has given me a more exacting view of human nature, but in fact this is my experience—with a significant qualification. Forgiveness shifts the basis on which I judge everything and everyone, from a "good/bad" or "right/wrong" basis to an ongoing questioning of my own perceptions. When I can relate to other people with that attitude of open questioning, I can actually see them more clearly.

A cynical view of human nature is one in which the qualities of other people have essentially been pre-decided as negative. If one believes that people are essentially evil, self-serving, or merely hapless, then virtually everything that other people do will fall into perceptual categories that reinforce such a bias. Likewise, a naïve assumption that everyone is vaguely "good" will be blinding in a different way. With either bias, anything people do that is difficult to categorize according to familiar prejudices will literally be difficult to see.

Where I tended toward a cynical bias earlier in my life, a discipline of forgiveness has enabled me to witness human behavior with a perspective that is much closer to a pure openness. I'm more capable of seeing everything that people do without having to pass judgment on their actions. When I do judge quickly, I'm much more likely to catch myself and "reopen the perception," as it were.

Part of this openness stems from the awareness that I cannot judge without projecting something about my own self-assessment at the moment. And I am better off admitting that I don't know exactly what I am than rushing to judgment of other people in order to feel more certain about myself. As the Course explains:

> The world can teach no images of you unless you want to learn them. There will come a time when images have all gone by, and you will see you know not what you are. It is to this unsealed and open mind that truth returns, unhindered and unbound. Where concepts of the self have been laid by is truth revealed exactly as it is. When every concept has been raised to doubt and question, and been recognized as made on no assumptions that would stand the light, then is the truth left free to enter in its sanctuary, clean and free of guilt. There is no statement that the world is more afraid to hear than this:
>
> *I do not know the thing I am, and therefore do not know what I am doing, where I am, or how to look upon the world or on myself.*
>
> Yet in this learning is salvation born. And What you are will tell you of Itself. (Chapter 31, V: 17)

A stronger sense of trust. Until I became ill in my early thirties, I lived the normal life of the ego—looking out for myself, trying to preserve my habits, and defending a number of strong, fixed opinions about other people and the world in general. I was more fearful than I was able to admit to myself, and I engaged in unconscious bargains with my fears in order to squeeze some enjoyment out of life. In this state of mind, daily life often felt risky and there were few people I genuinely trusted. But I could always compare myself to someone less fortunate and derive a kind of satisfaction from the idea that I was getting by better than others.

Embarking on a spiritual path of forgiveness meant undertaking a discipline of surrendering my habits and enlarging my worldview.

It also gave me an entirely different way of dealing with fear—as a part of my self-awareness that had to be honestly acknowledged, but was no longer allowed to dictate terms. In this consciousness I increasingly feel cared for by an ineffable, pervasive intelligence that I sometimes call God, but that can also simply be called love. And I trust everyone to be doing the best they can to uncover or rediscover that same foundation of love, even if some appear to be seriously misguided or tragically deluded in their pursuit.

In a day-to-day sense, I don't know if the way of forgiveness makes for an "easier" life than conventional egotism. In some respects it's more demanding. What has made the shift worthwhile is that my life makes sense to me now, and I feel consistently guided toward growth and service. In my pre-Course life I deeply distrusted myself and secretly believed that I had too many serious problems to be of real help to anyone.

A growing sense of peaceful strength. I could also identify this benefit of forgiveness as *resilience*, a kind of mental and emotional limberness that enables me to respond to life's surprises and challenges with equanimity and enthusiasm. That's not to say that I never get thrown off balance, but it does mean that I regain an inner and outer poise more quickly than I used to. When one first begins to deal seriously with the ACIM philosophy that the everyday material world is illusory, the initial effects can be quite disorienting, as described in Chapter 11. But over time, the growing awareness of a timeless, loving Source that transcends everything we see in the world provides a constant background reassurance. As one perceives the world with less of a sense of threat, and more with the knowledge that a response of love is possible in every kind of situation, a transcendent peacefulness grows within. The Course alludes to this process with the restatement of a biblical concept:

Remember that where your heart is, there is your treasure also. You believe in what you value. If you are afraid, you are valuing wrongly. Your understanding will then inevitably value wrongly, and by endowing all thoughts with equal power will inevitably destroy peace. That is why the Bible speaks of "the peace of God which passeth understanding." This peace is totally incapable of being shaken by errors of any kind. It denies the ability of anything not of God to affect you. (Chapter 2, II: 1)

Ultimately, the goal of the Course discipline of forgiveness is to free our consciousness from the time-bound world of the ego and the body entirely, returning us to the abstract infinity of what ACIM calls "knowledge," or oneness with God. But the way is gradual, usually involving a long series of awakenings. In fact, we are unlikely to transition directly from our current dream of the world directly into knowledge, because we will tend to be afraid of the loss of all we know in favor of a greater reality. "Fear not that you will be abruptly lifted up and hurled into reality," the Course reassures. "Time is kind, and if you use it on behalf of reality, it will keep gentle pace with you in your transition" (Chapter 16, VI: 8). Rather than shocking us into the full awareness of truth all at once, the Course regimen of perpetual forgiveness leads us from our current state of delusion into happier dreams.

Summary

The Workbook of *A Course in Miracles* starts out with very simple lesson repetitions that do not demand much time or effort from students. But its requirements rapidly intensify to a point where one's self-awareness is disrupted and redirected on a near-constant basis. The ultimate aim is to displace the normally fearful and egocentric outlook of the human psyche with a consciousness of perpetual forgiveness. The point of this mind-training is not to release the world from blame for all its apparent problems or shortcomings, but to make students aware that the world they see is entirely the projection of their own ideas. Instead of prejudging the world on the basis of ego-driven categorizations, students learn to see everything as either an expression of love or a call for love. In either case, their proper response is love, which is the true Source of their consciousness.

Over time, the discipline of perpetual forgiveness is far more practical than typical ego-driven strategies, no matter how strange or extreme it may seem at first. Benefits may include a healing self-awareness; greater creativity; a sharper yet more benevolent view of human nature; a stronger daily trust; and a growing personal resilience. Ultimately, the practice of "forgiveness 24/7" leads the Course student out of the common unhappiness of the human condition and into the "happier dreams" that precede a reunion with God, our Source in infinite love.

14.

Awakening to the Happy Dream

You will first dream of peace, and then awaken to it. Your first exchange of what you made for what you want is the exchange of nightmares for the happy dreams of love.

—*Chapter 13, VII: 9*

Perhaps because I began my writing career as an investigative reporter, I have a fairly high threshold of proof for what I consider a "miraculous" event. Finding a convenient parking space in San Francisco—no matter how unlikely that prospect, or how desperately I may be wishing for one—doesn't quite pass muster as a miracle. On the other hand, I'm not so skeptical that I feel the need to pick apart all surprising turns of good fortune, seeking reductive explanations or declaring them all to be meaningless accidents. Years of experience with the discipline of *A Course in Miracles* has taught me that there are certain kinds of incidents which occur when I'm "under the influence" of the internal guidance system that the Course calls the Holy Spirit. And those incidents, whether minor or major in effect, are suggestive of something more than mere good luck.

I had one such experience recently, during the writing of this book. On a Friday, my partner, Sari, had twisted her knee, leaving her hobbling about painfully by the next day. On Sunday morning, we decided that it would be best to get her a pair of crutches as soon as possible. Checking the Internet, I discovered that crutches were on sale at a local drugstore chain; we drove to the nearest one, which stocked only one pair of crutches, too large. The store manager directed us to another store in the chain, several miles across town, where they stocked several pairs—all of them too large. On the way back home, we attempted to stop at a local hospital to check its pharmacy, but couldn't find a parking place. Since merely walking around was a substantial challenge for her, Sari was beginning to tire of our adventure. I dropped her at home and drove another five miles to a large discount store with a pharmacy.

There were no crutches available there, and by the time I got back in the car I was beginning to feel exhausted. It didn't seem that it should be so impossible to find a rather common medical appliance, but my logical, step-by-step search for it was proving fruitless. There was obviously no sense in continuing to go from drugstore to drugstore. Suddenly remembering ACIM's observation that the goal of the ego is "seek and do not find" (Chapter 12, IV: 1), I closed my eyes and asked silently for less rational guidance: specifically, the input of the Holy Spirit. The exact language I used was "How can I do this differently? Help me to find the solution I cannot see by myself."

Immediately I had a distinct if undramatic vision: the mental picture of a shopping center less than a mile from the parking lot I was sitting in. I knew there was a drugstore there, but it was another franchise of the same chain I had twice visited already. So I thought, "That won't do any good; they'll have the wrong size too." But at that moment, a stronger inner voice prevailed: "Go there," it told me with certainty, "and you will find the help you need."

I drove the short distance to the shopping plaza I'd seen in my mind. There was no parking place close to the pharmacy that I knew about, so I had to walk some distance. Inside that pharmacy I found, as I'd expected, one pair of the wrong size of crutches. *So much for the Holy Spirit*, I thought ruefully, but I had a hunch that I should ask one of the pharmacists if they might have a smaller size somewhere in stock. "No, I'm sorry," the pharmacist said, "but check with the grocery store across the plaza. They have a pharmacy and I think they carry crutches there."

Okay, one more stop, I thought, *and then I'm giving up.* (Walking there, I noticed that I had parked very close to the grocery store I'd just been directed to; in fact, right outside the doors of its drugstore entrance. But I had not noticed that when I parked.) At the last pharmacy I would visit that day, there were two people working behind the prescription counter when I asked about crutches. One of them, the manager, said they didn't carry any. Even as he reported that, the woman standing directly in front of me blinked in surprise and said, "Well, I happen to have a pair in my car. I was going to donate them to a Goodwill store on Friday, but I forgot to drop them off. You're welcome to them."

Perhaps it's needless to say that this gift pair of crutches was in the right size range for Sari. And they were better made than any of those I'd seen for sale that day.

"The Miracle Is Always There"

There are several aspects of this experience that qualify it as a Course-style "miracle" to me. An obvious element is the synchronicity of what I was looking for with what the friendly pharmacist happened to have stowed in her car. A skeptic might say that it was just dumb luck, a coincidence that was bound to crop up sooner or later as long as I kept looking for crutches. To me, that conclusion strains credulity far more than the assumption that the pharmacist and I connected on a subconscious basis—not because we were trying to connect to each other in particular, but because we shared a common purpose of trying to help someone in need.

On the pharmacist's part, that purpose had led her to place a pair of crutches in her car to give away. Since she had forgotten to donate them on Friday, she was aware on Sunday that the crutches were in her car and she still intended to give them away. Meanwhile, at the point when I gave up on finding the right size of crutches through my logical search and invoked a deeper intuition, then I was able to sense that woman's intention and locate her.

A natural temptation is to believe that this is the purpose *A Course in Miracles* is meant to serve: teaching us how to access a magical intelligence called the Holy Spirit who will intervene in all our problems and instrument miraculous solutions, thereby smoothing the path toward fulfillment of all our earthly needs and desires. In fact, ACIM is sometimes mistaken for just such a New Age strategy, both by students and some critical observers. Based on my long experience with the teaching, I don't think that's how it works. Understanding how it *does* work is key to maximizing ACIM's benefits over the long term.

In the Text's opening pages, a listing of fifty principles of miracles sheds some light on the mechanism that might explain experiences such as my connection with the pharmacist:

Miracles occur naturally as expressions of love. The real miracle is the love that inspires them. In this sense everything that comes from love is a miracle. . . .

Miracles are natural. When they do not occur something has gone wrong. . . .

Wholeness is the perceptual content of miracles. They thus correct, or atone for, the faulty perception of lack. (Text 1, I: 3, 6, 41)

Later, the discussion of Workbook Lesson 91, "Miracles are seen in light," provides an important insight about how we perceive miracles.

It is important to remember that miracles and vision necessarily go together. This needs repeating, and frequent repeating. It is a central idea in your new thought system, and the perception that it produces. **The miracle is always there.** Its presence is not caused by your vision; its absence is not the result of your failure to see. It is only your awareness of miracles that is affected. You will see them in the light; you will not see them in the dark. (Emphasis mine.)

By asserting that "the miracle is always there," the Course is implying that we do not exactly "perform" miracles by learning how to manipulate the physical circumstances of the world to get what we want. Rather, we decide at every moment whether we want to see the whole and undivided truth of love behind the confusion and distortions of our fear-driven perceptions. As a rule, we do not want to. But when we do want to see the truth, even a little, our vision suddenly opens up to admit miracles.

Remember that ACIM asserts we are habitually attached to a profoundly deep delusion: We believe that we exist as separate bodies and minds in a chaotic world of light and darkness, time and space, isolation and suffering. Behind the veil of illusion that seems to limit and define our very existence, there is only light, infinite and eternal, extending from the subatomic level to the farthest reaches of the cosmos. Our real mind is synonymous with that light; its emotional content, or feeling quality, is what we know as love. Thus, an infinite and unconditional love is the "deep background" of our everyday world.

When we experience a miracle here on earth, I believe we are simply electing to see a glimmer of the infinite light and love that is the real matrix of our existence. When I found the pharmacist who just happened to have the crutches I was looking for, the "faulty perception of lack" that had been frustrating me was suddenly corrected. By surrendering my ego-driven search and asking for help from a deeper wisdom within my mind, I connected with another person's intention to be helpful. That enabled me to receive a reminder about the wholeness of spiritual reality.

Compared to the vastness of ultimate truth that the Course urges us toward, this miracle was a tiny reminder indeed—but it was still "enlightening" in the sense that it pointed toward a whole different order of reality than the one I was accustomed to. One might say that it was all the miracle that I could allow myself at the time.

"Advancing to Love's Meaning"

If it is always possible to see a miracle of wholeness behind our fractured sense of reality, it's worth asking why we don't elect to see them more often. Why, for instance, did Sari and I simply not see her as healed from her knee injury, and thus not in need of crutches at all? There are enough credible stories of miraculous healings to speculate that we could all perceive ourselves as whole and healthy if we really put our minds to it, and that begs the question: *Why don't we all make our lives much easier by experiencing miracles all the time?*

The short answer: We don't *want* to see miracles all the time, because experiencing more and more of them would eventually threaten our very sense of existence. If we progressively became free of our handicaps and illnesses, for example, we would reach the point of realizing that the body itself is a handicap on our spirit (as anyone who's ever had an ecstatic flying dream can attest). To surrender our bodies and egos to the infinite abstraction of God— even when returning to God promises an experience of eternal bliss—is perceived as a sacrifice we are unwilling to make.

I once interviewed an addiction counselor who likened the challenge of "going cold turkey" on drugs to telling a scuba diver deep under the surface of the ocean that his breathing apparatus would be suddenly removed, but not to worry—he'd be perfectly fine. To someone who has grown dependent on an addictive substance, its elimination seems to portend death, not freedom. We are all likewise addicted to the physical and psychological apparatus that defines our identity—so much so that we allow fear and isolation to define our lives, even to the point of regarding love itself as a fearful thing. As the Course suggests:

> Truth has rushed to meet you since you called upon it. If you knew Who walks beside you on the way that you have chosen, fear would be impossible. You do not know because the journey into darkness has been long and cruel, and you have gone deep into it.

A little flicker of your eyelids, closed so long, has not yet been sufficient to give you confidence in yourself, so long despised. You go toward love still hating it, and terribly afraid of its judgment upon you. And you do not realize that you are not afraid of love, but only of what you have made of it. You are advancing to love's meaning, and away from all illusions in which you have surrounded it. When you retreat to the illusion your fear increases, for there is little doubt that what you think it means *is* fearful. (Chapter 18, III: 3)

My own experience of the "advance to love's meaning" is often that of three steps forward and two back. There have been times, in fact, when it seemed that learning to forgive on a continuous basis only entailed progressively larger crises to be overcome. And yet, in retrospect, I can appreciate what might be called a "reservoir of peace" that owes to having settled certain issues in my life once and for all.

A major issue is the fear of death, which was of particular concern to me before I undertook study of the Course. When I was younger, I was not anxious about the actual experience of dying, or the idea of being snuffed out, but I did harbor the fear that I might die before I had done anything worthwhile or notable in the world. I didn't know exactly what was "required" of me in that respect, but there was an anxiety that somehow I wouldn't prove my worth or value to the world before I was gone. It was as if I had to earn the right to be here before I could feel comfortable with the idea of leaving someday.

In retrospect, I recognize this anxiety as the ego's basic insecurity about its own value and reality. And because the ego's victories tend to be short-lived and unsatisfying, I might have felt this misgiving indefinitely, had I not encountered the Course discipline. Although there was no particular lesson or passage from ACIM that settled this issue for me, it was fairly early in my study—at a time when I was still seriously ill with chronic fatigue syndrome—when I awoke one day with the peaceful realization that it would be all right to die. I knew from my diagnosis and my own gut feeling that I was unlikely to die anytime soon, even if I might prefer expiring to continuing to suffer. But the nagging feeling that I hadn't done enough to "call it a life" was suddenly gone, and there was a new element of serenity added to my baseline of awareness.

That doesn't mean that I never fear for my mortality or that I'm oblivious to physical dangers. But it does mean that I live without feeling that it's necessary to stave off death at all costs, largely because I've recognized that the "death" I used to fear was really the ego's resistance to surrendering its agenda of self-preservation. While I still have a personal identity and find it useful in getting through the day, I feel less besieged by any apparent attacks on it, or the need to confirm its worth once and for all.

When I do see myself acting in a defensive or self-serving manner to protect my egotistic concerns, I'm much more likely to see those behaviors compassionately, as if I were viewing a child acting out. And I also find that I have more understanding of other people who are obviously struggling with the ego's demands for self-preservation and confirmation. Whether it's myself or another who acts in a petty or fearful way, I'm more likely to handle the situation with tolerance than judgment. The growth of this instinctive response has helped me understand that the ego does not have to be battled or defeated so much as clearly seen without condemnation, and with care. For it is ultimately love that undoes the ego, whereas confronting it only tends to strengthen its defensive hold on consciousness.

The back-and-forth nature of spiritual growth, which involves advancing toward unconditional love only to fall back into egocentric habits and beliefs, is addressed by the Course as a process of learning that inevitably leads into awakening:

> Forget not once this journey is begun the end is certain. Doubt along the way will come and go and go to come again. Yet is the ending sure. No one can fail to do what God appointed him to do. When you forget, remember that you walk with Him and with His Word upon your heart. Who could despair when hope like this is his? Illusions of despair may seem to come, but learn how not to be deceived by them. . . . (Clarification of Terms, Epilogue)

The Course often refers to the end of the spiritual journey as the attainment of "knowledge," or total union with God, which is beyond our capacity to experience on earth. In a very real sense, you can't get there from here—because the last step on the journey is a mysterious attainment that we cannot undertake for ourselves. We can, however, learn to attune to the voice of the Holy Spirit, which helps us forgive all the illusions we live by and make ourselves ready for a last step, which is taken by God on our behalf:

> God honored even the miscreations of His children because they had made them. But He also blessed His children with a way of thinking that could raise their perceptions so high they could reach almost back to Him. The Holy Spirit is the Mind of the Atonement. He represents a state of mind close enough to

One-mindedness that transfer to it is at last possible. Perception
is not knowledge, but it can be transferred to knowledge, or cross
over into it. It might even be more helpful here to use the literal
meaning of transferred or "carried over," since the last step is taken
by God. (Chapter 5, I: 6)

Although we cannot directly awaken from the dreaming of this
world into the full awareness of God, what we *can* do on our own
is to improve the quality of our everyday dreams. The spiritual
journey that the Course would have us take is literally one of progressing through our own illusions, from the most terrifying to the
most gentle:

You are the dreamer of the world of dreams. No other cause it
has, nor ever will. Nothing more fearful than an idle dream has
terrified God's Son, and made him think that he has lost his innocence, denied his Father, and made war upon himself. So fearful is the dream, so seeming real, he could not waken to reality
without the sweat of terror and a scream of mortal fear, unless a
gentler dream preceded his awaking, and allowed his calmer mind
to welcome, not to fear, the Voice that calls with love to waken
him; a gentler dream, in which his suffering was healed and where
his brother was his friend. God willed he waken gently and with
joy, and gave him means to waken without fear.

Accept the dream He gave instead of yours. It is not difficult
to change a dream when once the dreamer has been recognized.
Rest in the Holy Spirit, and allow His gentle dreams to take the
place of those you dreamed in terror and in fear of death. He brings
forgiving dreams, in which the choice is not who is the murderer
and who shall be the victim. In the dreams He brings there is no

murder and there is no death. The dream of guilt is fading from your sight, although your eyes are closed. A smile has come to lighten up your sleeping face. The sleep is peaceful now, for these are happy dreams. (Chapter 27, VII: 14)

Seeing Through a "Flimsy Veil"

David Hoffmeister is a popular speaker on the ACIM circuit who spends nearly eleven months of the year on the road leading workshops worldwide. He discovered the Course at a humanistic psychology conference in 1986, after ten years as a "professional student" at the University of Cincinnati, where he majored in urban planning and general studies before beginning to gravitate to a study of the mind, philosophy, and spirituality. But nothing focused his attention like the Course, which he almost immediately felt to be his calling. "When I discovered the Course, it was like a tsunami of love washing over me," David reports. "It was a mystical experience just to open the book."

Soon David was studying ACIM for up to eight hours a day, a regimen he continued mostly alone for two years before beginning group work with a similar intensity, going to five study meetings weekly. At a large group that had no facilitator, people began to direct their questions to David as he felt "the Holy Spirit just coursing through me, and answers would come pouring out." In the early 1990s he began touring Course study centers around the United States, gradually finding himself to be more and more inspired to teach and facilitate various kinds of events related to experiencing Course principles.

To his own surprise, David undertook his journey of Course

teaching without much planning. "My ego freaked a little bit in the beginning," he admits, "because I was going on the road with no money in the bank, no organization behind me, and no practical support. I was afraid of ending up like a bag lady. But things turned out just the opposite. Once I was on the road people offered me places to stay, and enough food and gas to keep going. And it's been that way ever since; things just seem to work out in the way that Jesus suggests in the Course: 'When you perform a miracle, I will arrange both time and space to adjust to it.'" (Chapter 2, V: A: 11)

Thus, for David, one aspect of the Course-inspired happy dream is that "life gets easier at the practical level. Things just seem to click into place without a sense of effort or control. This is the complete opposite of the ideas I was raised with, that you've always got to work hard to get ahead, and even then things will go wrong so that you have to learn to make lemonade when you get lemons, and so on. It's not just that I'm more relaxed about difficult challenges, but that everything gets easier when I let go of planning what I should do."

David cites the following text from Lesson 135, "If I defend myself I am attacked," for clarification of this easier way of life:

> A healed mind does not plan. It carries out the plans that it receives through listening to wisdom that is not its own. It waits until it has been taught what should be done, and then proceeds to do it. It does not depend upon itself for anything except its adequacy to fulfill the plans assigned to it. It is secure in certainty that obstacles can not impede its progress to accomplishment of any goal that serves the greater plan established for the good of everyone. (Workbook 135: 11)

David has also experienced three revelatory encounters with a "blazing light" in which "the three dimensions we normally experience collapsed around me. Three times in my lifetime, the world has literally disappeared before me. I had read before about such mystical experiences, but it was only experiencing them firsthand that completely changed my perspective on reality. Afterward the world seemed like a flimsy veil, not nearly so substantial as it had looked before. And there was a sense of lightness, not an unsteady giddiness, but a light and stable joy that's always present underneath my emotions of the moment. That joy helps me see my emotions much more clearly, as interpretations or reactions to what I'm seeing, rather than the objective truth of the situation at hand.

"What all this has confirmed for me," David explains, "is that there's not actually an objective world outside our consciousness, but only a reflection of what's going on in our mind. The more you can let your consciousness be cleared, the more you will see a happy world regardless of what seems to be going on. I can now turn on the TV and see all the usual news, but I don't have negative judgments of it anymore. That's what has been washed away in my consciousness."

David concludes that "there's a correlation between the happy dream and the absence of expectations. Even mild expectations or subtle agendas of control, wanting a certain outcome to any degree, will block the happy dream from awareness. A sense of ongoing wonderment and innocence is what I've experienced. You finally yield to the simple idea of *peace of mind now* as the only goal worth having. This is very alien to our usual way of thinking, because we're used to setting a lot of goals that are all related to the future. But the happy dream has nothing to do with the future. It's feeling peace now as a way of being, rather than something to be achieved someday after a lot of effort to arrange the right circumstances in order to feel peaceful.

"I once heard this kind of peace described as 'being happy for no earthly reason,'" David muses. "That sums it up pretty well for me."

Forgetting the Course

While there are teachers and scholars of *A Course in Miracles* who have devoted their lives to parsing its language and clarifying its principles to students, there is no clear-cut definition of mastery in the field and not even a formal acknowledgment that one has graduated from this course. In fact, ACIM itself suggests that the full integration of its message will incur a readiness to leave the teaching behind:

> Simply do this: Be still, and lay aside all thoughts of what you are and what God is; all concepts you have learned about the world; all images you hold about yourself. Empty your mind of everything it thinks is either true or false, or good or bad, of every thought it judges worthy, and all the ideas of which it is ashamed. Hold onto nothing. Do not bring with you one thought the past has taught, nor one belief you ever learned before from anything. Forget this world, forget this course, and come with wholly empty hands unto your God. (From Lesson 189)

At the end of the Workbook of daily lessons, it is further suggested that the student can thenceforth depend on the "Voice for God" for constant guidance:

No more specific lessons are assigned, for there is no more need of them. Henceforth, hear but the Voice for God and for your Self when you retire from the world, to seek reality instead. He will direct your efforts, telling you exactly what to do, how to direct your mind, and when to come to Him in silence, asking for His sure direction and His certain Word. His is the Word that God has given you. His is the Word you chose to be your own. . . .

The end is certain, and the means as well. To this we say "Amen." You will be told exactly what God wills for you each time there is a choice to make. And He will speak for God and for your Self, thus making sure that hell will claim you not, and that each choice you make brings Heaven nearer to your reach. And so we walk with Him from this time on, and turn to Him for guidance and for peace and sure direction. Joy attends our way. For we go homeward to an open door which God has held unclosed to welcome us. (Workbook, Epilogue: 3, 5)

Of all the distinctions that set *A Course in Miracles* apart from conventional religious practice, this is perhaps the most significant. Once the discipline has been completed, there is no requirement that the student retain a loyalty to the teaching, join a church devoted to its spread and popularity, or tithe to support its maintenance. It's possible to invest no more than the original cost of the book to become and remain a student. (In fact, the Foundation for Inner Peace has always made copies of the standard edition of ACIM available without charge on a "scholarship" basis to people who write and request it.) While many students do invest more in supplemental study guides by a variety of teachers and join local study groups or one of the larger Course-related organizations, all such decisions about furthering one's study are left to the individual student of the Course. Many students have developed a lifelong identification with their study, but it's impossible to say how many other readers have turned away from an incomplete study or used only brief portions of the Course for guidance at a particular point in their lives.

By being available to all but forced on none, the Course has established itself as an unusually democratic, free-floating spiritual discipline in a world of hierarchical and sometimes warring religious institutions. Its thorough repudiation of the doctrine of sin, coupled with a thorough training in forgiveness as a reliable route to salvation or enlightenment, is likely to have more and more appeal as the popular identification with being "spiritual but not religious" grows. Recent polls have indicated that this self-description is accepted by at least a third of American adults, with one recent survey suggesting that 72 percent of the so-called Millennial Generation, currently aged eighteen to twenty-five, finds this perspective appealing.

While there has been criticism of this outlook as a self-serving "smorgasbord" approach to spirituality in which people sample various religious perspectives and adopt only the elements they are comfortable with, the Course itself does not fit this description. For those who choose to stick with it, ACIM offers an exceptionally demanding regimen of ego-confrontation along the way to attaining an experience of God as a selfless, unconditional love at the root of their own consciousness. Most students report a significant degree of discomfort with this "mind training" at some point in their study, sometimes for years. Yet these same students find reasons to continue their work with ACIM on their own, without the urgings of a priest, pastor, or other authority figure, or the peer or organizational pressure of a church. And upon completing the Course—or at any point in their study, for that matter—they are free to turn away from it and rely on their own sense of internal wisdom, identified by ACIM as the Holy Spirit, for further guidance.

"A Journey Without Distance"

When I encountered the Course in the midst of a serious illness, I was watching my prior way of life fall apart. I had long harbored the suspicion that something was not right about the world and that a herculean effort was needed from right-minded people to correct the almost infinite variety of things that were going wrong. (Right-minded people were those like me, of course, and the more like me the better!) It was as if I had exhausted myself by trying to devise and mount a single-handed assault on a vast, multifaceted conspiracy of wrongdoing "out there."

A Course in Miracles helped me recognize that this "conspiracy" was my own: a classic ego-driven war of projection on the world, a projection doomed to failure by its own grandiose, insubstantial delusions. I felt the world had gone wrong because I secretly believed that I had somehow gone wrong. Thus my assault on worldly wrongdoing was actually a twisted attack on myself—an attack which once seemed perfectly logical, but was in fact completely insane.

Not surprisingly, ACIM's emphasis on forgiveness first struck me as unwise and possibly dangerous. When it began to yield healing effects despite my initial skepticism and resistance, I was able to confront my prior perceptions of the world and recognize how little I had really understood. Accepting that an unconditional and infinite love lay behind the seeming chaos and suffering of the everyday world was an even bigger step, because I had been raised to believe that real love was limited, rare, and in constant need of defense. Perceiving the world as a dream was not a big leap for me, but in my early years I would have regarded that dream as a tragic comedy at best and an inescapable nightmare at worst.

I now see "the world" as a kind of Rorschach test for my own consciousness: whatever I think I see going on out there is a reflection of what's going on in my mind. Either I choose to see everything from the vantage point of love, or I choose to see it with something less. From day to day and moment to moment, my perceptions still vary from loving to doubtful to distressed. But one thing is consistently different in my consciousness from my pre-Course days: *I can quickly become aware of how I am choosing to see, and elect to change the basis of my perceptions.* Years ago, I was totally prey to my own projections. My frequent unhappiness painted itself onto the apparent world and seeing it there made me all the more unhappy, sick at heart, and even physically ill. As a rule I thought the world was making me distressed, and I was always losing the battle to undo its effects on me.

The Course suggests that the choice between seeing with love and seeing with anything less is the choice between living in truth and suffering from delusion. I can't vouch for everything ACIM claims about the ultimate nature of time, space, matter, and the body. I don't base my continuing study on an unquestioning belief in everything it says, but rather a daily test of its principles in action. I don't always forgive immediately, or even know how to do it in a novel situation. But whenever I can find the way, then forgiveness never fails to deliver a healing and transformative result. One by one, forgiveness exchanges the elements of my prior nightmares for the unified light of happier dreams. And I figure that the philosophy behind a spiritual strategy that has yet to fail me is probably sound as well, no matter how radical its propositions.

In a paradoxical way, *A Course in Miracles* doesn't demand much of its students. No one is required to fast or confess, go to church, pray on schedule, or travel to the remote cave of a guru to find enlightenment. In fact ACIM calls the search for God "a journey without distance" that requires only a shift in perception to be completed:

> The journey to God is merely the reawakening of the knowledge of where you are always, and what you are forever. It is a journey without distance to a goal that has never changed. Truth can only be experienced. It cannot be described and it cannot be explained. I can make you aware of the conditions of truth, but the experience is of God. Together we can meet its conditions, but truth will dawn upon you of itself. (Chapter 8, VI: 9)

Elsewhere the Course explains that "enlightenment is but a recognition, and not a change at all" (from Lesson 188). What this means is that at any moment, anyone can choose to perceive and act on the basis of love instead of fear, and in so doing "save the world" that he or she sees from unhappiness and condemnation. Even the most violent attack or tragic disaster can be seen as a call for love that deserves only love in response—and the particular way in which we choose to express that love can be guided from within by an intelligence that far surpasses our normal, individual resources. Whenever we can manage this simple yet saving change of perception, we will find that we are living in the midst of miracles.

Summary

What the Course calls a miracle is best understood not as a magical manipulation of our material circumstances, but rather the recognition of perfect love behind all the seeming difficulties and inadequacies of life on earth. When we witness a miracle that transforms our ordinary experience to any degree, it means we have become willing to recognize our spiritual reality to that same degree. The reason that we do not witness miracles constantly is that we still prefer to believe in our illusory existence as egos and bodies. This is what ACIM means when it claims that "Miracles are natural. When they do not occur something has gone wrong."

Progressing with the Course discipline does not abruptly lead us into salvation or enlightenment. Rather, we gradually evolve from our most nightmarish illusions to "happy dreams" that offer proof of our advancement toward the meaning of universal love. Along the way, Course students will not only suffer less from the typical pains of the human condition, but may also be gifted with revelatory "light experiences" that help them see through ordinary reality while growing less dependent on egocentric expectations and plans.

The ultimate aim of studying *A Course in Miracles* is not to become an expert on its theological principles or a walking collection of quotations, but to develop forgiveness as a ready response to all the world's challenges and attune to the Holy Spirit as a constant source of guidance. As these rewards of spiritual growth are realized, the need to identify oneself as a Course student will drop away. As an unusually democratic spiritual discipline that is both easily accessible and highly challenging, ACIM is likely to meet the needs of many who identify with the growing culture of those who consider themselves "spiritual but not religious." It demands neither defense nor devotion to its creed, only the student's willingness to "shift perception" from fear to love, from the ego to God, and from the mundane to the miraculous.

APPENDIX

RECOMMENDED RESOURCES FOR FURTHER COURSE STUDY

These resources are drawn from the books and other teaching media of ACIM *teachers quoted in this book.*

A Course in Miracles, Combined Volume (Third Edition). Foundation for Inner Peace, 2007. Includes Preface, Text, Workbook for Students, Manual for Teachers, Clarification of Terms, and Supplements. This is the standard version of ACIM footnoted in this book. At the Foundation's website (www.acim.org), you can find other authorized editions and a wealth of archival material.

Understanding A Course in Miracles: *The History, Message, and Legacy of a Spiritual Path for Today* by D. Patrick Miller. Celestial Arts/Random House, 2008. The author's first book on ACIM, detailing its history and cultural significance, including critical commentary. Find a variety of additional resources including links to Course groups worldwide at the author's website: www.fearlessbooks.com/ACourseInMiracles.htm.

The Works of Kenneth Wapnick: Editor of ACIM and one of its primary teachers, Ken Wapnick has a number of books and classes available through the Foundation for *A Course in Miracles* at www.facim.org.

Books and other media by DavidPaul and Candace Doyle are available at www.thevoiceforlove.com.

Books and other media by Nouk Sanchez and Tomas Vieira are available at www.takemetotruth.com.

For more information about Philip Urso, see www.saltpondyoga.com.

Books and other media by David Hoffmeister are available from the Foundation for the Awakening Mind at http://global-miracles.net.

INDEX

joining beyond bodies, 145–48
realization of holy instant,
147–48
release of self-judgment, 160
and special relationship,
vacillation between, 149–53
transformation of special
relationship into, 146–47, 157
unilateral experience of, 153–55,
157, 161
Holy Spirit
access to, through forgiveness, 3,
57–59, 136–37
in achievement of innocent
confidence, 233
as ambassador from God, 25
categories of judgment, 251
change of perception, 154, 158
choice to hear and follow,
26–27
correction of errors, 113, 131,
140, 219
definition of, 57–58
fulfillment of true needs, 58,
136–37
guidance to encounter ACIM, 44
healing and wisdom through,
137–40
as internal teacher, 22, 26,
64–65, 68
as link between God and
ego-driven self, 57–59
teaching through holy instant, 147

illness. See sickness
illusory world. See material world
immaterialism, 2
inner voice
beneficial advice from, 79–80
ego's, 82
forgiveness and, 81–82

guidance in large and small
decisions, 80–81
versus hallucination, 75–76
historical role of, 73–75
manifestation of, 76
summary, 83
variety of ways to access, 76–79
See also Holy Spirit
innocent confidence
allowing for plurality of truths, 231
loss of, through living in adult
world, 233–35
versus self-confidence, 232–33
Institute of Noetic Sciences, 2
internal teacher. See Holy Spirit

Jesus Christ
authorship of ACIM, 64, 67–68,
206–9
Christian versus Course notions
of, 207–8
first-person references in ACIM,
2, 16, 60–61, 90–91
as role model, 20, 70–71, 88–89
Sonship, 61, 65
Jones, Jim, 75
Jung, Carl, 131

King, Martin Luther, Jr., 74
Koresh, David, 75
Krishnamurti, Jiddu, 232

language of ACIM
incomprehensibility, 63–64
masculine references, 62–63
as product of Schucman's mind,
50–52
prose style, 45, 49
religious terminology, 26,
54–57, 65
Shakespearean rhythms, 51–52

language of ACIM *(cont.)*
  summary, 65–66
  words as symbols of symbols,
    47–49
learning
  during childhood innocence,
    230–31
  end of, in adult material world,
    232–35
  miracle as substitute for, 228
  regaining of open-mindedness,
    236
  See also spiritual growth
lessons. *See* Workbook, citations to
Liester, Mitch, 74, 75–76
love
  advance to meaning of, 269–73
  as basis for thoughts and actions,
    26, 281
  as choice, 27, 28, 266
  ego's search for, 124–26
  versus fear, 80, 110–11
  forgiveness as messenger of, 251
  Holy Spirit's categories of
    judgment, 251
  impediments to, 3–4
  miracles as expression of, 266
  as natural inheritance, 3
  through release of fear and ego,
    220
  as spiritual reality, 4
  unity with others at level of
    mind, 18
  See also God

Mandela, Nelson, 168
Manual for Teachers, citations to
  (Manual, 3: 5), 156
  (Manual, 4, I: A), 160
  (Manual, 4, I, A: 3–5), 241
  (Manual, 4, I, A: 6), 242

(Manual, 4, I, A: 7), 242
(Manual, 4, I, A: 8), 243
(Manual, 8: 3–4), 250
(Manual, 16: 5), 195
(Manual, 24: 1, 5), 229
(Manual, 26), 57
(Manual, 28: 1), 192
(Manual, 29: 5–6), 81
(Manual, 4-A: 4), 227
(Section 21), 47
Master Teacher (MT; Charles Buell
    Anderson), 211–13
material world
  body as part of, 186
  God's lack of concern for, 24–25
  helpful occurrences, 227
  problems in, as choice of
    perception, 18–19, 82, 136,
    249–50
  as product of imagination,
    248–50, 275, 280
  quantum mechanics and, 119–20
  riddles and mysteries, 118
  shift in beliefs about, 36, 196, 247
  summary, 121–22
  time as illusion, 119
  transcendence of, through
    forgiveness, 17, 87, 88, 91,
    117, 167, 248–50
  unreality of, 4, 18–19, 104,
    116–18, 120
Miller, D. Patrick, "On
    Sleeplessness," 95–97
mind
  body's influence on, 184, 198
  categories of judgment, 250
  as consciousness of God and love,
    106–9
  creation of material world,
    248–50, 275, 280
  ego's conflict with, 105–6